GREED
&
GLORY

Books by William Houston

BALLARD (1984)

INSIDE MAPLE LEAF GARDENS: The Rise and Fall of the Toronto Maple Leafs (1989)

MAPLE LEAF BLUES (1990)

PRIDE AND GLORY: 100 Years of the Stanley Cup (1992)

GREED
&
GLORY

The Fall of Hockey Czar Alan Eagleson

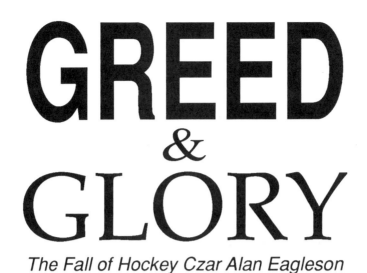

William Houston • David Shoalts

Warwick Publishing Inc.
Toronto   Los Angeles

Published by the Warwick Publishing Group
Warwick Publishing Inc., 24 Mercer Street, Toronto, Ontario M5V 1H3
Warwick Publishing Inc., 1300 N. Alexandria, Los Angeles, California 90027

ISBN 1-895629-24-1

Distributed in the United States by:
Firefly Books Ltd.
250 Sparks Avenue
Willowdale, Ontario
M2H 2S4

Cover design: Dave Hader, Studio Conception
Text design: Nick Pitt
Editorial services provided by Word Guild, Toronto.

Printed and bound in Canada.

To my mother, for her encouragement,
support and love. And to my nieces
and nephews — Andrew, Ben, Christopher,
Collin, Emily, Jennifer and Laura.
— W.H.

To Yvonne, Rebecca and Matthew.
— D.S.

Table of Contents

Acknowledgements

IN EARLY 1993, we worked on a series about R. Alan Eagleson for *The Globe and Mail*, along with freelance reporter Stevie Cameron. Out of that investigation came the idea of writing this book.

The series was initiated by Edward Greenspon, then a deputy managing editor of the newpaper and now the Ottawa bureau chief, along with Colin MacKenzie another *Globe* deputy managing editor. Dennis Anderson oversaw the project as principal editor and was assisted by Paul Knox. We were also helped by *The Globe*'s sports editor, David Langford, as well as reporters Al Strachan, Dan Westell and James Christie. Before us, Brian Milner and Larry Millson of *The Globe* did some good research on Eagleson in 1991. We owe them all many thanks. To Stevie Cameron, who encouraged us to do the book, opened some doors for us, and provided us with her own research material, we owe a special thanks.

Several probes into Eagleson's business and union activities preceded this book. In 1982, Deidra Clayton wrote an unauthorized biography of Eagleson titled *Eagle: The Life and Times of R. Alan Eagleson*. In July 1984, *Sports Illustrated* published an investigative report by John Papanek and Bill Brubaker titled "The Man Who Rules Hockey." In 1991, the book *Net Worth*, written by David Cruise and Alison Griffiths, examined the National Hockey League's history of labour-management relations, with a particular emphasis on Eagleson's role as head of the NHL Players' Association. Finally, Russ Conway, a journalist with *The Eagle-Tribune* in Lawrence, Massachusetts, published two investigative series on Eagleson in September, 1991, and February, 1993.

The work of Clayton, Papanek, Brubaker, Cruise, Griffiths and Conway, along with reports from other newspapers, books and magazines, were used as secondary source material in this book and are credited in the Endnotes. These journalists were the ground-breakers and deserve credit as such.

To Don Loney, a thank you for his valuable work in editing the manuscript. Our gratitude also to Don Broad, Heather Somerville and Linda Stoewner at McGraw-Hill Ryerson; Jim Williamson and Nick Pitt at Warwick Publishing; Marian Hebb, who handled our contract; Sue Foster, who kept us pointed in the right direction; and journalists Alan Adams and Earl McRae for their assistance.

We would also like to thank Celia Donnelly and Rick Cash of the Globe and Mail's library staff for doing our corporate searches, digging up odd bits of information and being unfailingly helpful.

There are a number of people who deserve our thanks for supplying valuable information but must go unnamed. Thanks to you all, we could not have managed this without you.

From William Houston, a special thanks to his wife, Janet , for her generous support and for putting up with long absences in front of a computer terminal. Janet's editorial advice was invaluable.

Thank you from David Shoalts to the Forskin family — Martin, Elaine, Marysha and Elden — for helping to care for two very active children during a chaotic time. You couldn't ask for better in-laws. Thanks too, to his father, Roy Shoalts, for shouldering some of the burden of home renovations while the bulk of this was written, and to his mother, Vivian Shoalts, whose faith never wavered.

Finally, an especially grateful thank you to his wife, Yvonne, for giving up her own vacation and her own activities to look after home and family and allow him the freedom to write. It is a debt he can never repay.

GREED
&
GLORY

(Courtesy of Ed Garvey)

Chapter One

THE ANTAGONISTS

FOR THE BETTER PART of two years, the members of the grand jury have been gathered in a courtroom at the John W. McCormick Post Office and Court House in Boston, Massachusetts. They met once a week, usually on a Thursday, and they listened to testimony from people who knew or had done business with R. Alan Eagleson, a prominent Canadian who at one time was the most powerful hockey executive in the world.

As in all U.S. grand jury investigations, the courtroom was sealed to the public and the press. Even the witnesses entered the courtroom alone, their legal counsel left to wait in the hall outside. Inside, the 23 jury members learned of Eagleson's activities as executive director of the National Hockey League Players' Association, the players' union that he founded in 1967. They were told of his role as an international hockey impressario and hockey agent. And they have heard about his power, influence and important friends.

Those who testified include some of the biggest names in hockey: Phil Esposito, a first-team All-Star centre with Boston six years in a row and one of the heroes of the 1972 Canada-Soviet Union hockey series, which was organized by Eagleson; John Ziegler, the former president of the National Hockey League; and Bryan Trottier, a past-president of the NHLPA.

Eagleson's friends, associates and business partners appeared before the grand jury, and so have his enemies. Among the latter are Rich Winter, an Edmonton lawyer who initiated an investigation of Eagleson by the players in his role as head of the NHL Players' Association, and Ed Garvey, a lawyer and former head of the National Football League Players' Association who wrote a scathing report on Eagleson's conduct as union boss that shocked and dismayed the players at their annual meeting in Florida in 1989.

Grand juries are powerful investigative tools. If a witness refuses to appear, he or she can be forcibly brought to court and then charged with contempt, the result of which is imprisonment for the life of the grand jury. An agreement between Canada and the United States, called the Mutual Legal Assistance Treaty, empowers the United States Justice Department to question witnesses who reside in Canada and have refused to appear before the grand jury. Through diplomatic channels an order is issued, the witness is brought before a judge in Canada, and a sworn deposition is given.

During the grand jury process, members who are selected randomly from a census list learn from the prosecutors about the laws that apply to a particular case. If an investigation unearths apparent violations, the prosecution informs the jury of the crimes and proposes indictments. The ultimate power lies with the jury. It decides if charges will be laid.

Among the laws that may apply to the Eagleson case is the RICO statute, an acronym for Racketeer Influenced and Corrupt Organization. The RICO law provides powerful civil and criminal penalties for people in an organization who engage in a pattern of activity that is illegal. If the Justice Department can show three separate criminal events engaged in by an organization, it has a RICO violation. A person guilty of a minor RICO offence faces up to 20 years imprisonment. For anything more serious the maximum penalty is life. The minimum sentence for a minor offence is three to five years.

There is also the ERISA, the Employee Retirement Income Security Act, which is a federal law governing pensions in the United States. If pension fund improprieties are discovered in a union with members in both the United States and Canada, the U.S. Justice Department can lay charges under ERISA, even if all the activities have taken place in Canada.

That Eagleson, who turned 60 in April, 1993, might be charged, convicted and imprisoned, seems to many unfathomable. He is a famous Canadian and has been honoured innumerable times during his career in hockey. He is a member of the Canadian Sports Hall of Fame and the Hockey Hall of Fame. In 1989, he was appointed an Officer of the Order of Canada. He won the Vanier Award in 1968 and the Lester B. Pearson Peace Award in 1987. He is on the board of governors of several Toronto hospitals. He is a Queen's Counsel, a former member of the Ontario legislature, a pal of Canadian supreme court justices, federal cabinet ministers and more than one prime minister.

Eagleson is a long-time member of the Progressive Conservative Party, but he also has well-placed friends in the Liberal Party. In late 1992, Dennis Mills, the Liberal member of Parliament for Broadview-Greenwood in Toronto, met John Turner, a former Liberal prime minister of Canada, for dinner in Ottawa, during which Turner casually asked Mills what he had been doing. Mills mentioned that he was looking into the Eagleson case on behalf of several retired players.

Turner, most strenuously, advised Mills not to get involved. Says Mills, "It's not a big secret that he and Eagleson are close friends."

In 1988, however, there began an unfolding of events that even Eagleson, with all of his connections and important friends, was powerless to stop. A move in June, 1989, to overthrow him as executive director of the NHLPA had succeeded; he was forced to apologize to the players and later announce his early retirement. In January, 1990, the Law Society of Upper Canada received a 51-page complaint about Eagleson from Rich Winter, the consequence of which was a slow-moving but inevitable probe of Eagleson's conduct as a lawyer.

The most damaging development, however, turned out to be a series of articles published by a suburban Boston newspaper, *The Eagle-Tribune* of Lawrence, Massachusetts. *The Eagle-Tribune* has a weekday circulation of only 52,000, which makes it a small player in the Boston market compared with the two metropolitan dailies, *The Boston Globe* and *The Boston Herald*. But, despite its size, *The Eagle-Tribune* commits large resources to investigative journalism. In 1988, it won a Pulitzer Prize for a series of articles on the parole system of Massachusetts. The articles dealt specifically with the case of Willie Horton, a convicted murderer who, after a furlough from prison, invaded a Maryland home and raped and tortured a woman.

In the late 1970s, Russ Conway, a sports reporter with *The Eagle-Tribune*, wrote a series of articles on race-fixing at New England thoroughbred tracks. His revelations resulted in a federal grand jury investigation, indictments, convictions and prison sentences. The series earned Conway awards, won friendships with Federal Bureau of Investigation agents and federal prosecutors, and was a factor in his promotion to *Eagle-Tribune* sports editor in 1981.

Conway's years of NHL coverage and his connection with players, specifically former members of the Boston Bruins, led to his investigation into the affairs of Eagleson. Members of the Bruins had been vocal in questioning Eagleson's conduct as head of their union. In 1982, Brad Park, then a Bruin defenceman, complained that the union was being run "by an inner circle of yes-men for Eagleson." For years Mike Milbury, another Bruin defenceman, had carried on a running battle with Eagleson over his stewardship of the NHLPA.

Eddie Johnston, a former Boston goaltender, became suspicious of Eagleson's relationship with Chicago Blackhawks' owner Bill Wirtz (then the powerful chairman of the NHL's board of governors) when Johnston was fired as the Blackhawk coach after dismissing Eagleson as his agent.

Other ex-Bruins, such as Greg Sheppard, Steve Kasper and Phil Esposito, were also vocal Eagleson critics. But the most noteworthy antagonist, the man who hated Eagleson the most and seemed to live for the day that his enemy would be brought down, was one of hockey's greatest stars. More than anyone else, Bobby Orr was responsible for Eagleson's spectacular rise as a super-agent. Orr was not only Eagleson's most famous client, but he was also his business partner and close friend. However, when he split with Eagleson in 1979, Orr claimed to have been left with virtually nothing, his debts amounting to more than his assets. To this day, Orr despises Eagleson and it was with his assistance and support that Conway, a reporter Orr had known for 20 years, began his investigation in June, 1990.

There is no hard and fast rule applying to a reporter's relationship with law enforcement officials while working on a story.

Generally, however, a reporter does not divulge information to authorities unless there's a q*uid pro quo*, and even then he does so reluctantly. In Conway's case, he willingly passed on his information to FBI officials he knew in the Boston area. He started doing this months before his first stories appeared.

Conway insists he has received nothing in return from the FBI sources and explains his decision to assist the Bureau by saying, "I think it's a responsibility if you're going to be a good citizen, and if you see something that may constitute a crime, that you bring it to the attention of the authorities."

Acting on information acquired from Conway, as well as complaints from former players whom Conway had interviewed, the FBI started interviewing hockey people about Eagleson in January, 1991. A few months later, the FBI asked for a legal opinion from the U.S. Department of Justice in Washington concerning the allegations presented by various players. If these allegations were proven to be true, would they constitute criminal offences? In April, 1991, the Justice Department replied in the affirmative.

Conway, meanwhile, continued to work at his investigation. After several delays, his articles finally ran in September, 1991. His five-part series was kicked off under the headline "Big-time hockey: A study in conflicts of interest. Did union chief Alan Eagleson help the players or himself?"

Conway wrote, "The head of the players' union, Eagleson, has repeatedly placed himself in a position of conflict of interest between players and team owners and between union and personal business. Some players and other agents charge the players have wound up the losers.

"Meanwhile, they contend, Eagleson has won the favour of the league and team owners and advanced his own career, becoming perhaps the most powerful man in hockey."

Conway's series was comprehensive, exhaustively researched and impressive enough to place second in its category of news beat reporting for a Pulitzer Prize in 1991. It was a damning indictment, not only of Eagleson and his web of business and union activities, but also of the NHL and its monopoly in professional hockey.

The degree to which Eagleson was in trouble became known in December, 1992, when the FBI and U.S. Justice Department announced their investigations, while at the same time serving subpoenas on NHL president John Ziegler and NHL club owners. The subpoenas asked the owners to turn over club and players' association records dealing with insurance, pension funds and other union-related activities.

Assistant U.S. prosecutor Paul Kelly, who was in charge of the public corruption unit, was assigned to head up the NHLPA investigation, which by now not only involved Eagleson but, in the words of Kelly, "various people associated with the NHLPA, including Eagleson — and other people as well."

As the investigation progressed, one of the curious pastimes in hockey came to be speculation as to what Eagleson would do if he were charged and faced the possibility of spending a significant part of his remaining years behind bars. When Conway's articles appeared, he said that on advice from his lawyer, Edgar Sexton of Toronto, he would not reply to specific questions pertaining to information in the series. However, he did lash out, accusing the FBI of feeding Conway information and leading a witch hunt. To Scott Morrison, the sports editor of the *Toronto Sun*, Eagleson said, "This all came from Bobby Orr. It had to. A lot of material that has been presented, it could only have come from him. . . ."

"There have been at least 100 grotesque distortions (in the media reports)," continued Eagleson. "They claim they're using facts, but they don't use all the facts. With each attack you want to counter-attack with the facts. . . . You have to wonder. This has become a public attack orchestrated by the people doing the investigating. It's frustrating."

Eagleson theorized that Conway and the prosecutor, Paul Kelly, had, in effect, been deployed by the vengeful Bobby Orr to destroy him. Indeed, there were rumours, circulating widely, that Kelly had entered the investigation as a less-than-objective seeker of the truth, that in fact he knew Orr, was a great admirer of the former hockey All-Star, and even had a picture of Orr hanging on his office wall.

Kelly is a short, stocky 37-year-old Bostonian with the "determination of a bulldog," according to a witness who testified at the grand jury. He is a hockey fan who, in his youth, followed the Bruins when they were the dominant team in the NHL, led by the brilliant Orr. He played hockey as a child and later in high school and at Boston College where he was a member of an intramural team. While in law school, he coached minor hockey and continued to coach after graduation.

In Kelly's office hang two framed newspaper reports, one above the other. On top is a story published in *The Boston Globe* in 1989. With an accompanying photograph of Kelly, it tells of a federal prosecutor who was able to find time to coach a successful high school hockey team.

On the bottom is a clipping about Orr visiting a kids' team in 1986. "Orr offers tips to Pee Wees," the headline reads. Kelly, after coaching a season of high school hockey in 1986, decided to conduct a series of clinics for local teams, for which he hoped to enlist prominent former players to assist, such as Orr.

"I made a random call out of the blue to Bobby Orr, and to my surprise he agreed to come out," Kelly says. "He spent a couple of hours with us in a clinic and I was extremely impressed.

"In fact, I remember vividly arriving at the rink a half-hour before the kids set up, just to make sure things were in place and I had my paperwork together. It was kind of dark in the rink and they hadn't even flipped the lights on above the rink. I was rummaging around in the locker room and, bam, five minutes after I got there, in the door walked Bobby Orr. I'd never met him before and we kind of exchanged greetings. He was very relaxed, very easy-going. He made you feel very much at ease.

"My two assistant coaches arrived a few minutes later and three of us tied on our skates, as did Bobby, and we spent about 15 minutes on the ice, passing the puck around and taking a few shots and kind of having a good time until the kids arrived on the ice. Then we were swarmed under by about 60 little kids. I have a very fond memory of that day."

Kelly says he did not see or talk to Orr again until he was asked to head the Eagleson investigation in 1991. "I'm sure when they asked me to handle this matter my superiors took into account that I was a person who was a hockey fan and a hockey coach," Kelly says. "To me, it was not a dry subject, but a very interesting subject. If I had not been a hockey and sports fan, I'm not sure how I'd react. But I love hockey and have taken a very keen interest in the case."

In Toronto, meanwhile, another lawyer took a keen interest in a different case that indirectly involved Eagleson. In 1990 a group of seven retired hockey players, led by former NHL defenceman Carl Brewer and including two of the greatest players in the history of the game, Gordie Howe and Bobby Hull, retained Mark Zigler to represent them in a lawsuit against the NHL over a dispute involving pension funds.

Two years later, Mr. Justice George Adams of the Ontario Court, agreed with the players that the NHL clubs and the NHL Pension Society had misappropriated a total of $21.1 million in surplus pension benefits in 1982 and 1986. He ruled that the money should have been reinvested in the players' pension plan. Most of the pension surplus was earned in the 1980s when annuities, bought to finance the pension plan, produced a higher rate of return than expected.

In the months that followed Justice Adams's October 22, 1992 decision, Eagleson's antagonists continued their pursuit. Conway was working on a second series, assisted by Bruce Dowbiggin of CBC, who had done a follow-up to Conway's first series. Brewer and Rich Winter, who had led the 1989 player revolt, pressed for a Canadian investigation, something the players had been asking for since 1990. Until its official announcement of an independent probe in January, 1993, the RCMP had been merely assisting the FBI in attempting to determine whether any criminal acts were committed in Canada by Eagleson, specifically with the pension funds.

The Eagleson antagonists charged that the RCMP, the Law Society of Upper Canada and various levels of law enforcement were dragging their feet, in effect stonewalling the process. In July, 1992, Winter sent a letter to Howard Hampton, then the attorney general of Ontario, complaining about the slow work of Thomas Lockwood, the acting senior counsel in charge of discipline for the Law Society of Upper Canada. Winter wrote: "Close to three years have passed since The Law Society received this complaint. Despite my ongoing advice to Mr. Lockwood that he investigate this matter thoroughly and expeditiously, he has not. For example, he did not travel to the United States until after the FBI announced its investigation and subpoenaed records (which) Mr. Lockwood could have had access to had he acted in a timely manner as he was advised to do initially. Also, on numerous occasions, I advised him of the fact documents may be being destroyed. He did not appear to act on this at all. His refusal to do so may have made it next to impossible for The Law Society to completely investigate this matter. Now, at this late stage, they may never be able to do so. In fact, he has yet to speak with virtually all of the witnesses I have suggested he contact.

"Basically, the investigation has proceeded as if a lawyer who proved himself influential is presumed innocent until the victims can display pictures of him at the scene of the crime."

In a sharply worded letter to Lockwood three months later, Winter wrote, "I continue to wait for you to question even a small number of the witnesses you have been invited to meet with by individuals such as Carl Brewer . . . as we approach entering the fourth year of The Law Society's 'so-called' investigation of this matter.

"In the three years since I filed my complaint, the Pittsburgh Penguins have won two Stanley Cups, Mario Lemieux has scored about 300 points, the Iron Curtain has fallen, and seven retired NHL players have had the time to retain legal counsel, commence a complex action against the National Hockey League, try the action and receive a favourable verdict."

If Lockwood was moving slowly, he was also keeping a low profile. In a column in *The Globe and Mail*, December 21, 1992, Stevie Cameron, a freelance investigative reporter, quoted Bruce Dowbiggin as saying Lockwood had failed to return "at least 20" of his telephone calls. Carl Brewer said he had left six unanswered messages. Cameron noted that Lockwood had not returned her calls, either. Immediately after Cameron's column appeared, Lockwood started taking his calls. He assured everyone that the investigation was, indeed, proceeding.

For his part, Brewer's chief concern was the limited scope of the RCMP's investigation into Eagleson's activities which, as far as the public knew, was restricted to assisting the FBI. Specifically, Brewer wanted the RCMP to probe Hockey Canada, the government supported non-profit agency controlled by Eagleson. At the very least, he wanted Hockey Canada to release its financial statements, something it had refused to do even though it was supported in part by public money.

In the fall of 1992, Brewer sought help from his member of parliament, Dennis Mills. In October, Mills sent letters to Pierre Cadieux, the minister of Fitness and Amateur Sport; Otto Jelinek, the minister of National Revenue and former minister of Sport;

and Kim Campbell, then minister of Justice and attorney general of Canada.

A few weeks later, Mills sent a copy of his letter to Doug Lewis, the solicitor general of Canada, asking him to look into the concerns of Brewer and other players. In a letter to Mills dated November 25, Lewis replied: "Thank you for providing me with a copy of your letter of October 23, 1992, addressed to the Honourable A. Kim Campbell, Minister of Justice and Attorney General of Canada, regarding your constituent, Mr. Carl Brewer, and his concerns about the various activities and relationships of former National Hockey League players with Hockey Canada.

"The Commissioner of the Royal Canadian Mounted Police (RCMP) has informed me that the RCMP . . . are currently reviewing your specific concerns. Once this review is completed, I will write to you again.

"I trust this information will be of assistance."

Mills and another Liberal MP, David Dingwall, of Cape Breton-East Richmond, decided not to wait for Lewis's next advisory. In December, in the House of Commons, Mills read a statement: "Madame Speaker, Hockey Canada had been involved in international hockey for 20 years. NHL players donate their service.

"I have asked several ministers repeatedly for the complete books and records of Hockey Canada: revenues, expenses, tax receipts, sponsorships, rinkboard advertising, et cetera.

"The U.S. government through the FBI has been gathering this information on Hockey Canada for three years. Why is the government of Canada not interested in satisfying the NHL players who were involved in these tournaments and who want to see the records?

"I believe taking three years to react on the Hockey Canada file is too long."

During question period, Dingwall followed up with a question to Pierre Cadieux: "The minister will know that today in Florida governors of the National Hockey League are discussing the future of the league, while in Canada, the hockey tradition, whether it be professional or amateur, goes on.

"However, many serious questions have been raised recently about the financial dealings of the non-profit federal agency Hockey Canada and certain individuals.

"I ask the minister responsible if the government will provide to this House a full financial disclosure other than the annual one-line item expenses and income reports for Hockey Canada since Hockey Canada has been incorporated?"

Kim Campbell chose to respond to the challenges: "Madame Speaker, I will take that question on behalf of my colleague, the solicitor general, who has indicated that this matter is currently being investigated by the RCMP. The government of Canada will offer no further information until the RCMP has concluded its investigation."

Campbell's implication that the RCMP was now independently investigating Eagleson and Hockey Canada was a point not lost on Bob Kilger, the Liberal MP of Stormont-Dundas in Ontario, and a former NHL referee, who said: "Madame Speaker, I welcome the minister of Justice telling the House that the RCMP have an ongoing and I would hope an independent operation and not simply an operation in conjunction with the FBI. I would like to ask the minister why the government has hidden the RCMP's involvement for so long in this matter?"

Pierre Cadieux replied: "Madame Speaker, I think my honourable colleague would know that the RCMP does not necessarily advertise the investigations it is undertaking."

The next day, Hockey Canada fired off a news release refuting the statements of Campbell and Cadieux. The agency said it was not being investigated by the RCMP, but it was cooperating with the joint FBI-RCMP probe of Eagleson. In an attempt to prevent further damage, the Hockey Canada board of directors met in Toronto on February 11, 1993, to decide if Eagleson should stay on as a board member. Eagleson survived the vote, but the board decided to conduct an internal investigation. Hockey Canada chairman H. Ian Macdonald also said that Eagleson's duties as a dealmaker in international hockey had been transferred to Hockey Canada president Ron Robison. Macdonald said that Hockey Canada was "tired of being perceived as a secret society with something to hide," and said it would open its books and financial records to the public.

The RCMP eventually did announce in February, 1993 that it had started its own independent probe of Eagleson, after which Mills met with an RCMP officer who asked him asked what had caused the perception the RCMP wasn't working on the case. Mills says he replied, "When you're given a file three years ago, and nothing seems to happen with it, and you pass it on to the Toronto fraud squad and nothing seems to happen there, and then there's a three-and-a-half-year delay in the investigation by the Law Society, after a while the hockey players thought the service was slow."

Hockey Canada's decision not to remove Eagleson as a board member raised eyebrows. Al Strachan, a sports columnist for *The Globe and Mail*, wrote: "Now that Hockey Canada has decided to keep Alan Eagleson on its board, the time has come to answer another question.

"Why should we keep Hockey Canada?

"After all, what does Hockey Canada do that the Canadian Amateur Hockey Association could not?

"The fact that the Hockey Canada board held a full meeting on Thursday and allowed Eagleson to stay on is a clear indication that it is out of touch with the realities of the hockey world. At the moment, Eagleson is under investigation by the RCMP, the FBI and the Law Society of Upper Canada.

"In the legal world, he's innocent until proved guilty and so he should be. But in the real world, he no longer has any clout or any real credibility. His presence on the Hockey Canada board is being portrayed as a matter of due process, but that's a red herring.

"The real question is whether in Eagleson, Hockey Canada has the best available person in the role of international negotiator. The simple answer is they do not. Whether it is legally just or not, Eagleson is no longer that person."

Strachan's column was relevant not so much for what it said, but that it had been written at all. For more than three years, the Canadian media, with the exception of the CBC in Toronto, had ignored the Eagleson story. However, Stevie Cameron's column in *The Globe and Mail* on December 21, 1992, had sounded an alarm when she wrote, "Tidings of comfort and joy are not on Canada's hockey agenda this winter. A hockey story that has been years in the making may well shake up the country within a few weeks."

A few weeks later, *The Globe* began its own investigation of Eagleson, racing to catch up with the collaborative effort of Conway and Dowbiggin, which was expected to run in mid-February. When it was learned that Conway's series would begin

Sunday, February 21, *The Globe* scheduled its release a day earlier. When Dowbiggin heard *The Globe* was starting its series on Saturday, he went on the air Friday night with the first part of his series.

All three news organizations led with the story that was viewed the most newsworthy and sensational — Eagleson's unusual business agreement with Peter Karmanos, the chairman and chief executive officer of Compuware Corp., a computer software company based in Farmington Hills, Michigan, a suburb of Detroit.

Karmanos is a millionaire and staunch hockey fan who has been attempting for several years to buy an NHL franchise. In October, 1988, he hired Eagleson to help him acquire a franchise. Karmanos told *The Globe*, "Eagleson helped us form a relationship with the league and helped us talk to a few teams about where they were at. . . . We got to know some people because of our relationship with Alan. . . . I thought and still think he was the finest guy to be representing us in that situation because of his abilities and contacts."

Eagleson's contacts included owners, such as Bill Wirtz, the chairman of the NHL's board of governors, and John Ziegler, who was then president of the league. Eagleson had an extremely close relationship with both men, as well as other NHL owners.

But, at the same time, Eagleson was also the head of the players' union. He was the person the players paid to negotiate the best possible collective contract for them with the club owners. Eagleson, in effect, was doing business with the people who were supposed to be his adversaries.

Karmanos says that Eagleson assured him the players knew of his involvement with Compuware and that they had given their consent. But neither *The Globe* nor *The Eagle-Tribune* could find any evidence of this. Two members of the NHLPA's executive at the time, Bobby Smith and Rick Vaive, said they had known nothing about Eagleson's involvement with Karmanos. Bryan Trottier, the NHLPA president at the time, refused to comment because similar questions had been asked of him when he had testified before the grand jury. Conway reported that 18 players, active at the time, whom he had contacted, knew nothing of Eagleson's deal with Karmanos.

When asked by *The Globe* about the Eagleson-Karmanos deal,

Vaive said, "This is completely new to me."

"I can't say I really knew anything about it," said Smith, who was a supporter of Eagleson and still defends his actions as head of the NHLPA.

As it turned out, Eagleson was unable to broker a deal between Karmanos and an owner willing to sell a team. But if he had, he would have earned a flat U.S.$1-million salary from Karmanos, as well as substantial bonuses determined by how much Karmanos had to pay for the team. The lower the price, the larger the bonus for Eagleson.

Lawyers noted that Eagleson's deal with Karmanos did not breach laws in Canada. But the notion of a union leader working in secret, without the knowledge of his membership, wheeling, dealing and wooing owners — the people he was supposed to go toe-to-toe with during labour negotiations — shocked many in and out of hockey. Paul Kelly, the U.S. prosecutor, says, "Most of the people I've spoken with, owners and players, were absolutely repulsed by this."

Eagleson's reaction to the Karmanos story was not reported. He did tell his friends in the media that the months of investigation had taken their toll in his family.

Elsewhere, things had not gone well for Chris Lang, Eagleson's old friend who was an original member of the Hockey Canada board and the agency's secretary general. *The Globe* reported that Hockey Canada paid out $926,000 for "consulting, management, secretarial and other office services" from 1989 to 1992 to at least two directors of the agency — Eagleson and Lang. H. Ian Macdonald told *The Globe*, "since [Eagleson's and Lang's] firms did provide management services of one kind or another, that's the only explanation I can think of, but I just don't know."

Lang, who had told *The Globe* that Hockey Canada should not say anything "until we get our stories straight," suffered a heart attack after the series ran. He spent March, 1993 in recovery. Also in March, Eagleson sent a letter of resignation to the board of Hockey Canada. In June, the directors accepted his resignation. In the months that followed, Eagleson stayed out of the public eye, awaiting the decision of the grand jury.

Chapter Two

THE LEGEND

ON A COLD DAY in February, 1993, Billy Harris, a former Maple Leaf player, met Alan Eagleson and his accountant Marvin Goldblatt by chance outside Eagleson's Maitland Street office in downtown Toronto. Eagleson and Goldblatt were on their way to lunch and asked Harris to join them. Harris, who had known Eagleson since the late 1950s when they had been business partners and friends, excused himself and said he had other plans. "I didn't want to have anything to do with him," Harris said later.

In 1959, Eagleson had included Harris in his first important hockey deal when he had set up the Blue and White Investment Group. Three other Leafs were in the group — Bob Pulford, Carl Brewer and Bobby Baun — along with two of Eagleson's law partners, Bob Watson and Irv Pasternak, as well as George Graham and Pat Savage of Ostranders Jewellers and Hearn Kerney of Hearn Pontiac. In addition to investing money in mortgages, the Blue and White group functioned as a social club in which businessmen had the privilege of rubbing shoulders with Leaf stars. For their part, the players, Eagleson included, got deals on cars as well as jewelry for their wives or girlfriends.

From the beginning, Eagleson impressed everyone with his skills as a deal-maker. He knew where to get a bargain, he knew every angle, how to make a buck and how to save a buck. He was brazen, bold and indefatigable. At an early age, he had told his parents he wanted to be a minister when he grew up. "Only, I won't make the sermons. I'll just collect the money and leave."

Robert Alan Eagleson was the third of four children and the only boy born to James Allen Eagleson, an immigrant mill worker from Northern Ireland, and his wife Agnes, in St. Catharines, Ont. The Eaglesons became enthusiastic followers of hockey soon after emigrating to Canada in 1930. Agnes often said the excitement of listening to Foster Hewitt describe Ken Doraty's historic overtime goal for the Leafs in the fifth overtime period in the 1933 playoffs brought on her labour and the birth of another hockey legend, young Alan — this despite a three-week gap between Doraty's goal on April 3 and the baby's arrival on April 24.

In Deidra Clayton's 1982 Eagleson biography, she described young Al's hard upbringing, which was underlined by Agnes's Irish Protestant principle of "potatoes and pointing." The family members at the dinner table could eat as many potatoes as they wanted, but only the breadwinners got the meat, which usually meant the men. There are few better motivators than an empty stomach, and Alan, who grew up poor, vowed at an early age that he would someday make a name for himself.

As a child, he was neither significant in status nor stature. He was small and scrawny, but mouthy, and he would regularly come home in tears after getting in fights with the neighbourhood kids. He fantasized about becoming a boxer and fighting under the name "The Eagle," but his mother dismissed the notion saying he was too small, although she conceded that he looked a little like a bird. The nickname "Eagle" would stay with Al for the rest of his life. Eagleson might have been overmatched in the school yard, but in the classroom, few could compete with "Wee Alan." He finished his lessons quickly and was accelerated twice in elementary school. At the age of 14 he weighed only 80 pounds, but was already in grade 11. One of his high school teachers described Al as precocious, but boastful and "mischievous."

"If the rest of the class took 30 minutes to do an assignment, it only took Alan five," said Marguerite Weir. "Then he would clown. He would even stand on his desk. . . . He had to get attention some way and he certainly couldn't get it on the football field or with girls. . . . He simply couldn't compete."

That didn't stop Eagleson from getting involved in other sports both as a participant and an organizer. After the family moved to New Toronto in Metropolitan Toronto's west end, Al swam and worked at Gus Ryder's famous Lakeshore Swim Club which included swimmers Marilyn Bell and Cliff Lumsdon. One of his jobs was to look after the transportation of the students to swim class, collecting the money for the bus as they got on. Young Al was able to negotiate a group rate for the passengers and reward himself with a commission.

"He was a regular little monopolizer," his mother told Clayton. "If a kid showed up without his money a second time, Alan took it upon himself not to let him on the bus."

By the time Al finished high school, he had his goals clearly set. He wanted status, power and fame. He once said, "Whenever I read in the society pages of the newspapers about the wealthy sons going to Ridley College or Upper Canada College, I pledged to myself: I'll get a crack at you guys one day."

Al viewed law school as a level playing field and one that would send him on the road to success and wealth. But it also meant hard work and sacrifices. He worked for a year after graduating from high school and supported himself while at the University of Toronto by assisting his father in cleaning oil furnaces.

In 1954, he graduated from the University of Toronto with a B.A. and then stayed at the university to study law. It was a dynamic and pivotal time in the history of the University of Toronto law school. The faculty included giants in the field of law such as Bora Laskin, later to become chief justice of the Supreme Court of Canada, and Cecil (Caesar) Wright, a brilliant legal scholar who had left hallowed Osgoode Hall to set up the breakaway school at the U of T. Wright waged war against Osgoode which tried to dominate his upstart law school and feuded with the Law Society of Upper Canada, requiring U of T law graduates to attend Osgoode Hall for a year before they could be admitted to the Bar. In this atmosphere, Eagleson and the other students at the U of T saw themselves as rebels and bonded in a spirit of common cause.

At university, Eagleson was no longer a scrawny, undersized child, but a strong young man, 5-foot-10 and a muscular 170 pounds. In his autobiography, Eagleson wrote, "University days were a dream come true for me. I had been small for my age . . . and suddenly felt invincible." Eagleson's sense of invincibility not only meant defending himself, but also playing the role of an aggressor. It was as if he were waging war against, or paying back, the bullies, particularly the athletes, who had made life miserable for him as a child.

Robert Mackay, a friend of Eagleson's and at the time a lecturer at the U of T law school, told David Cruise and Alison Griffiths, the authors of *Net Worth*, that he would occasionally give Eagleson a ride to school. On one occasion, after a car passed them a great speed, Mackay caught up to it at an intersection. Suddenly, Eagleson jumped out of Mackay's car and pounded on the driver's window. When the driver made the mistake of rolling down the window, Eagleson punched him several times and ran back to the car.

Mackay recalled another attack sparked by a motorist cutting Eagleson off. Eagleson followed and at the first stop, leapt out, dragged the offender out of the car window and beat him. He then calmly walked back to the car and drove away.

Eagleson had a different version of the story when interviewed by *The Globe and Mail* in 1991. "Can you imagine pulling a guy out of the front window of his car and hitting him? Can you imagine pulling a guy out of the front window of a car when he's under the steering wheel? I don't give a shit how small he is. It makes a great story. I don't remember that I might have grabbed him or I might have punched him, but I didn't bring him out the window."

Al was heavily involved in university athletics and many of his battles were fought on or near the playing field. Lacrosse was his best sport and one day he arrived at U of T's Hart House, with other players, for a practice. When a group of basketball players showed no sign of leaving the court, Eagleson shouted that the "faggot" basketball players had better hand over the gym. One of them said, "Where's you're permit?" Eagleson marched up to him and decked him. As the basketball player laid on the floor, Eagleson stepped over him and said, "There's my permit."

Bob Watson, a schoolmate and former law partner of Eagleson, told Cruise and Griffiths, "Al told me that he worked on the premise that if you hit them with everything you had with the first blow, they really questioned coming back at you."

Eagleson's pugilistic nature didn't end at graduation. There was an incident a few years later at a Leaf game with some friends of Bob Pulford. When Eagleson heard a fan booing Pulford, he exchanged words with the needler after which he took off his glasses, handed them to someone in his group, and then leapt at the man's throat.

Even after Eagleson became a famous hockey promoter, there were fisticuffs. In 1984, during Team Canada's training camp for the Canada Cup hockey tournament, Eagleson and some associates went to dinner at a posh restaurant in Banff, Alberta. When Eagleson's loud profanities upset a man and a woman at a nearby table, the man asked Eagleson to desist. Words were exchanged and a fight broke out. In 1987, there was a confrontation in the stands of the Eisenstad in Vienna during the world hockey championship.

Despite Eagleson's aggressiveness, he wasn't viewed by everyone as a brawling misfit. His friends saw him as resourceful, ambitious and sometimes charming. His roots as a sports organizer can be easily traced to the U of T where, among other things, he managed the senior basketball Varsity Blues, headed the lacrosse committee, coached a lacrosse team and the varsity girls' lacrosse team.

Managing the basketball team, which spent 26 days a year in Florida in training, was a plum assignment that Eagleson pursued with vigour. To get the job he needed to win over the basketball coach John McManus. Included in Eagleson's campaign for the job was cleaning, for free, McManus's furnace. "He was a belligerent little rooster, but he knew how to handle a dollar," McManus said. "When he went into a hotel everything was taken care of right away — the rooms, meals, everything."

When the team was in Florida, it stayed near a beach. During the day, Eagleson would collect a dollar from each sunbather for a party that night. He would use the money to buy pop and chips, and then pocket a percentage of his take. Once when the team was in New York, he devised a way to save money by cramming six players in a cab from the airport, even though the legal limit was four. He would grab a cab at the end of the line and shove in two players. When it got to the front, four more jumped in. Snowbound on a train between Buffalo and Rochester, Eagleson had the players singing Christmas carols, after which a collection was taken, apparently, for a charity.

In the summers, he ran carnival games at country fairs in

Southern Ontario. He guessed ages and weights and ran bingo games. Once, at the Woodbridge Fair, he took wedding gifts belonging to one of his sisters, who was on her honeymoon, unwrapped them and displayed them as prizes at his booth. Winners were given cheaper merchandise and, at the end of the day, the gifts were returned and re-wrapped.

Eagleson told *The Globe and Mail* in 1991, "Guessing weights and ages were the easiest games to win. You have to come within two years or three pounds. It sounds that way but you really have five years and you have seven pounds because you've got three on either side. If you're careful you don't lose any big prizes. Even then, you have a series of big prizes and a series of little prizes and you try to make sure everybody wins a little prize. For a week at the Western Fair and two weeks at the CNE, I could make $2,000. That was big money in the 1955, '56, '57."

At an early age, Eagleson cultivated contacts and friends, one of whom was an usher at Varsity Blues and Argonaut games. With the help of the usher, he devised a way of sneaking into the Argo games, with his friends, by using an usher's arm band. Once in, the intruder would toss the arm band over the fence for the next free admission.

When Eagleson was called to the Bar in 1959, his chutzpah and bravado not only landed him a job but a partnership, something quite unusual for a graduating law student, with J.D.W. Cumberland, Queen's Counsel, in New Toronto. A year later, he married Nancy Fisk of Collingwood, Ont., whom he had met at the U. of T. Nancy majored in physical education and taught school after graduation. In 1961, the Eaglesons had their first child, Trevor Allen, and in 1964 their second and last, Jill.

Al didn't last long at Cumberland's law firm. He was there only a year before joining Bob Watson and three other young lawyers in Blaney, Pasternak, Smela, Eagleson and Watson. Like Watson, Smela had played lacrosse with Eagleson.

He began his career in law as a general practitioner, dealing with police court cases, traffic violations and probating wills, gradually spending an increasing amount of time in real estate, processing mortgages and practicing re-zoning law. The Blue and White Investment Group was a product of Eagleson's interest in real estate and dealt mostly with mortgages. A large part of Eagleson's future wealth would be tied up in real estate investments.

In the early 1960s, Eagleson's two passions were hockey and politics, and not necessarily in that order. His fascination with politics was whetted in university by the 1957 victory of John Diefenbaker's Progressive Conservative Party ending 22 years of Liberal government. Eagleson called the Diefenbaker-led Tories, "a beautiful ride 'em cowboy contrast to old-line stuffed-shirt Liberals who'd been in power so long they treated it as their divine right."

In 1962, he became friendly with John Hamilton, who was the federal Tory MP for his riding, York West, and agreed to work for him in the federal election that year. Red Kelly, a standout for the Maple Leafs and Detroit Red Wings, captured the riding for the Liberals, but the Tories did win the four seats for which Eagleson and his workers had canvassed.

Diefenbaker's minority government lasted only a year, and for the 1963 federal election the Tories asked Eagleson to run against Kelly. Eagleson agreed, but his decision split the Maple Leaf hockey club down party lines. Harold Ballard, who was one of the three principal owners of the club, had known Eagleson from his lacrosse days and actively supported him during the campaign. So did the members of the Blue and White Investment Group — Pulford, Harris, Baun and Brewer. Other members of the Leafs worked for Kelly, who won easily.

The defeat did not lessen Eagleson's interest in politics, and when he was asked a few months later to run provincially for the Progressive Conservatives in the new riding of Lakeshore, which included Eagleson's old stomping grounds of New Toronto, he agreed. The working-class area had been Tory country for years, but Eagleson, in his biography, portrayed himself as the underdog because of New Toronto's union ties.

Still, Eagleson had a high profile in the riding because of his activities in local athletics. It didn't hurt that his father was a union steward at the local Goodyear plant and, of course, Eagleson had been busy attempting to improve the lot of professional hockey players. While Eagleson campaigned, his law partners covered for him at the firm and wrote political speeches for him.

Bob Watson told Deidra Clayton, "We literally subsidized him for several years while he did virtually everything but practice law . . . certainly as long as he was in politics."

During his 1963 campaign, Eagleson also enlisted the help of a local youth lacrosse team. He told them that if they agreed to hand out pamphlets he would treat them at the Dairy Queen when they were finished.

"We took 'em, went door to door, handing those pamphlets out. Every one of them, too," recalled Tom McKean, who is now a Toronto dentist. "At five o'clock, we were at the ice cream stand waiting for him. He never showed up. Just left us there waiting. I never forgot that."

Eagleson won the 1963 election and served in the Ontario legislature until 1967. He quickly became a member of a group of Tory backbench hecklers dubbed the "Chicago Gang" by Vern Singer, the Liberal deputy leader from Downsview. During his four years, he was regarded a liberal MPP. He supported legalized abortion, interfaith adoption and divorce reform.

In 1967, Eagleson was defeated by New Democratic Party candidate Pat Lawlor. On election night, Al's wife Nancy was interviewed, and the next day was quoted in the newspapers as saying, "The reason my husband lost was the Lakeshore has too many poor people." After that comment, there was no need for Eagleson to run again in that riding, although he stayed active in the party, serving as president of the Ontario Progressive Conservative Association and later as a high-profile fundraiser. By the mid-to-late 1960s, however, he was devoting more and more time to his principal line of work — the representation of professional hockey players.

Eagleson's entry into the world of professional hockey was facilitated by Bob Pulford; they had been chums since childhood in New Toronto. Their families were friendly and Bob and Al had played for the same Ontario Lacrosse Association team, the Woodbridge Dodgers. After Pulford joined the Leafs, he introduced Al to his Leaf teammates and the young lawyer quickly became part of the inner circle. He socialized with the players, provided legal services, occasionally *pro bono*, recommended investments and, of course, advised them as to where they could get a deal.

Billy Harris, who lived next door to the Eaglesons in the Toronto suburb of Etobicoke in the 1960s, remembers Al as being aggressive and dominant in social gatherings. "He was loud and his language was unbelievable," Harris said. "He was incapable of speaking softly and his profanity often got him into trouble. I know at one time, three or four of the very popular restaurants in downtown Toronto told him they didn't want to see him again. I was always afraid he might drop by the house when my mother was visiting. That's a real fear I had."

In an interview with *The Globe* in 1991, Eagleson said he didn't think his swearing was any more frequent than that of an average professional athlete. "I think a lot of it came from sports. It's because I'm not a professional athlete and that I adopt the language in other spheres, that people jump back. To me it's just accentuated slang. . . . I can control it, I can turn it on and off. I wish I could control my temper the way I control my language."

By 1964, Eagleson and his law partners were doing legal work for at least half the Leaf team — providing advice on contract negotiations behind the scenes, investing money or simply offering general legal services. Carl Brewer became particularly close to Eagleson, and after Al and Nancy had their second child, Jill, Carl and his wife accepted the Eaglesons' request that they be her godparents.

Brewer, a star defenceman with the Leafs, was not a typical player of his era. He was inquisitive, was rebellious and fought several times with the Leafs' coach and general manager, Punch Imlach, over his contract.

When the Leafs refused to reward Brewer for being voted to the NHL's first All-Star team in 1962-63, Eagleson advised him to quit hockey and enroll in university courses at McMaster University in Hamilton. After seeing a photo of Brewer in a McMaster football uniform, the Leafs dispatched King Clancy, Imlach's assistant, to make peace with Carl and settle up.

A year later, Brewer quit the Leafs again and returned to school after the club refused to compensate him for being unable to work during the summer because of an injury suffered during the hockey season. Again, the Leafs blinked and Brewer was duly compensated.

By the summer of '65, Brewer's hockey career in Toronto was almost over. Imlach refused to negotiate with Eagleson while Brewer insisted that Al was his representative in contract negotiations.

"Can he play hockey?" Imlach asked Brewer one day.

"No," said Brewer, with a trace of condescension. "He's a lawyer."

"If he can play hockey, I'll talk to him," snapped Imlach. "If he can't, I'm not wasting my time talking to him."

During the Imlach-Brewer confrontations, Eagleson boasted

that there were two names Imlach particularly hated to hear —
his and Brewer's.

Finally, at the start of the 1965-66 season Brewer decided to
retire permanently and enrolled at the University of Toronto,
where he earned a B.A. Imlach said later that Eagleson was to
blame for Brewer's shortened career in Toronto. "He (Brewer)
needed somebody who instead of aggravating his problem would
cool his problems down. But this guy Eagleson aggravated the
problems, made them bigger. I mean, the game itself aggravated
Brewer enough without having somebody standing behind him
always giving him the rebel treatment."

Brewer, however, says it was his decision to leave the Leafs,
not Eagleson's. "All the ideas I've ever had have been my own. . .
A few lackeys have followed around behind Eagleson, but my
ideas justify playing the game under Punch Imlach. . . . That was
it. At that time I didn't want to ever play again."

Brewer jumped from one field of battle to another by asking for
reinstatement as an amateur so he could play hockey for Canada's
national team. With the help of Eagleson, he did win his amateur
status which allowed him to play for Father Bauer's Canadian
team at the world hockey championships in 1966 and 1967.

Eagleson's contribution to Brewer's petition for amateur status is debatable. Brewer says Al provided mostly "moral support." The key player, says Brewer, was his own father-in-law, W.
Harold Rea, a prominent Toronto businessman with important
friends in Ottawa and in amateur sport. In 1968, Rea was one of
three people appointed by federal Health and Welfare minister
John Munro to a task force on sport, along with skier Nancy
Greene and Quebec physician Paul Desruisseaux. One of their
objectives was to inquire about and report on the "prevailing
concepts and definitions of both amateur and professional sport
in Canada and the effect of pro sport on amateur sport."

During Brewer's self-imposed exile, he earned a university
degree. In terms of money, he ended up making more in 1967-68
as the player-coach for Muskegon of the International Hockey
League, which was semi-pro but officially amateur, than most
NHL players. Brewer's salary that year was $22,000 which was
well above the NHL average of $15,000.

At the end of that season, he returned to Toronto, called
Eagleson, and over dinner at the Granite Club in Toronto told

him he would no longer be retaining as an agent. There were no hard feelings on Brewer's part. He simply felt that he could now adequately represent himself. Eagleson's response, however, puzzled Brewer.

"He almost begged me to not say anything bad about him to other players," Brewer says. "He said he was just getting started in the business of representing players, and if players heard I had been unhappy with him, it would hurt his business. This surprised me because I had no complaints. I always wondered what he was concerned about."

.   Eagleson's attitude toward players has always a subject of debate. When, in 1984, he told *Sports Illustrated*, "we're not dealing with a series of Einsteins," in referring to hockey players, many felt that was Al's honest appraisal of the men upon whom he had built his empire.

Billy Harris feels Eagleson *did* respect the members of the Blue and White Group. After all, they were a cut above the average player — Brewer, Pulford and Harris had earned university degrees. "We had gone to university and could speak to him at his level," Harris says. But generally, says Harris, "Eagleson looked down on hockey players. I think underneath he thought we were all a bunch of dummies."

Harris's friendship with Eagleson ended in the fall of 1967 after a late night phone call from Eagleson. That summer, Harris had been acquired by the Oakland Seals, one of several former Maple Leaf players to join the team. Bert Olmstead, the Seals' coach and general manager, asked Eagleson to survey players he knew to find out what they wanted to be paid.

This, in itself, was a curious role for Eagleson to play — working for team management while, at the same time, acting as head of the newly formed players' union, the National Hockey League Players' Association. Frank Selke, Jr., who was the president of the Seals that year, says he doesn't recall whether Eagleson was formally retained by the club or if he was working for Olmstead.

Harris recalls, "I got the phone call from Al about eleven-thirty at night, and we talked for about five minutes. He said Olmstead had eight or nine guys from the Toronto area on the team, guys like Baun and Wally Boyer, and he wanted to get some idea of what kind of money we were hoping to make.

"I told him I had made $18,000 the year before in Detroit and I was aiming for $25,000 a year for two years."

During the Seals' training camp in Port Huron, Michigan, Harris met twice with Olmstead over his contract and once more in Oakland before signing. Eagleson did not advise Harris on his contract and, in fact, had never been retained by Harris to represent him. Harris had always negotiated his own deals.

Eagleson did not even inform Harris that Baun, whom he had also called, was asking for (and received) a $70,000 annual deal from Oakland. Had Harris known that, he would have asked for more than $25,000.

In November of that year, Harris received a bill from Eagleson for $750. Given that Eagleson was on the phone with Harris for five minutes, his legal fees worked out to $8,000 an hour. But Harris had not retained Eagleson, and on the night the call was made, Eagleson had phoned Harris, not the other way around.

Harris says, "On my first trip back east, I phoned him and said 'What's going on here? I negotiated my own contract.' He hemmed and hawed. He said, 'Put 100 bucks in the mail and we'll forget the whole thing.' I didn't send him anything, but I'd like to know what kind of bill he submitted to the Oakland Seals. He was working on their behalf."

As for Brewer, he eventually returned to the NHL after playing a year in Finland in 1968-69. He spent a season in Detroit and another in St. Louis with the Blues. He would come out of retirement one more time, in 1979, to play for the Leafs. Then, in 1980 there was a final, bitter severance with Eagleson. As the 1980s progressed, Brewer would rival Bobby Orr for the role of Eagleson's chief antagonist. Billy Harris says of Brewer, "I don't know anybody who wants to see Eagleson assassinated more than Carl."

Of the original Leafs in the Blue and White Investment Group, only Pulford kept Eagleson as his agent, and they remained friends. It was a fortuitous relationship for both. Pulford became the first president of the NHLPA. He played out the final two years of his hockey career in Los Angeles with the Kings before taking over as coach in 1972. In 1977, Eagleson negotiated a deal that made Pulford coach and general manager of the Chicago Blackhawks. Pulford remains the team's general manager.

Eagleson has enjoyed a warm and mutually supportive relationship not only with Pulford, but also with Blackhawk owner Bill Wirtz, for a long time the most powerful member of the NHL's board of governors. The fact that Wirtz faced Eagleson from the opposite side of the table in collective bargaining negotiations over a period of 20 years did not diminish the relationship. If anything, that friendship only deepened.

Chapter Three

THE EMANCIPATOR

THE CRITICS OF R. Alan Eagleson offer an account of the National Hockey League that cannot be found in any authorized history or official record book. It is the story of professional hockey players who for years were poorly paid, who had no rights or any means of representation. They were ruled by autocrats — greedy, hypocritical businessmen, some of whom associated with criminals or were themselves felons.

But then a saviour arrived. He organized the players. They formed a union. The players rallied behind their leader to fight for their rights. But, as the years passed, the players saw only marginal gains. The emancipator, the man who was supposed to liberate them, had failed. The prospect of freedom had been only an illusion.

At the time Eagleson and his supporters founded the National Hockey League Players' Association in 1967, players were without the rights most workers outside of professional sport take for granted. When a player signed a standard player's contract, he was an NHL club's property until the club decided otherwise. The "reserve clause" of the contract stipulated that a player belonged to his NHL team for life, even after retirement, unless traded to another team. If a player was unhappy with the amount of money he was offered in a contract, he could not take his services to another team. He could either accept what was on the table, hope that he was traded, or quit.

Players also could be demoted on the whim of a coach or manager, and performance was not necessarily the determining factor. In the 1960s, an award-winning defenceman was demoted after he began dating an usherette who had been sleeping with the team's coach. He was powerless to stop the demotion or seek another opportunity with another team.

Players, as set out in the standard player's contract, also were obligated to promote the club. In 1957, Maple Leaf Gardens Ltd., was paid $9,300 from the St. Lawrence Starch Company and the Parkhurst Bubble Gum Company for the rights to the Leaf players' pictures. The players received nothing. But if players decided to moonlight by charging for public appearances or sponsoring products, they needed "written consent from the club."

If a player found himself in trouble, there was no due process or union to advise him. He appeared, unrepresented, before the NHL president, who was hired and paid by the owners, and the president decided the player's fate. In 1948, president Clarence Campbell suspended Don Gallinger and Billy Taylor from the NHL for life for allegedly gambling on games when, at the same time, the two most powerful owners in the league were notorious gamblers.

Conn Smythe, the principal owner of the Maple Leafs, boasted for years that he had doubled his severance pay from the New York Rangers by betting on horses, the gains from which provided him with enough money to head a group that bought the Toronto franchise. A few years later Smythe acquired King Clancy, a star defenceman with the Ottawa Senators, for $35,000 by using winnings from a bet on a long-shot horse called, ironically enough, Rare Jewel.

Smythe was a tough, snarling dictator who usually got his way in league matters. But in the 1930s and 1940s, the most powerful family in hockey was the Norris clan, headed by patriarch Jim Norris. Big Jim wielded more control over the NHL than any other owner before or since. Indeed, no proprietor in any North American sports league has ever exercised such dominance.

Norris virtually controlled four NHL teams. He owned outright the Detroit Red Wings and Chicago Blackhawks and their arenas. He was the principal owner of Madison Square Garden and the Rangers. And he controlled the Boston Bruins and Boston Garden through unpaid loans made to Bruins' owner Charles

Adams. Big Jim and his son Jimmy were also heavy gamblers who controlled professional boxing in the United States for the better part of three decades, and who counted among their friends some of the most notorious crime figures in America.

Norris, whose Canadian family had accumulated wealth from shipping on the Great Lakes, made his fortune as a grain speculator on the trading floor of the Chicago Board of Trade building. He expanded his empire to include railways, real estate and cattle, and eventually sports and entertainment. By the 1930s, he was among the wealthiest men in the United States.

To run his entertainment division, in the 1930s Norris teamed up with Arthur Wirtz of Chicago, who had accumulated significant wealth of his own in real estate. Together, Wirtz and Norris either bought or promoted circus acts, such as Ringling Bros. and Cole Bros. Circus, as well as ice shows and countless vaudeville productions.

Norris's acquisition of arenas facilitated his move into boxing, where he quickly became a major figure. In 1935 he showed how powerful he was by unilaterally moving the centre of boxing from New York to Chicago where he hired matchmakers Nate Lewis and Jim Mullen to arrange fights. In a period of only four months, Lewis and Mullen set up four championship fights in Chicago and one in Detroit.

By the late 1940s, Big Jim, now in semi-retirement, was succeeded by his son, James D. (Jimmy) Norris, who had few of his father's business smarts but shared his love of gambling and boxing. In 1949, Jimmy, along with Arthur Wirtz and Joe Louis, solidified the Norris control over boxing by forming the International Boxing Club, based at Madison Square Garden.

By 1951, IBC owned or managed almost every important boxer in the United States. It also packaged the television deals and sold the rights. If IBC didn't own the fights outright, friends of Jimmy Norris did. For example, crime figures Blinky Palermo and Frankie Carbo owned lightweight champion Ike Williams; Eddie Coco controlled Rocky Graziano; and Carbo controlled Jake LaMotta.

By the early 1950s, Jimmy Norris was known as "Mr. Big" in boxing. By 1954, he had been accused of fight fixing, consorting with known criminals and operating a monopoly. But only one charge was laid, an anti-trust suit, and it was thrown out of court.

Through all of this, Jimmy insisted his first love was hockey and he would take a Stanley Cup championship ahead of a boxing crown any day.

At NHL board of governors' meetings, owners grew accustomed to seeing mob figures hanging around the halls waiting for their pal Jimmy to come out. One of Norris's friends was described as "a tall, slender, bespectacled man with the mien of a minister and the voice of a confessor." The man booked rooms for Norris, stayed by his side, ordered drinks and arranged female companionship. His name was Sammy (Golfbag) Hunt, a notorious hitman from the Al Capone era who earned his nickname apparently from toting a machine gun in a golfbag and yelling "Fore" before each execution.

Another Norris pal was Frankie Carbo, with whom he partied, gambled and did business. Carbo, as a member of Murder Inc., had helped Ben (Bugsy) Siegel execute in 1939 Harry Greenberg, who had been threatening to turn state's evidence on Siegel. Later, in one of the most famous gangland killings, Carbo murdered Siegel in his Hollywood home on orders from Mafia bosses Meyer Lansky and Lucky Luciano.

After Jimmy Norris's death 1965 (of natural causes), Arthur Wirtz assumed complete control of the Chicago Blackhawks and immediately appointed his son, Bill Wirtz, president of the club. In the 1970s, and until his death in 1983, it was rarely mentioned on the sports pages that Arthur had been a partner in the infamous International Boxing Club and had associated with and cut deals with major U.S. crime figures. Instead, he was referred to as a wealthy Chicago real estate investor. The Wirtz family, with an estimated wealth in the billions, regularly made *Fortune*'s list of the wealthiest families in the United States.

In Detroit, Big Jim's other son and Jimmy's half-brother, Bruce Norris, owned the Detroit Red Wings from the mid-1950s to 1982 when he sold the team to Mike Ilitch, the owner of Little Caesars pizza chain. Bruce was a weak man and heavy drinker who presided over the downfall of a once-great franchise and squandered most of his $200-million inheritance before his death in 1986. His most significant contribution to the NHL was recommending John A. Ziegler, Jr., a Detroit lawyer and the Red Wings' chief legal counsel, as Clarence Campbell's replacement as president.

In the 1960s and 1970s, Arthur Wirtz's closest friend among the owners was Harold Ballard of the Toronto Maple Leafs. Although there was no evidence that Ballard associated with mobsters, he was, himself, a convicted felon. In 1971, both Ballard and his business partner Stafford Smythe, the co-owner of the Gardens and son of Conn Smythe, were charged with income tax evasion as well as multiple counts of fraud and theft in connection with alleged improprieties as officers of Maple Leaf Gardens Ltd. Smythe died of stomach cancer before his day in court, but Ballard stood trial and was convicted of 47 of 49 counts of fraud and theft. He was sentenced to three, three-year concurrent prison terms, of which he served one year. In the 1950s, Conn Smythe also had problems with the federal revenue department, but was never charged.

Today, Big Jim Norris, sons Jimmy and Bruce, Arthur Wirtz and Harold Ballard are all honoured members of the Hockey Hall of Fame.

With Ziegler's coronation in 1977, it came to pass that the two most important powerbrokers in the NHL during the 1970s and 1980s were Bill Wirtz, the chairman of the NHL's board of governors, and John Ziegler, the new president. It was not a coincidence that both owed their rise to power to one family.

The NHL's third kingpin during this period had taken a different route. Instead of owning a club, he controlled the players. But in terms of influence, Alan Eagleson matched or perhaps even surpassed both Wirtz and Ziegler.

Eagleson became a hero to players when he went to war against Eddie Shore in 1966. Shore had been a brilliant but brutal defenceman with the Boston Bruins in the 1920s and 1930s, and had permanently maimed several players during his career, one of them Ace Bailey, an All-Star forward with the Maple Leafs. Shore ended Bailey's career in 1933 when he sneaked up behind him and knocked him to the ice. The back of Bailey's head smashed against the hard surface and he almost died during brain surgery.

In 1939, Shore bought the Springfield Indians of the American Hockey League and quickly became prominent, not only as an innovator, but also as a somewhat sadistic eccentric. He taught goaltenders how to "visualize," stopping imaginary pucks and he used tap dancing as a training device. But he also initiated bizarre and torturous training regimens such as using rope to hobble players whom he thought were skating with their legs too far apart. When he felt one goaltender was falling to the ice too often, he tied a rope around his neck and fastened it to the rafters above the net.

But what most upset the players on the Indians was Shore's ministrations as the team's self-appointed medical expert. When a player, who suffered a deep cut in his knee, was told by doctors to stay in the hospital for four days and wait several weeks before skating, Shore ordered the player to immediately rejoin the team on threat of being fired. After another player had fractured his ribs, Shore refused to let him get an X-ray. Then there was the player who was sidelined with a double fracture to the jaw and told by Shore to attend practice and made to pull a jersey over his plaster head cast.

In *Net Worth*, the authors reported the story of goaltender Jacques Caron who had a fist-fight with Shore when he was refused a trip home to visit his sick wife. Caron was also subjected to extreme abuse. Caron said, "When I first arrived in Springfield, I took a size 13 skate. This was interfering with my leg exercises and tap-dancing, according to Mr. Shore, because they were too large. I was given a pair of skates size 11 and thus lost all my toenails when I stopped a shot with my skates." Four years later, when Caron could barely walk, Shore agreed to let him wear a size 13 skate.

In December, 1966, Shore had a full-scale uprising on his hands after he suspended three defencemen: Bill White, Dale Rolfe and Dave Amadio. The three players had held out at training camp for more money and, to their surprise, Shore had given it to them. But a few weeks before Christmas, Shore suspended the three for "indifferent play," which didn't affect the team's standing because the team was off for seven days. It did mean, however, the players would not be getting paid for a week, which basically nullified their raise at training camp.

In a move of solidarity, all the players on the team walked out. Shore countered by bringing in replacements and then sued the striking players for breach of contract. The strikers were unsure of their next move, but during a meeting Bill White suggested contacting Eagleson, "the guy who had signed Bobby Orr and did the Brewer thing."

Eagleson immediately agreed to fly to Springfield with two of his law partners, Ray Smela and Bob Watson, to meet the players. They told Eagleson what they wanted from Shore: to be reinstated; to have new equipment to replace Shore's ancient hand-me-downs; and to have the right to visit a doctor if they were hurt. Eagleson had them swear out affidavits outlining Shore's mistreatment.

According to Shore's nephew, Jack Butterfield, who was the team's general manager and also the acting president of the American Hockey League, Eagleson never did meet directly with Shore. Instead, Butterfield acted as the go-between. To the players, Butterfield issued the threat of expulsion from the league if they stayed out. When he met Shore, he begged him to reconsider his hard line, reminding him that his health was poor and if he died the players would win by default anyway.

Suddenly and unexpectedly, Shore resigned as president of the club and Eagleson, not surprisingly, was hailed as the shining knight who had slain the dragon by newspaper reports of the day. But it wasn't that way at all. The credit, although somewhat suspect, is Butterfield's. (The three defencemen were allowed to return, but the players did not receive new equipment and the club's medical services were not improved.) When Shore got around to resigning, he promoted his 20-year-old son Ted from team errand-runner to president, an obvious signal from Shore that nothing had really changed. He was still running the show.

That summer, Shore sold the team to Jack Kent Cooke, the owner of the expansion team Los Angeles Kings which, to Eagleson, was confirmation that he had been instrumental in removing Shore from the game. Eagleson told Deidra Clayton, "I ended up negotiating Shore's retirement. Getting Shore and Butterfield out of hockey (Butterfield was until 1993 president of the AHL) was the best thing that ever happened to it."

But, as it turned out, Shore had cut the deal with Cooke in November, 1966, one month before the December players' strike. Years later, just to make a point, perhaps, Shore bought the team back from Cooke, ran it for a year and then resold it. Still, the time that Eagleson had spent working on the Eddie Shore case had been well worth it. His combined legal fees from the players on the Springfield Indians amounted to $6,000.

Eagleson's role in facing down Shore also heightened his profile in the hockey world and set the stage for his most important achievement, the formation of the National Hockey League Players' Association. It would be, or appear to be, mutually beneficial. The players would finally have the support of a union and they, in turn, would serve as Eagleson's base of support, giving him unprecedented power within the NHL and also in international hockey.

The year 1967 was ripe for change. The old six-team era was over, the league was doubling in size, and the grip of the NHL owners seemed to be loosening. Eagleson's move to organize a union followed a decade of bitterness and resentment that had been sparked by the NHL's success in busting a short-lived players' association in 1957.

The players' movement of 1957 had been initiated by Ted Lindsay, the Detroit Red Wings' captain and one of the superstars of his era. When Lindsay, with help from Doug Harvey of the Montreal Canadiens, looked into forming an association, his first move was to meet with two New York labour lawyers, Norman J. Lewis and Milton Mound, who had negotiated a contract on behalf of the baseball players. After hearing Lindsay's recounting of labour relations in the NHL, Lewis called the players' plight "Plain and simple indentured servitude. Conditions far worse than any other sport."

Thirty years later, Mound told the authors of *Net Worth* that hockey in the 1950s was, "Outrageously corrupt, outrageously wrong — far worse than baseball. Hockey was so medieval it was as if it were a dynasty. When you were born, you were already indentured to the lord and he could tell them what they had to and what they shouldn't do. The fellow who was the president of the team was God to them."

In addition to the constraints of the standard player's contract, the hockey players in the 1950s were grossly underpaid considering the revenue the owners were making from the gate and in broadcasting. Bruce Norris, as owner of the Detroit Olympia and the Red Wings, earned profits during the 1950s of $2 million a year from the operation of the Red Wings as well as the arena. Five of the league's six arenas consistently sold out — Chicago Stadium being the exception — and television revenue was already increasing on a yearly basis. During the 1955-56 season, for example, CBS paid the NHL's four American teams a total of $100,000 for televising 10 games. Hockey was a hit in most U.S. cities, even in the south, and for the following season, CBS increased its commitment by paying $210,000 for the rights to 21 games. Meanwhile, in Canada the Maple Leafs and Canadiens were each receiving $331,000 a year from CBC for their hockey rights. The players received no portion of this money.

In baseball, however, the players had negotiated a deal in which 60 per cent of the $9.75 million in World Series broadcast revenue would be turned over to the players' pension fund. Salaries were also higher in baseball than hockey, which was understandable because there was more revenue to be made in baseball. But the disparity was disproportionate.

In 1957, the average salary for a baseball player was $20,000 compared with hockey's average of $8,000 — only 40 per cent of baseball's average. Twenty-two years later, at the height of the rivalry between the World Hockey Association and the NHL, hockey salaries were only slightly below those of baseball. In 1979, the average salary in baseball was $113,558, and the average salary in hockey was $101,000. While baseball had a succession of star players who were paid $100,000 a season, beginning with Babe Ruth and followed by Joe DiMaggio, Ted Williams, Mickey Mantle and Roger Maris, there was none in hockey. In fact, the NHL's stars were often paid a salary below that of lesser players or even rookies.

In the 1940s and 1950s, Montreal's Maurice "Rocket" Richard was the league's top gate attraction along with Detroit's Gordie Howe, but when the Canadiens finally signed Jean Beliveau to a contract in 1953, Beliveau made more in his rookie year ($15,000) than Richard was making ($12,000).

The Red Wings, knowing that Gordie Howe was a modest man, gave him a contract at the beginning of each year but left his salary open. Gordie was allowed to write in his own amount and he, being a modest man, would give himself a $1,000 raise. In the 1960s, Bruce Norris promised Howe he would always be the league's highest paid player. Howe's faith in the Red Wings' word was shaken in 1966 when Bobby Orr agreed to a rookie contract that included a $25,000 signing bonus and $25,000 in his first year.

Then, in 1968, Bobby Baun, who had just joined the Wings, sat Gordie down and explained to him that he wasn't close to being the highest-paid player in the game. "The other players are laughing at you," Baun said.

Howe that year was earning $45,000 a season, while Baun was making $67,000 and Carl Brewer, who had just joined the team, was earning more than Baun. Howe was bitterly upset, and, after talking to Bruce Norris on the telephone, renegotiated a contract that paid him about $100,000.

But in 1957, the players were less concerned about salaries than basic benefits, such as some percentage of television money going into the pension fund and compensation if an injury suffered during the season prohibited a player from working at a summer job. They made no demands and even objected to the word "union" used to describe the association.

On February 11, 1957, the association was announced, along with its executive committee, Lindsay, Harvey, and Jim Thomson and Tod Sloan of the Leafs. Lindsay was quoted in *The New York Times* as saying, "The association will be news to the NHL owners, I believe, but we get along fine with them. We are very happy, but we want to make the league so popular that youngsters in both Canada and the United States will want to grow up and play professional hockey."

The NHL, however, had no intention of co-existing with a union and moved quickly to discredit the founding members and erode the association's support. Detroit made the stunning decision to trade Lindsay, one of the most colourful and violent players of his era, hated in arenas around the league but revered at home. The Red Wings also made it clear that friends of agitators would be punished. Marty Pavelich, who was Lindsay's partner in a business, was demoted (a year earlier he had been described in the Wings' media guide as "untradeable"), and since neither partner could run the business while playing in another city, Pavelich quit hockey.

In the press, Jack Adams, the Red Wings' general manager, disparaged Lindsay, calling him "a bad apple" and a "cancer on the team." Sports writers accepted Adams's character assassination of Lindsay and wrote articles quoting anonymous players as saying Lindsay's selfishness had destroyed the team.

The same sort of warfare was waged in Toronto. Leaf owner Conn Smythe, in fact, led the league's fight against the union, stressing to the other owners that nothing short of total victory would be acceptable. Jim Thomson, the Leafs' captain, was called into Smythe's office where Smythe denounced him as a traitor and a communist. The Leafs released Thomson a few months later. In August, 1957, he was claimed by Chicago. A year later, Sloan was sold to the Blackhawks.

In the spring of 1957, the Leaf players received a visit in the dressing room from not only Conn Smythe, but his son Stafford, the Gardens' legal counsel Ian Johnston, whom Smythe had assigned full time to fighting the union, and Clarence Campbell, the president of the league.

Conn Smythe began the harangue by saying the New York lawyers, "these outsiders" retained by Lindsay and the others were trying to destroy hockey. Campbell followed with a speech about "the fragility of hockey" and how the players were jeopardizing "the finest pension plan in sport." Stafford warned the players that Lindsay and the other dissidents were out to help themselves and nobody else.

In Detroit, Adams and Bruce Norris used the same strategy, during which Adams, in tears, implored the players to give up their fight. In Chicago, Jimmy Norris, already under investigation by the FBI because of the International Boxing Club, told Lindsay if he didn't cancel the union, he would fold the Blackhawks. "I'm losing money anyway, so I don't give a fuck."

Ultimately, the association died. The players did win a few concessions from the owners, such as a $7,000 minimum salary, an increased playoff pool and moving expenses for traded players. But for the most part, nothing changed.

In the early 1960s, Eagleson's friends on the Leafs — Carl Brewer, Bob Baun and Bob Pulford — talked extensively about forming a players' union and, naturally, felt Eagleson should be the man to lead them. Not everyone, however, endorsed Eagleson. Allan Stanley, a veteran defenceman on the Leafs who would later be part of the retired players' class-action suit against the NHL in the dispute over the pension fund surplus, for one, had concerns.

"His school buddies on the Leafs said 'What do you think?' I said, 'I don't know.' They said, 'He's a good man.' I said, 'One thing I'm against is him being a player agent and head of the association. That doesn't seem right at all.' But nobody did anything about that."

In early 1967, Eagleson paid a visit to each NHL team and most of the minor pro teams in the United States and Canada and gave his pitch for a union. The players, almost to a man, were eager to get involved. They wanted information on their pensions, increased benefits and better money. In Eagleson, they saw a man who could relate to them. He talked in simple terms, he was blunt and he swore a lot. He was young, fit and looked like an athlete. He seemed like one of them.

The attitude of the owners toward Eagleson and the proposed union seemed almost ambivalent. They did not want a union and would have jumped at the chance to crush it. But with Eagleson, they felt they could do business. He wasn't a labour lawyer, had no experience in labour negotiations and showed no sign of militancy. Better him, the owners felt, than the frightening Marvin Miller, the head of the baseball union and a man with 16 years' experience with the United Steelworkers of America. Or Jimmy Hoffa and the Teamsters, who in 1966 had announced plans to unionize all of professional sports. Clarence Campbell would eventually endorse Eagleson as executive director of the NHLPA, saying, "I don't like unions but I'm glad it's Eagleson at the head of the players' association rather than somebody else."

Just as Eagleson would share a close relationship with John A. Ziegler, Jr., he got along famously with Ziegler's predecessor, Campbell. The two men were a study of contrasts — Eagleson, the aggressive hustler with a working-class background; Campbell, the tall, aristocratic Rhodes scholar, decorated hero of World War II and prosecutor at the Nuremberg Trials. One executive friendly with both called it a "curious, mutually respectful and warm friendship. Almost like a father and son."

Eagleson's depth of loyalty to the NHL president was evident even after Campbell's death in 1984. Several years earlier, Campbell had been charged with conspiracy and influence peddling along with Liberal senator Louis Giguere and businessmen Louis Lapointe and Gordon Brown in the so-called "Sky Shops Affair." The men were shareholders in Sky Shops Export Ltd., which ran a duty-free shop at Montreal's Dorval Airport. Giguere was acquitted and Lapointe died shortly before his trial was to have begun, but Campbell and Brown were found guilty. Each was sentenced to a "symbolic" day in prison and fined $25,000. The judge said he was handing down a light sentence to Campbell because of his age and poor health.

In 1984, along with Campbell's obituary, *The Globe and Mail* ran a photograph of Campbell standing beside Giguere during their arraignment, which Eagleson, among others, felt inappropriate, given Campbell's service to his country, and record as a jurist and sports administrator.

There were no public complaints. Nothing was made of it by the league office in Montreal or by executives working for Canadian-based NHL teams. But in Toronto, Eagleson, as executive director of the NHLPA, fired off a letter to *The Globe* that read: "I was very disappointed with the photograph you used to accompany the obituary of the late Clarence Campbell.

"Mr. Campbell did a great deal for hockey not only throughout Canada, but throughout the world and his obituary described quite reasonably his career. It is unfortunate that you could not have used an accompanying photograph that would have been more sensitive to the circumstances."

Chapter Four

THE BROTHERS

AS A GUEST SPEAKER at law schools in the 1970s, R. Alan Eagleson was inevitably asked the key to being a successful player-agent. Eagleson's standard reply was, "Find yourself another Bobby Orr, do a good job for him and you will get carried along on his coattails for a while. . . . Then you expand."

Eagleson became a success and he did expand, but it is difficult to imagine Orr viewing his relationship with Eagleson as anything less than disastrous. After Orr split from Eagleson on Labour Day weekend of 1979, he discovered that he was virtually broke. After 12 years in the National Hockey League, Bobby Orr, the greatest player of his era and a man who had made more money in his rookie season than Gordie Howe had earned in his 20th year in the league, had assets totalling $456,600. His taxes, legal and accounting bills amounted to $469,550.

Years earlier, not long after he teamed up with Orr, Eagleson boasted that his client would be worth a million dollars in five years. When that didn't materialize, Eagleson said Orr would be a millionaire at age 30. Orr was 31 when he had his last telephone conversation with Eagleson, but there was only one millionaire on the phone that night — and it wasn't Orr.

The itinerary of the relationship between Orr and Eagleson is one of hockey's most compelling and disturbing stories. Wayne Parrish, the former sports editor of the *Toronto Sun*, once noted, correctly, that the relationship spanned hockey's most turbulent period, from 1966 to 1979, the 13 years during which the NHL expanded from six to 21 teams and fought a seven-year war with the World Hockey Association. It was a partnership between a superstar who revolutionized the game and a lawyer who became its most influential figure.

Born March 20, 1948, Orr was Canada's first sports hero of the television age. In the 1950s, Canadians saw star athletes such as Gordie Howe, Maurice Richard, Bobby Hull and Jackie Parker in action through the new medium of television. But unlike Howe, Richard and the others, Orr became an intimate part of Canadians' lives at an early age. When he was barely 12 years old, the country was alerted to the fact that a phenomenally talented boy was tearing up minor hockey in Parry Sound, Ontario, a small town on Georgian Bay, Lake Huron. In a cover story feature on Bobby, *Maclean*'s magazine reported, "He is a swift, powerful skater with instant acceleration, instinctive anticipation, a quick accurate shot, remarkable composure and unrelenting ambition, a solemn dedication, humility, modesty and a fondness for his parents and his brothers and sisters that often turns his eyes moist."

At the excruciatingly young age of 15, Orr moved from home to play major junior hockey in Oshawa, Ontario, with and against young men 18, 19 and 20 years old. A year later, at the age of 16, Bobby led his team to the Ontario Hockey Association major junior championship. As a teenager playing in Oshawa, he was interviewed on "Hockey Night in Canada," CBC's nationally televised Saturday night game. The public witnessed a shy young man who was soft-spoken and self-effacing. He revealed how much he missed home and how he would cry on the telephone when he talked to his family back in Parry Sound. Leaving home at an early age was the price young hockey players paid to chase a dream. But in Orr's case, playing in the NHL was more than a dream. In media and hockey circles, Orr was already projected to be hockey's next superstar, perhaps the greatest of them all.

Doug Orr, Bobby's father, first met Eagleson in the summer of 1953. Al had worked as a recreational director at MacTier, a hamlet located south of Orr's home town, and had played fastball against Doug, a good athlete with the Parry Sound team. Ten years later, as a Tory MPP, Eagleson was asked by Alistair Johnson, the MPP for the Parry Sound riding, to attend a sports banquet in the town and to bring with him one of his high-profile friends from the Maple Leafs.

Eagleson took Carl Brewer, who had just been voted to the NHL's first All-Star team. At the banquet they met 14-year-old Bobby, who was captain of the minor baseball league team to which Eagleson was to award a trophy. Bobby and Al talked briefly and then Doug Orr reminded Eagleson of their playing days 10 years earlier. Orr also mentioned that his son had done very well in his first year with Oshawa and might need some legal advice down the road when he turned pro.

At the time Orr met Eagleson, he was already the property of the Boston Bruins. Prior to the establishment of the universal amateur draft, the NHL clubs signed prospects on a first-come first-served basis to contracts called "C Forms" that made the players the club's property for life. In the case of Orr, Bruins' scout Wren Blair was so impressed with the 13-year-old that he arranged for a blanket sponsorship of Parry Sound minor hockey by the Bruins, which meant the rights to all players in the Parry Sound system belonged to Boston.

As Eagleson noted in his biography, the cost of financing minor hockey in a small Canadian town was minimal — sticks, tape, sweaters and a $1,000 donation to minor hockey. Years earlier, the Maple Leafs had used the same strategy to acquire a young Frank Mahovlich. The Leafs had bankrolled the minor hockey system of Schumacher, a Northern Ontario mining town where Frank happened to play hockey.

By the time Bobby Orr was 18, he had reached near legendary status in Canada. No defenceman had dominated junior hockey the way he had and followers awaited eagerly his NHL debut, as did the Bruins, who were the perennial doormats of the NHL during 1960s. The Maple Leafs reportedly offered Boston $1.5 million for the rights to Orr in 1965, but were turned down flat. Hap Emms, the Bruins' crusty general manager, growled, "We wouldn't trade Bobby Orr for $1.5 million and all the players on the Toronto hockey team. Orr will make the Boston franchise a winner and keep it that way for years."

The Bruins would have turned Orr professional at the age of 16, had that been allowed. Watching the Leafs trounce the hapless Boston team in a game in the early 1960s, Boston scout

Harold "Baldy" Cotton said, alluding to the mediocre defensive corps, "We have a 15-year-old kid in Oshawa better than any of those guys."

But the Canadian Amateur Hockey Association insisted a player had to be 18 before turning pro, and even after that age, amateur hockey was still an option. A young player could choose to join Father David Bauer's Canadian national team. Eagleson was well aware of this alternative as he prepared to negotiate Orr's first professional contract with the Bruins.

In the summer of 1966, Orr spent time at Eagleson's summer cottage on Lake Couchiching in the Central Ontario region near Orillia. Other frequent visitors to the Eagleson cottage that summer were Carl Brewer, who was in the process of acquiring his amateur status so he could play with the Canadian national team, and Bauer, the coach and manager of the team. Bauer tried mightily to convince Orr to play one year for the nationals, a point that wasn't missed by *Sports Illustrated* when it published a lengthy article on Orr and Eagleson. The magazine noted that Orr would not come to the Bruins cheaply and that he could opt for the Canadian amateur team.

This was the leverage Eagleson was seeking and would need if he hoped to extract a record contract for his client from Hap Emms, a tough taskmaster of the old school who made it known he would not be negotiating Orr's contract with "a goddamn lawyer." Weeks dragged on during which Eagleson broadly hinted that Orr would be attending university in the fall and playing for Father Bauer's national team.

But then, in the middle of August, Eagleson met Emms at Lock 42 of the Trent-Severn waterway near Lake Couchiching by chance. Eagleson and his family were in a 14-foot craft with a small outboard and Emms, who lived in Barrie, Ontario, during the summer, was aboard his 42-foot cabin cruiser.

Eagleson once described Emms as a "scary old bugger," but on that day, after he spotted the Eaglesons in the little boat, Emms beckoned the family to pull up alongside. After boarding the yacht, Nancy and the kids were served refreshments by Hap's wife, while Emms and Eagleson talked contract. Eagleson and Emms met several more times aboard the yacht until a deal was finally hammered out. On Labour Day weekend, just before the opening of the NHL training camps, the contract was signed.

By the standards of the day, it was a monstrous deal, described by one sports writer as "an obscene precedent." In total, it was a two-year pact worth $80,000. It included a $25,000 signing bonus for Orr, a $25,000 salary the first year and $30,000 the second year. By comparison, hockey's two biggest superstars of that period, Gordie Howe and Bobby Hull, were earning $35,000 and $40,000 a season respectively.

But the Bruins' huge investment was really a bargain. The young defenceman exceeded even the loftiest of expectations. During a rush at training camp, Orr deked Ted Green, the Bruins' talented but rough and ill-tempered defenceman, after which Green skated furiously over to him and said, "Kid, I don't know what they're paying you, but it's not enough."

Orr almost immediately transformed the Bruins from an incompetent club which regularly fell short of selling out the Boston Garden into an exciting contender that played before packed houses. By Christmas of Orr's first year, the Boston club's box office receipts had increased by almost $100,000.

In Orr's first season, he easily won the "Rookie of the Year" award and was also voted to the NHL's second All-Star team. When Harry Howell was awarded the Norris Trophy as the NHL's best defenceman, he noted that he was fortunate to be voted the award that year, "because I got a feeling Bobby Orr is going to be winning this for next decade or so."

Orr would capture eight consecutive Norris Trophies, and would revolutionize the position of defence more than any player before or since. With his speed, mobility and break-neck acceleration, he would jump into offensive rush and then retreat to his defensive position before the opposition could counterattack. He was a beautiful skater, an uncanny playmaker and a brilliantly accurate marksman. With his enormous skills he controlled the game at both ends of the ice. He won the NHL scoring championship twice, something no other defenceman has ever done, and the most valuable player award three times. In 1971, *Sports Illustrated* selected him its "Sportsman of the Year." Orr, wrote *SI*, is "the greatest player ever to don skates; not the greatest defenceman, the greatest player at either end of the ice."

Orr's former teammate Eddie Johnston once said, "He could thread a needle with the puck, shoot it like a bullet or float it soft. Orr was the only player who could dictate the tempo of the game, speed it up or slow it down. He could see the whole ice the way a spectator sees it from above. He's the best player I've ever seen."

Orr was joined on the Bruins by prospects Wayne Cashman and Derek Sanderson, as well as Phil Esposito, Ken Hodge and Fred Stanfield, who were acquired from Chicago, and goaltender Gerry Cheevers, who was claimed from the Toronto organization. These young players along with veterans such as Johnny McKenzie and Ted Green made the Bruins into the NHL's most powerful and feared team of the late 1960s and early 1970s. They were a tough, flamboyant group that dominated the league for seven years and won two Stanley Cups.

The impact of the Eagleson-Orr partnership on players around the league was profound. They envied Orr's special relationship with Eagleson and longed for similar guidance. Orr, the greatest hockey player in the world, became, it was said, a "walking advertisement for Alan Eagleson." Allan Stanley, a veteran of the 1940s, 1950s and 1960s, says, "I thought Bobby Orr was the luckiest man in the world. He had everything. He had legal advice, investment advice. He was the guy who was going to make the big money."

Players flocked to Eagleson for representation. By the early 1970s, his firm represented more than 150 players, roughly half the number in the NHL. In addition to Orr, his headliners included Marcel Dionne, a young superstar in Detroit; Paul Henderson, the hero of the 1972 Canada-Soviet Union series; Dale Tallon, a junior star who was the second player taken in the 1970 amateur draft; Steve Shutt, one of the Montreal Canadiens top forwards; and two talented young players on the Leafs, Darryl Sittler and Lanny McDonald.

In her biography of Eagleson, Deidra Clayton listed some of the contracts 1973 Eagleson negotiated for athletes:

* Mike Walton, Minnesota Fighting Saints: $100,000 to $125,000 a year over three years for a total salary of $405,000 plus potential bonuses which could bring the amount to $450,000.
* World figure skating champion Karen Magnusson, Ice Capades: $500,000 over three years.
* Bill Harris, New York Islanders [not to be confused with Billy Harris of the Leafs]: $300,000 over three years.
* Syl Apps, Jr., Pittsburgh Penguins: $750,000 over three years.

Eagleson's burgeoning clientele represented the foundation of the Eagleson empire. In 1972, Eagleson formed Sports Management Ltd., a player agency that offered complete financial management for players. It was run by Marvin Goldblatt, an old friend of Eagleson's who had worked as an accountant in the 1960s for Blaney Pasternak, the law firm in which Eagleson was a partner. Players paid as much as $100 an hour for financial advice from Sports Management and, by 1978, company billings were $500,000 a year.

In 1975, Eagleson established Rae-Con Consultants Ltd., with wife Nancy as sole owner and Goldblatt as treasurer. In addition to being a vehicle for Nancy's interior design business, Rae-Con also offered financial planning services of its own for 60 professional athletes including Sharif Khan, the world champion squash player at the time. In 1978, Goldblatt estimated Rae-Con's annual billings to be $250,000.

Eagleson built a web of companies which, if not owned by himself or a member of his family, were controlled and operated by friends and, of course, interconnected with Eagleson businesses. Eagleson's high-profile athletes, for example, were referred to Sports Representatives Ltd., a company that handled endorsements and off-ice employment for players in public relations and advertising campaigns. The company was run by Bobby Haggert, who had been a Maple Leaf trainer in the 1960s and had operated as one of Eagleson's sources inside the Leaf dressing room. It was generally assumed that Eagleson had bankrolled Haggert's business and perhaps even owned it. That was the impression left with Leaf owner Harold Ballard, who was a friend to both Eagleson and Haggert. And in 1976, *The Toronto Star* reported that Eagleson and Haggert had set up the company together. Eagleson and Haggert, however, always denied that Eagleson had an interest.

Another member of the inner circle was Arthur Harnett, a former Toronto radio broadcaster who ran Eagleson's 1969 campaign for the presidency of the Ontario Progressive Conservative Party. In 1972, Eagleson had brought in Harnett to sell advertising for the Canada-Soviet Union series. Harnett's company, Harcom, subsequently brokered the TV and rinkboard advertising rights to Eagleson-organized tournaments in the 1970s and 1980s. In 1980 Eagleson became a 50 per cent partner with Harnett in selling the advertising rights for Exhibition Stadium in Toronto. Six years later, Harnett bought him out.

Irving Ungerman, a Toronto businessman and fight promoter, began a long-time relationship with Eagleson in 1971 when the two (Eagleson using Orr's money through Bobby Orr Enterprises) bought the Canadian closed-circuit television rights to the Muhammad Ali-Joe Frazier fight from sportsman Jack Kent Cooke. Through Eagleson's contacts, Ungerman's profile in the fight game grew significantly during the 1970s. In 1975, Eagleson solidified his relationship with Ungerman by setting up a law firm with Irving's son, Howard, who had recently graduated from law school, as his sole partner. The firm was called Eagleson Ungerman.

Eagleson's departure from Blaney Pasternak was not without hard feelings. Outside of the original partners, Eagleson had an uneasy relationship with the members of the firm and finally said he would stay only if the practice was downsized to include only the original members which, at that point, was impossible.

The fact that Eagleson took his real estate business with him when he left was resented by the partners. They felt they had covered for Eagleson when he had been pursuing outside interests and with Eagleson's departure would never be repaid. Bob Watson, a partner and Eagleson's old friend from law school, told Deidra Clayton, "We spent a lot of time making it happen when Al was going to meetings with the players' association. There would be months when he wasn't doing much legal work; in fact, when he wanted to go somewhere we paid for it, so when he left he more or less took a debt with him."

Watson continued, "[The partners] didn't know what each other was billing, no one really went into it so we were very vulnerable. Whereas if we knew he was leaving we would have made sure we had continuing contact with his clients. That's where the hardship arose because we felt we'd been very supportive in developing Alan Eagleson. . . .

"During the early years, Al could have been a very large business getter in other areas which would have been much more lucrative [than his particular interests]. . . . When he left, his department was finally growing and anyone would just have to look to see it was a very lucrative area. . . . and for whatever reasons he didn't feel he wanted us to share in it. . . . That was really hard to accept."

Initially, Eagleson's relationship with Bobby Orr seemed a match made in heaven — "hockey heaven," as the sports writers said. It was close, intense, complex, evolving but, near the end, not always what it seemed to be. Paul Mooney, the former president of the Boston Bruins, said, "I don't think you could characterize the relationship Alan Eagleson and Bobby Orr as anywhere near that of athlete and agent. It was very personal, very emotional, very complex. They vacationed together, they lived at each other's houses, they came and went as members of the same family. The passion level was incredible."

Initially, it was a big brother, little brother relationship. Fifteen years separated the two men in age, and in the early years Orr relied on Eagleson almost entirely. Eagleson was best friend, confidant, mentor and advisor. Orr was shy, retiring and sometimes touchy, especially with the media. Eagleson, loud and aggressive, was Orr's buffer, his fixer for making things he didn't like go away.

But there was much more to Orr than the stereotypically reclusive athlete. Like Eagleson, he was ego-driven, hot-tempered and ambitious. Like Eagleson, he used profanities constantly, loved to tell jokes and sought the company of sycophants. As Orr grew into manhood, he became more self-absorbed and more demanding of Eagleson, but trusted him totally and paid little or no attention to what Eagleson was doing with his money. Eagleson viewed Orr as "the perfect client" because he gave him a free hand.

For years, the two shared a standing joke. Eagleson would tell a crowd at a sports banquet, "Bobby and I split his earnings 90-10 . . . and Orr lives very well on the 10 per cent." Orr would tell the same joke with a different punch line. "Al lets me keep 10 per cent."

In 1966, Bobby Orr Enterprises was incorporated, with Orr as the 18-year-old president and Eagleson as vice-president, as a tax shelter and an investment vehicle for Orr. The first important acquisition was a 180-acre tract of land on the east side of Lake Couchiching near Orillia, upon which sat an old resort called Owaissa Lodge. The Orr-Walton Sports Camp was established at the site, and Mike Walton, a young prospect on the Leafs and an Eagleson client, was brought in as Orr's partner.

Bill Watters, a Toronto high school teacher who grew up in Orillia, was hired to run the camp and, in the years that followed,

Watters would grow in the empire to become Eagleson's chief recruiter of players and right-hand man in Sports Management Ltd. Watters, and later Rick Curran, another camp employee, also developed a close relationship with Orr. Orr and Walton became best friends. Rounding out the family was Bobby's father Doug, who was convinced that he should quit his job with CIL in Parry Sound to take on an undefined role at the camp, and Mike Walton's father, who was appointed head of "clean up."

The people of Orillia looked upon Orr and the young hockey players at the camp as something approaching gods. For a drink, Orillians, living in a conservative Central Ontario town that disallowed licenced establishments, had to drive a mile outside of town across the bridge that spanned the Narrows between Lake Couchiching and Lake Simcoe, to the rural hamlet of Atherley. There were two hotels in Atherley — the Atherley Arms and the Lakeview — both of which were just a few miles down the road from the Orr-Walton camp. A visit by Orr and his entourage to the Atherley Arms, which catered to a roll 'n roll crowd and was better known as "The First," or the Lakeview Hotel, which was called "The Second," was viewed as one of the more important events of the summer, especially to a young girl if she got a chance to dance with Orr or one of his friends.

In the late 1960s and early 1970s, Orr thrived both on and off the ice. Eagleson decided that Bobby Orr Enterprises (BOE) would invest in real estate companies, one of which was called called Nanjill Investments. Nanjill was named for Eagleson's wife (Nancy) and daughter (Jill) and was owned by the Eagleson family. In 1973, BOE also funded a $125,000 mortgage on Eagleson's Rosedale home in Toronto. BOE invested in Marty's Custom Clothiers, a high-end men's retail store in downtown Toronto run by Marty Alsemgeest, a close Eagleson friend. There were also investments in a car wash and Pony Sporting Goods Ltd. In terms of personal endorsements, Orr became a pitchman for Standard Brands, General Foods, Coca-Cola and General Motors.

During this time Orr says he knew little and cared less about what was happening to BOE. In 1970, a reporter visiting Orr in Parry Sound wrote, "Bobby seemed to have trouble concentrating on the papers Eagleson brought for him to sign. He was more concerned whether his father had brought the breakfast cereal for the fishing trip." Orr told an interviewer in 1976, "Frankly, I leave all that (business) stuff up to Al. There are people who think I could do more, yet, as I see it, my job is playing hockey."

Playing hockey, of course, had its special rewards. In 1971, the Bruins signed Orr to his first corporate contract. It was a five-year deal worth $1 million that was intended to shelter his personal income and reduce Orr's tax rate from more than 50 per cent to 25 per cent. On a annual basis, Orr personally received $120,000 from Boston, with the Bruins also buying $80,000 yearly in BOE shares. In 1974-75, Orr's contract with the Bruins was renegotiated to $200,000 a year.

Orr appeared to be living every Canadian boy's dream. He was the greatest hockey player in the world, he was famous and his "big brother" agent was making him rich. In 1973, Eagleson said, "I suppose either of us could be called millionaires if one of us wanted to turn everything into cash, but we're not about to do that. We're like brothers in our relationship. Money has never been the primary consideration."

At that point, nobody would have foreseen trouble, but the signs were there, beginning with Orr's chronic knee problems. Orr suffered the first injury to his left knee while still in junior hockey. During his early years with Boston, he was relatively injury free. But by 1971-72 he was hurting again and a major operation in the off-season denied him an opportunity to play in the September, 1972, Canada-Soviet Union series.

Four years later, Orr at the age of 26, played his final full NHL season. In 80 games in 1974-75 he set a record for goals by a defenceman — 46 — and points — 135. And for the second time in his career, he had led the league in scoring. It had been a brilliant season — arguably his best — but, for all intents and purposes, it was also his last.

Despite the fragility of Orr's career, he received two substantial contract offers from the Bruins prior to the termination of his contract in 1976. The first came from the Storer Broadcasting Company, owned by the Weston family, for $355,000 annually over five years. After the club changed hands and was bought by Jeremy Jacobs, who had made his fortune from the ownership of thoroughbred race tracks and a concessions business in arenas and stadia, Jacobs put another offer on the table — $295,000 a year for five years with Orr also to receive in 1980 either a $925,000 payment or an 18.5 per cent ownership in the Bruin club.

Eagleson, however, turned down both deals, a decision confirmed by a letter dated January 23, 1976, sent by Eagleson to Paul Mooney, the president of the Bruins, which read:

> As you are well aware, Bobby is anxious to finalize his agreement with you. I am sure your records will indicate that our last offer from you was as follows:
>
> Salary: $295,000 a year for five (5) years, plus a payment of $925,000 on June 1st, 1980 or 18.5 per cent of the hockey club in lieu thereof.
>
> You are also no doubt aware that Storer Broadcasting offered the sum of $335,000 per year for a five (5) year contract commencing on the 1st day of September, 1975.
>
> These offers were both declined by me and my client.

Fourteen years later, Orr said Eagleson never informed him of the specifics of the Jacobs offer — that the deal included an 18.5 per cent ownership position in the club by 1980. Orr told Russ Conway of *The Eagle-Tribune*: "There's no way I was given the details of that kind of offer. I think anyone would remember if he was offered over 10 per cent of a National Hockey League club."

Eagleson, however, says he did keep Orr apprised of the negotiations. According to Eagleson, the Bruins' interest in re-signing Orr dropped off precipitously following another injury to his knee on November 29, 1975, which ended his season. After the injury, the club did not bargain in good faith, Eagleson says, adding that it reduced its offer from $2.4 million over five years to $1.75 million, with Orr needing to pass a medical examination before he would get paid anything.

Eagleson said later that he rejected Jacobs' offer because he was advised by a U.S. tax consultant that the $925,000 payoff would have posed tax problems for Orr in 1980, but gave no reason for rejecting the 18.5 per cent ownership in the Bruins club in lieu of the $925,000 lump sum.

In fact, 14 years later, for one of the first times in his life, Eagleson admitted publicly that he had erred. "I wish I'd made the deal [with Boston]," he told Wayne Parrish of the *Toronto Sun*.

When the season ended, Orr's contract with Boston expired and he signed with the Chicago Blackhawks. In the years that followed, it was frequently suggested that Eagleson's rejection of the Bruin offers had been part of the plan to "deliver" Orr to Eagleson's close friend, Blackhawk president Bill Wirtz. It's an accusation that Eagleson denies. "The fact is," he said, "I went to Bill Wirtz and told him he owed me, and since Boston was throwing Bobby to the wolves with no guarantee, Bill Wirtz should do the right thing. Wirtz stepped up to the plate and paid $500,000 a year for a player we all knew wouldn't be able to play at any level of tough hockey."

Although it's unclear why Eagleson felt Wirtz should be in-debted to him, Chicago obviously felt Orr could still play. Making the deal more desirable for Wirtz was the fact that the Blackhawks would be stealing him from the Bruins, the team that had fleeced the Blackhawks in probably the most one-sided trade in league history. In 1967, Chicago traded Phil Esposito along with Ken Hodge and Fred Stanfield to the Bruins for Gilles Marotte, Pit Martin and Jack Norris. Norris turned out to be a fringe player; Marotte, an average defenceman with limited mobility; and Martin, an effective but small centre.

Esposito, on the other hand, became a superstar with the Bruins, the dominant centre of his era and a Hall of Famer. Hodge, too, had some great years in Boston as Esposito's right winger. Stanfield fulfilled the role of an effective second-line centre who happened to also play the point on the power play. The Bruins' heist infuriated Chicago owner Arthur Wirtz, who felt Boston general manager Milt Schmidt had plotted to take advantage of his Chicago counterpart Tommy Ivan by catching him off-guard with the trade offer. Nine years later, the signing of Orr was seen as a means of paying the Bruins back.

In fact, the Blackhawks wanted so badly to sign Orr that they began negotiating with him while he was still under contract to Boston. The NHL forbids clubs from talking to players under contract and a club guilty of "tampering" can be fined up to $500,000. But that did not stop Bill Wirtz from meeting with Eagleson and Orr several times in the spring of 1976 to talk contract while Orr was still being paid by the Bruins. Bruins' general manager Harry Sinden was suspicious and accused Bill Wirtz of tampering with Orr, and even requested that Wirtz be given a lie detector test by the league, but eventually dropped the idea. Instead, he challenged Orr's move to Chicago in federal court. The case, however, was dismissed by a federal judge in Chicago.

Orr's contract with Chicago appeared generous; $3 million

over six years, $1.5 million of which was guaranteed even if he could not play out his contract. But Orr's decision to move to Chicago marked the beginning of the most troublesome period of his hockey career.

"He didn't want to leave Boston," said Sinden, who says he would sometimes get a call from Orr in the early hours of the morning during the stalled contract negotiations. "He'd break down and cry on the phone over the prospect of leaving the Bruins. His mind was in an awful state."

As it turned out, Orr's farewell performance as a player took place in September of 1976 when he helped lead Canada to victory in the Canada Cup tournament. He was brilliant and was selected the player of the tournament, but only his teammates in the dressing room knew about the pain he endured. He would sometimes arrive for the games on crutches and after the games would be unable to walk at all. "He basically played on one leg," Bobby Hull said years later. "It was the most remarkable performance I had ever seen by a hockey player."

Orr's knee problems limited him to only 20 games for Chicago in the 1976-77 season after which it was decided he should take the entire year off in the hope that his damaged knees would heal. During that time, Orr worked as Blackhawk coach Bob Pulford's assistant, but he had problems dealing with the players. Eagleson said, "It got sticky then. Bobby had trouble communicating with the players. He'd give them hell if they didn't measure up to his standards. It got to where he wasn't talking to them. Bobby seemed to forget that his talent was God given, that others had to work. It got to where the players were so uptight they had trouble performing. One of the players went to Pully and said get that guy off the ice or there'll be a full-scale riot. Pully took him off."

Dale Tallon, an Eagleson client and a top NHL prospect who had played below expectations in Vancouver before being traded to Chicago, where he continued to perform at a pedestrian level, was one of the players who had trouble with Orr. Tallon said, "I used to be great friends with Bobby. I used to help at his hockey school, I golfed with him. But in Chicago, he changed. I couldn't do anything right as far as he was concerned. He began isolating himself from the players and a resentment built up toward him. He stopped talking to me. He hasn't talked to me since."

The regret, the bitterness, the resentment — Orr, to those around him, was a mass of frustrations boiling barely below the surface. Not only was his playing career all but over, but he had financial problems. Because he was unable to play, he had volunteered to take a cut in his salary. Instead of earning $500,000 a year as the $3-million contract called for, he accepted a $200,000 interest-free loan from the Blackhawks to buy a house in Chicago and then agreed to accept $150,000 annually until the $1.5 million guarantee had been paid. Then, in 1978, he learned that he had tax problems. Bobby Orr Enterprises was not recognized as a tax shelter by the Internal Revenue Service.

Orr seemed ready to break emotionally at any time. In March, 1978, he got into a fight in a Vancouver bar where the players from the Blackhawks and Canucks met after a game. One of the players was Hilliard Graves, a tough, hard-nosed winger with Vancouver. Graves told journalist Earl McRae: "Bobby was giving the Vancouver players hell for not putting out. He was very belligerent, very mean. Then he started on me. He said I shouldn't hip-check guys, it damages their knees. I said I only weighed 170 pounds, so hard checking was the only way I could make it in the NHL.

"He then said if he ever came back, he was going to get me. He was really mad. I said if he did, I'd take his knee right off. He punched me in the chest, knocked me off my stool. I threw him to the floor, but he jumped up and punched me under the eye. I nailed him twice, one on the nose and one on the eye, and he went down. Some guys broke it up and, a few moments later, I see him standing at the door to the washroom and he's calling me over. His eye was nearly shut, he looked terrible. I thought he wanted to continue the fight, so I said no. But he said he just wanted to talk to me, so I went over.

"He invited me into the washroom. We were in there alone. I could hardly believe my ears. Bobby was almost in tears. 'I'm really glad you hit me,' he said. 'I deserved it. I've been acting crazy lately, I don't know what the hell's wrong with me. I'm so frustrated. I've been looking for something, I don't know what.' Then he apologized and we shook hands. I felt so sorry for him because I always liked Bobby. He's a supernice guy."

In 1978-79, Orr made one last attempt at a comeback, but could play only six games. As a result, the Blackhawks moved him into the front office to work as an assistant to Pulford who was also the general manager of the team. But that arrangement did not work out. Pulford and Orr did not get along. Orr second-guessed several of Pulford's decisions and at the end of the season, Orr, who had announced his retirement as a player earlier in the season, left the Blackhawk organization and moved back to Boston.

In the early years, Orr had been the star player on the Eagleson-Orr team. He had been a world-famous superstar and Eagleson, as he often noted, hung onto his coattails. But by 1978, Eagleson had not only exceeded Orr in wealth, but also power. He had other high-profile clients, such as Darryl Sittler, the star captain of the Maple Leafs to whom Eagleson was very close. Orr, who had not played a full season since 1974-75, heard less and less from Eagleson, to the extent, Orr says, that Eagleson sometimes would not return his telephone calls. When they did talk on the phone, the conversation often regressed into yelling and profanities.

Eagleson said, "A large part of it is that Bobby couldn't understand or appreciate that things happened that made me a success, perhaps because of him, but often unrelated to him. Instead of a guy walking behind Bobby Orr in his shadow, [it became] more of a two-man deal, then [Orr was] a little bit in my shadow. I don't think he liked that and I can't blame him."

Said Orr: "In the beginning, Al was working for me. In the end, I was working for him. Somewhere along the line, it got inverted in his mind."

One of the disputes that led to the Orr-Eagleson split was Dave Hutchison's free agency in 1978. Hutchison was a tough defenceman who had played well for Pulford when he coached in Los Angeles. Orr and the Chicago front office wanted Hutchison, who was represented by Eagleson, to join the Blackhawks and thought they had an agreement with Bill Watters, Eagleson's employee. Eagleson, however, interceded and made the deal with Toronto, which also coveted Hutchison's services. Orr saw this as a betrayal and, according to Eagleson, viewed this a sign of Eagleson's shifting loyalty to Sittler.

At the same time, Orr was feeling the squeeze from the IRS. He owed $300,000 in back taxes. His assets weren't what he thought they should be. And he blamed Eagleson. In 1982, Eagleson offered his recollection of the final telephone call between him and Orr on Labour Day weekend, 1979: "He called me at home late one night yelling and cursing about how I had mistreated him, how I didn't care for him anymore, how I wasn't doing this, doing that, how things were going wrong for him. He said it was all over between us. He was making no sense, so I told him I'd call him the next day and hung up." The following day, a meeting was set up at the apartment of a mutual friend in New York and according to Eagleson it didn't go well. "It was bad. Lots of shouting. At one point he said I didn't give a damn about people. That did it. I said if that's the way you feel, it's over."

Over the next several months, Orr began the process of extricating himself from Eagleson, during which he lived on deferred money from an earlier contract with the Bruins. His only guaranteed income was a five-year endorsement deal with Standard Brands, a food conglomerate now owned by R.J.R. Nabisco, that paid him about $100,000 a year. It was money he needed, because when everything was added up, Bobby Orr Enterprises, once described by Eagleson as "the best pension plan I could have given Orr," was worthless.

Eagleson, in trust, bought the assets of BOE for about $620,000. Those assets included $150,000 for Orr's interest in Walker Heights, which principally owned seven acres of land near Collingwood, Ontario; $100,000 for his interest in a Toronto car wash; $40,000 for his interest in Nanjill, Eagleson's real estate investment company; and $330,000 for the Orr-Walton Camp. But with a $285,000 in outstanding mortgages on the camp plus bank loans totalling about $450,000, BOE showed up in the red.

In the 1980s, the Walker Heights and Nanjill real estate holdings increased substantially, and Eagleson also did well with the Orr-Walton Camp, flipping it for $500,000 a few months later. After the new owner defaulted on the mortgage, he bought it back and sold it again in 1988 for $900,000. Eagleson says he strongly advised Orr to hold onto the properties, but by then Orr insisted on a complete severance. "I just wanted him out of my life," Orr said.

Orr's income-tax problems were the result of Eagleson's recommendation that Orr use BOE as a tax shelter. Both Revenue Canada and the IRS came to the conclusion that Orr had stepped on the ice to play for the Bruins from 1971 to 1976 and not Bobby Orr Enterprises. As a result, Orr had to pay up and settled for a net reassessment of about $300,000.

Orr blames Eagleson for his tax problems, but many lawyers

and accountants were giving similar advice to their clients during the period. Toronto accountant Lyman MacInnis, who was Orr's accountant in 1971, strongly opposed Eagleson's decision to put Orr on a corporate plan, but admits tax experts were about equally divided on whether it was sound financial advice. Still, Harvey Strosberg, a Windsor, Ontario, lawyer working for Orr in the early 1980s was harshly critical of Eagleson for not accepting MacInnis's offer to sit down with Orr and explain the risks involved in setting up a corporate plan, especially considering the uncertainty of Orr's money-earning potential because of his knee problems.

Eagleson says BOE was a failure because of Orr's excessive spending. Orr didn't have any bad habits, but he lived well, probably too well, and was especially generous to his family, giving members more than $200,000 in cash gifts during his playing days. Between 1971 and 1979, Orr withdrew from BOE a total of $1,134,741, most of it in after-tax dollars.

So, was Eagleson to blame for Orr's difficulties or was it a shared responsibility? Orr admits the blame has to be shared. But there is something wrong when an athlete of Orr's status, one who signed precedent-setting contracts with NHL clubs, one who did not have a personal problem — drugs, drinking, gambling or an expensive divorce — ends up with virtually nothing.

Eagleson did some good things for Orr. The Standard Brands endorsement deal that Eagleson arranged through his pal Ross Johnson, the company's flamboyant CEO, was a life saver for Orr. Moreover, Eagleson argued in his biography that Orr didn't work hard enough at selling himself and even refused to promote some products that he recommended. Certainly Orr's decision to break with Eagleson was badly timed and perhaps misguided. The real estate boom of the 1980s was several years away and as a result Orr lost heavily when he cashed in his chips in 1979.

But some obvious questions linger. Should Eagleson have not kept a tighter rein on Orr's spending, given the fragile nature of Orr's career, and especially after 1976 when it was apparent that Orr's playing days were rapidly winding down? When Orr needed Eagleson the most, in the mid-to-late 1970s, was he there, or was he too busy?

Did Eagleson invest Orr's money wisely? Did Orr's interests always come first? For example, was it beneficial for Orr that his money was used for a mortgage on Eagleson's Rosedale home?

Was it in Orr's best interests to have his money invested in Marty's Custom Clothiers, which was owned by Eagleson's good friend, Marty Alsemgeest? Was it wise to put Orr's money in a Toronto car wash? Was Eagleson a bona fide financial manager or did he use Orr's money to solidify relationships and expand the Eagleson empire?

In an April 12, 1979 letter to Orr, Eagleson made note of Orr's $130,000 interest in the car wash and an additional $50,000 in Marty's Custom Clothiers. But when Orr and Eagleson settled up in April 1980, Orr received only $100,000 for his share in the car wash and $40,000 from Nanjill. Sometime in 1979, Orr's shares in Marty's Custom Clothiers had been shifted to Nanjill. That added up to a net loss of $40,000 for Orr. Athletes, as a rule, expect their financial advisers to encourage investments that produce equity, not lose it.

Orr says, "Al was looking after everything and I believed him. When he told me we were investing in something, I just said 'Great.' I didn't check anything and that's *my* fault."

When Orr did ask a question, he says Eagleson's response was, "What's the matter? Don'tcha trust me?"

Orr trusted Eagleson during his bitter contract dispute with Boston and his subsequent signing with Chicago — $3 million over six years or a guaranteed $1.5 million. But even that didn't work out. After agreeing to accept only $150,000 a year until the guaranteed $1.5 million portion of his contact was paid to him, he had, by 1980, received only $150,000 from the Chicago club. At that point the Blackhawks refused to pay him anything more, arguing Orr had voided his contract with Chicago by appearing at the Pittsburgh Penguins' training camp. Orr was forced to sue the Blackhawks and in 1983 received a settlement of $450,000.

Orr eventually got back on his feet and today he is financially secure. The money has been paid back, he's reportedly a millionaire, lives in the posh Boston suburb of Weston with his wife and two sons. He also owns a home on a South Florida golf course and according to his friend, Russ Conway, "enjoys golf and fishing in his spare time."

With a partner, Orr owns Can-Am Enterprises which handles endorsements. He also does promotional work for several major companies and with partners helps run Pandick Press, a New England financial printing company.

Orr and Eagleson don't speak, but they have exchanged volleys in the Toronto newspapers. One skirmish was over a $90,000 pledge made by Eagleson in 1978 on Orr's behalf to a sports medicine clinic at York University. Orr did not follow through with his obligation, because he said he could not afford it. He also claimed Eagleson had pledged the money without his knowledge. Eagleson, however, produced a letter from Orr's lawyer in Boston that stated that Orr would honour the commitment, had visited the clinic and was "very impressed." The first story written on the matter, by *The Globe and Mail*, made it clear that Orr had broken his word to York University. "It's sad," Eagleson was quoted as saying.

Others found it strange that Eagleson would pledge $90,000 of Orr's money, given that his client's hockey career was over, that his peak earning years had ended, that Bobby Orr Enterprises was cash strapped and that Orr was having tax problems.

After two major stories on the Orr-Eagleson feud in *The Toronto Star* and *Toronto Sun*, Orr dropped his profile even lower and rarely gave interviews. But he continued to work behind the scenes to discredit Eagleson. He assisted Ed Garvey and Rich Winter during the NHL players' revolt in 1989, talking to Garvey almost every day on the telephone during the critical June NHLPA meetings in Florida. Later, Orr assisted his friend Russ Conway, when he embarked on his series of articles on Eagleson and his conduct as head of the NHLPA for *The Eagle-Tribune*. Orr remains to this day Eagleson's fiercest enemy.

Chapter Five

THE PATRIOT

IN 1969, the year Hockey Canada was born, R. Alan Eagleson was far from a force in international hockey. He was occupied at the time with building the fledgling NHL Players' Association. Hockey Canada was the child of men such as Harold Rea, a Toronto businessman who headed a task force on sport initiated by the Trudeau government in 1968; the late Charles Hay, a Calgary oilman; newspaper tycoon Max Bell; and newspaper columnist/politician/civil servant Douglas Fisher.

Rea's task force, which was formed to investigate all aspects of sport in Canada, recommended the formation of a non-profit corporation to raise money and operate a national team program for Canada. By 1969, the amateur teams sent to the world championships and the Olympics were not competitive with the powerful Soviets, or even the Czechoslovaks, Swedes and Finns. Since the International Ice Hockey Federation, the governing amateur body of the sport, and the International Olympic Committee forbade professionals to play in the Olympics and the world championships, Canadians were becoming increasingly frustrated at their international hockey record and demanding that the policitians do something about it.

The answer was Hockey Canada, which was officially formed on February 24, 1969 in Ottawa, at a gathering presided over by John Munro, the federal minister of Health and Welfare. The meeting brought together most of the influential hockey people in Canada: among those present were Eagleson; Stafford Smythe, part-owner of the Toronto Maple Leafs; David Molson, boss of the Montreal Canadiens; Douglas Fisher (who had co-authored Rea's task force report); Father David Bauer, the driving force behind Canada's national team; and Earl Dawson and Gordon Juckes from the Canadian Amateur Hockey Association, heretofore the governing body of amateur hockey in Canada, which became a reluctant partner in Hockey Canada.

The Hockey Canada organization was handed a two-fold mandate from the Trudeau government:

> 1. To support, operate, manage and develop a national team or teams for the purpose of representing Canada in international tournaments and competitions.
> 2. To foster and support the playing of hockey in Canada and, in particular, the development of the skill and competence of Canadian hockey players.

But to the majority of Canadian hockey fans, Hockey Canada had but one aim: to get the best players, the NHL professionals, into the world championships or any other competition against the Soviets to show that Canada really was the best hockey nation on earth. It was the realization of this goal that had Eagleson dominating both Hockey Canada and international hockey by the dawn of the 1980s.

At the end of that first meeting in 1969, Max Bell was elected chairman of Hockey Canada, Charles Hay was president, and the chief fundraiser was Ian Sinclair, then chairman of Canadian Pacific. He was to use his contacts in the business community to raise money. The board of Hockey Canada was made up of representatives from every level of hockey in the country: Clarence Campbell, president of the NHL, Dawson and Juckes from the CAHA, and eventually representatives from the Canadian Inter-University Athletic Union, among others. As executive director of the NHL Players' Association, Eagleson also had a seat on the board, but not a conspicuous one. Jim Coleman wrote that "with an ironic twinkle in his eye, Alan Eagleson professed to be satisfied when the newly appointed governors urged him to be chairman of the public relations committee."

Hockey Canada was established as a non-profit corporation

and a registered charity. While it would receive a portion of its funding from the federal government, the goal was for the private sector to provide the lion's share of the money needed to run the national team, and to support the various coaching clinics, player clinics and hockey library that eventually became part of Hockey Canada's mandate.

By the end of 1969, the rest of the hockey playing nations of the world were well aware that the ultimate goal of the Canadians was to see their best professionals compete with them. At the time, the IIHF was under the control of its president, John Francis "Bunny" Ahearne, an Irish travel agent whose blunt tactics bore a remarkable resemblance to Eagleson's. For instance, anyone who wanted to take part in international hockey events always seemed to have a much smoother ride when the bookings were handled by Ahearne's travel agency. Ahearne was long considered an enemy of Canadian hockey for his opposition to letting NHL players enter the world championships, but by the end of 1969 he was telling the world he had cast the deciding vote at a meeting that allowed Canada to use nine minor-league professionals and reinstated amateurs in the 1970 world championship, set for Winnipeg. According to Coleman, "not one of the Canadian delegates who was present on that memorable occasion has found fit to corroborate Ahearne's version of history."

But Ahearne earned himself the enmity of all Canadian hockey fans at a follow-up meeting of the IIHF on January 4, 1970 in Geneva. By the time the Hockey Canada delegates, led by Charles Hay, arrived at the meeting, they were informed by Ahearne that a motion had already been passed which rescinded the use of professionals. Moreover, the world tournament had been moved from Winnipeg to Sweden. While the impetus for the move had been a change of heart by the Soviets, Canadian hockey officials had no doubt Ahearne's hands were just as bloody. Hay and his colleagues had no choice but to pull Canada out of all further international competition, including the world championships and the Olympics. This was the way things stayed until the historic Summit Series of 1972, when a team comprised of the NHL's best players finally met the Soviet national team and, in the process, launched Alan Eagleson on his path to the top of the hockey world.

More than 20 years later, most Canadians still believe the

series was created and produced by Alan Eagleson. In his biography, Eagleson wrote: "Between 1969 and 1972 I kept pushing the Canada-Soviet series idea, and suddenly, after all that work, the dam broke. Charlie Hay was the chairman of Hockey Canada at the time, with Douglas Fisher, an important member of the board. The 1972 world championships were in Prague that year. I was intending to go over for the last three or four days to help keep my contacts alive. One day, just before they were to start, Doug Fisher phoned me from Ottawa and said, 'I think you should get over there right away, I think something's going to happen and we have to make sure — the Russians have to know that the NHL players will agree.' He meant, agree to the big series I was working on. That call came, I think, on a Friday. Could I be in Prague at the International Hotel on Monday? It turned out that from Hockey Canada and the CAHA, Lou Lefaive, Joe Kryczka and Charlie Hay had been meeting with the Russians and the deal was pretty well set as long as there was no doubt about the NHL players agreeing. When I got there I could give that assurance."

This version has always been supported by Aggie Kukulowicz, an Air Canada employee and good friend of Eagleson's who has been, among other things, a translator for Eagleson in his talks with the Soviets ever since he became a force on the international hockey scene. Through Kukulowicz, Eagleson has booked all Team Canada travel on Air Canada and in return has received Kukulowicz's undying loyalty (along with more than one free ticket).

Kukulowicz told the authors of *Net Worth* that Eagleson was the man who negotiated with the Russians for the series, cursing and bullying them into the deal, peppering the talks with his customary foul language and telling Kukulowicz to "tell them every fucking word!"

This version doesn't jibe with what was observed in Prague in the spring of 1972, both by members of the CAHA and Hockey Canada. Derek Holmes, who was coaching the Swiss team at the world championship, spent a great deal of time at the International Hotel in Prague and said that Eagleson never played a direct role in the talks. In fact, he was told to butt out.

The negotiations in Prague were actually carried out by two CAHA officials: its president, Joe Kryczka, a Calgary lawyer who later became a judge on the Alberta Supreme Court, and the CAHA's executive director, Gordon Juckes. Hay was relegated to a seat in the hall. Kryczka, who spoke Russian but did not inform the Soviets of this, had actually been negotiating with them, along with Juckes and others, for a best-versus-best series since becoming CAHA president in 1971. But it wasn't until the Prague world championships in April, 1972, which were held in conjunction with the IIHF's annual meetings, that the Soviets agreed in principle to playing a team of NHL players. It was the job of Kryczka and Juckes to finalize the deal, not Eagleson.

"It was at that time that (Lou) Lefaivre and (Douglas) Fisher approached me to come back to Canada because I coached and played internationally, and I played for Father Dave (Bauer), so they asked me to come back and be executive director (of Hockey Canada)," Holmes said. "While all these negotiations were going on, lo and behold if Al doesn't show up. But he was always on the fringes. If you read Scott Young (who co-wrote Eagleson's authorized biography), or if you ever talked to him about it, he was integral in the whole thing, when in fact he wasn't even in the room."

Hay, who had come to be the *de facto* head of Hockey Canada because of the failing health of Max Bell, was also in Prague. But not even he, the president of Hockey Canada and a driving force for the sport, was a part of the final negotiations, although he had worked with Juckes in earlier meetings with the Soviets.

Fred Page, a veteran hockey executive who served on the board of the IIHF, said that Eagleson was never invited to the Prague meetings but turned up at the hotel anyway as Kryczka and Juckes were completing the deal. When Page asked Eagleson what he was doing there, Eagleson replied, "Oh, my wife and I just happened to be touring in Europe and we thought we'd drop by." Page's reaction: "What a crock!"

Kryczka, who died at the age of 55 from cancer in January, 1991, had little use for Eagleson. Men like Kryczka and Lou Lefaive, an original Hockey Canada board member, were pushed aside by Eagleson, a painful experience. But Kryczka said this mattered little in the long run: "The credit — the credit doesn't really matter. I knew what I did. I was proud, really proud to be a part of it."

Eagleson and eight other officials were named to a committee by Hockey Canada to run the series, but because of his bond with the players as the head of the NHLPA, and the force of his personality, Eagleson was soon running the show himself, along with a select group of associates and employees from the NHLPA and his sports management firm. Harry Sinden was chosen as the coach by the committee, with John Ferguson as his assistant. But Eagleson brought two associates aboard: Bob Haggert, whose Sports Representatives Limited handled endorsements and promotions for players, and Mike Cannon, his assistant with the players' association. This group became known as Team Five and soon operated independently of the committee.

The rosy glow that surrounded Eagleson and the players after the series was not in evidence early on. First, there was the Bobby Hull controversy. Hull had just jumped from the Chicago Blackhawks of the NHL to the Winnipeg Jets of the new World Hockey Association, but as the game's reigning superstar he was named to the team. However, under pressure from the NHL owners, who were furious at seeing Hull defect to the competition, Eagleson agreed to drop Hull from the team. The Canadian public complained loud and long, but the NHL owners held firm.

Eagleson, by putting up no public resistance to the exclusion of Hull and several other stars who had gone to the WHA, was branded the villain. In his defence, Eagleson said the NHL owners had left him little choice because they threatened to drop insurance coverage on the players if the WHA stars were allowed on the team.

"What happened was a peculiar set of events," Eagleson said. "We split the team up among four or five of us. Sinden, Ferguson, Haggert, Cannon and me. Each guy was to call five or six players to find out if they would come.

"I remember calling Dallas Smith (of the Boston Bruins) and he declined because he was a farmer and it was a thick crop. I think it was Fergie or Sinden that called Hull, and the condition was that you can't talk about it, and I had my reasons. But at a banquet somewhere Hull announced he'd been chosen for the team and that gave the NHL the chance to cut him off at the pass. So I took the rap for it, but that's the price you pay. We had five players in that category: Hull, J.C. Tremblay, Derek Sanderson, Bernie Parent and Gerry Cheevers. They just said no WHA players or we drop the insurance guarantee on the players."

What Eagleson didn't mention was that if the insurance guarantee was the only problem, there should have been little difficulty allocating some of the series budget for coverage. There was certainly enough money realized from the sale of the television rights to pay the relative pittance needed to insure the players against serious injury.

For it was through the television deal that Eagleson, and the rest of the hockey world, discovered just how much money could be had in international hockey. When the television rights came up for bids, there wasn't a great deal of interest. The only prospective bidder was MacLaren Advertising, which held the rights to "Hockey Night in Canada." When Eagleson, who was among those in charge of selling the TV rights, heard MacLaren was only going to offer $500,000 for the eight-game series, he called his friend Harold Ballard, the owner of the Toronto Maple Leafs. He and Ballard formed a company, Ballard-Orr Enterprises Ltd., which made a successful offer of $750,000 for the rights. The "Orr" in the company was Bobby Orr, Eagleson's most famous client. But he did not know that Eagleson had committed $375,000 of his money to the project.

When the series quickly caught the imagination of the country, the television deal turned into a bonanza. Sixteen million people, more than three-quarters of the population of Canada, watched the seventh and final late-game heroics on television. Ballard boasted that he and Eagleson "turned that $750,000 into a $1.2-million profit."

The television image of Eagleson imprinted upon Canadians was his being escorted across the ice during that final game, after he had been involved in a confrontation with some Soviet soldiers. As several of the Team Canada players took over and guided him to safety, Eagleson raised his middle finger to the Russian crowd, a gesture that both roused and embarrassed Canadians watching back home.

But the financial success of the series, with much of the money coming from television, gave the board of Hockey Canada, an organization struggling to escape government handouts, an appreciation of what Alan Eagleson could bring to the table. "I think Eagleson got his toehold during the '72 series," said Derek Holmes, "by the fact he could bring the players to the table and no one else could. At the time, the feeling in the country was it was reasonably important to beat the Soviets but we're better than them anyway. I think as the feeling for the series started to mount that Eagleson started to gain a stronger foothold. I think that really changed his position in hockey."

It took the next international series, the 1974 meeting between the best of the WHA and the Soviets, for Eagleson to be completely accepted around the Hockey Canada board table. "During that time (the WHA and Hockey Canada) tried and tried to get a television contract and couldn't," said Holmes, who by this time had joined Hockey Canada as executive director, its top administrative position. "During that time, Eagleson just sort of sat at the table and didn't help or hinder them. Finally they came, cap in hand, to Eagleson and asked him to help get them a contract, which he did, finally. That was the first inkling he could bring more to the table than just the players. He could obviously crank up a television contract."

By that time, Eagleson had volunteered to work on a long-time dream of his, a tournament that would be hockey's equivalent of the World Cup of soccer. In 1975, the federal government named Eagleson as Hockey Canada's international negotiator, a post which he would use to gain unprecedented power in hockey. By 1976, Eagleson had put together the Canada Cup, a tremendous tournament that brought together the top six hockey playing nations and became an overwhelming athletic — and financial — success. The first Canada Cup, won by the Canadians in overtime against the Czechoslovaks (Eagleson's friend and client, Darryl Sittler, scored the winning goal), brought in a profit of more than $3 million, which was shared between Hockey Canada and the NHLPA. The sight of this money pouring in soon made the directors of Hockey Canada become tolerant of Eagleson's excesses.

Once again, to deliver the players to the Canada Cup, Eagleson negotiated their release in the May 1976 collective bargaining agreement. But to get the owners' approval, the NHLPA paid a steep price, allowing the owners a clause in the agreement calling for compensation from any team that signs another team's players. The restrictive compensation rule called for a team losing a free agent to be compensated with a player of equal value. This effectively kept free agency out of the NHL. The only way the deal could be renegotiated was if the NHL and WHA merged. In return for the privilege of playing international hockey for token sums and giving the owners a share of the profits, the players were given a small increase in their pension plan contributions. But half of the cost of the $500-per-player annual increase was paid from the international hockey profits, which lessened the financial obligation of the owners.

This was a sweet deal for the owners, but it tightened Eagleson's grip on the game. As one NHL general manager told *Sports Illustrated* in 1984: "Al delivers us the players and we give him international hockey."

Eagleson also cut a deal with the IIHF to get its stamp of approval for the Canada Cup, which was needed if the Soviets and the rest of the top hockey nations were to play. He agreed (with Hockey Canada's okay) to send Canadian teams to the world championships, beginning in 1977, and to various other international events, for the first time since the Canadians had pulled out in 1970. The IIHF would also get a cash payment, $25,000 in 1976, which grew to $2.1 million by the 1991 Canada Cup.

As both the international negotiator for Hockey Canada and the head of the players' union, Eagleson now controlled every major international hockey effort for Canada. And with the increasing numbers of Swedes, Finns and Czechs coming to the NHL, Eagleson controlled the participation of those players as well.

"So then things started to get on the road," said Derek Holmes, who worked closely with Eagleson in the late 1970s. "He became increasingly more powerful as the years went on, in '77, '78 and '79. We weren't yet back in the Olympics; there was only the world championships, and, of course, the other commitment we had was the Isvestia tournament at Christmas time. It became increasingly more Eagle's show."

As Eagleson came to be the most important player in Hockey Canada, he didn't hesitate to tell the board just how he was going to spend the money. "You know that famous quote, 'If I raise it, I'll tell you how I'm going to spend it,'" Holmes said, referring to an oft-quoted statement by Eagleson. "That was one he sort of used."

But the Hockey Canada directors were in no position to put any clamps on Eagleson. Nor were they inclined to, for many of them still wanted to see Canada back in the Olympics. With Eagleson bringing in hundreds of thousands of dollars, the directors saw a way to get back in the hunt for Olympic gold.

"For the most part, the government was starting to cut back on the money Hockey Canada would have toward the Olympic program," said Holmes, who was also keen about an Olympic team. "The other people on the board, for the most part Father Dave Bauer, were very interested in coming back for the 1980 Olympics. Part of agreeing to some of the extravagances — the 1977 and '78 world tournaments, and, of course, the Canada Cup — is that a large portion of that money would go to the Olympic program in 1980.

"I think for the most part, people said we'll put up with what he has to say and do, if we'll get a pot of money. So I think a lot of people turned sort of a blind eye to what he was doing because they thought we'll get our money for the Olympic program and that's far more important."

When Hockey Canada saw its initial guarantee of a $600,000 share in the 1976 Canada Cup grow to more than $1 million, it was easy for the directors not to question just how Eagleson was going about the television deals, the advertising deals or why the expenses for the tournament were approaching a million dollars.

"Deals were deals. He did the television thing and all at once it ended up Hockey Canada got a million dollars," Holmes said. "No one questioned what he was going to do, how he was going to do it. This was the deal: You'll get this amount of money, the players' association will get this amount of money, and after a couple years of combating the government trying to get money, this was manna. This was tremendous.

"I could see how the people felt at the time who were interested, like Bauer, Professor George Lariviere, the guy from the CIAU, Bob Pugh and Lou Lefaive — people like that — felt boy, if we can get this kind of money then we're not beholden to the government."

Holmes is quick to say he never saw Eagleson do anything illegal. Nor did anyone else. But it was a little difficult to accept the sight of Eagleson proclaiming himself to merely be a great patriot serving his country for practically nothing when members of the board knew he was receiving money for office expenses (he ran the tournaments out of his Toronto law office), secretarial staff, employees at Sports Management Ltd., and for consulting work. Not to mention his large and growing entourage of employees and cronies who were a fixture from the first tournament in 1972 and ate up hundreds of thousands of dollars for their care and feeding.

"I think everybody thought this was Al's ego trip, he'll put on these shows and he'll do his act with his gang and that's part of what you have to pay for," Holmes said. "I'm a little sympathetic, but latterly I'm not so sympathetic to the board because they were sheep when things started to get out of hand, and he became a little bit — what's the word — he would lambaste people publicly, embarrass them and do things like that.

Eagleson, of course, maintains that everything he did, every deal that went to a friend of his, or consulting contract he awarded himself, was scrutinized by the full board of Hockey Canada.

"The board at Hockey Canada is a pretty sound group of people," Eagleson said. "Every contract is approved by them."

But Holmes, who attended the board meetings, remembers things differently.

"[Eagleson] was given carte blanche to run the Canada Cup. It was, in effect, given to him and he ran the thing. He would come back and report on an interim basis to the board of Hockey Canada, here in Ottawa, saying we've done this, this and this," Holmes said. "There was always intermediate kinds of reports on what we've done. Invariably, it was Al saying 'I've done this and I've done that,' that kind of thing, everybody would just sort of nod in unison. When he used to get opposition he was oftentimes very aggressive."

Any board member who dared to question one of Eagleson's moves would find himself "verbally smacked and frozen out," Holmes stated. Those who raised questions soon found themselves under a personal attack, Holmes said, "in whatever way that was necessary. A flip answer. Never physical, but in a verbal sense he would embarrass them into silence. He always had an answer whether it was adequate or not.

"For the most part, people came to the board for the benefit of hockey. They just became sort of tired and didn't want to be embarrassed. I felt a lot of disappointment in a number of people who sat on the board."

One of Eagleson's favourite targets was Bill Hay, the son of Charlie Hay, a player in the NHL with the Chicago Blackhawks in the 1960s and later president of the Calgary Flames. Perhaps resenting success in a man who was born into better circumstances than he, Eagleson was often cruel in his treatment of Bill Hay, who had devoted a good part of his life to Hockey Canada.

"[Eagleson] used to say 'Gee, it's nice to have Bill here,' and some sly little thing like 'No one's saying you're on the board here, Bill, because your Dad was former president, but . . . ' and Bill used to sit there and seethe," Holmes said. "I said to Bill, 'Maybe you should grab him some time.' Bill was a big, slow-moving guy, but tough as whalebone.

"Eagleson would say those kind of things and then he'd just laugh. Or he'd say, 'Go fuck yourself — oh, excuse me Father Bauer, will that go in the minutes?' People would put up with that because they knew he could deliver."

Nowadays, with Eagleson under investigation, Hay doesn't want to talk about him. "The Eagleson mess, you know, I'm not really interested in chatting about it," he said. "It's a mess, I hope it goes away. We've gotta get on with the game and other programs that work. There's a lot more to the game than Alan Eagleson."

Holmes himself ran afoul of Eagleson after the 1977 world championship, Canada's first foray back into the tournament since 1970. That was the year of "Team Ugly," as the press came to call the group of players who — because their NHL clubs hadn't made the playoffs — went to Vienna and played like thugs, finishing fourth. When Don Ramsay of *The Globe and Mail* asked Holmes, executive director of Hockey Canada, what he thought of the team's performance, he was candid.

"I said it was terrible. I didn't think it was the kind of hockey we needed. From that time on it was downhill for me. I had a lot of people in my corner on the board who liked the things I tried to do. I certainly pushed hard to get the Olympic team back (it returned to the Olympics in 1980). But Al certainly had strength. He had the strength to keep me out of Team Canada latterly, but not the Olympics. I can't remember Al coming to the board and apologizing for (the '77 team's) behaviour, because he certainly initiated much of it."

By 1981, tired of being frozen out by Eagleson, Holmes resigned his post with Hockey Canada and was replaced by Lou Lefaive, who returned from the civil service. The title Holmes had served under, executive director, was changed to president, but the position was still one of the few full-time, salaried jobs with Hockey Canada.

Chapter Six

THE HOCKEY CZAR

DURING THE LATE AFTERNOON of February 11, 1993, a small group of reporters gathered in a meeting room at the convention centre attached to the Westin Harbour Castle Hotel on Toronto's lakefront.

The scene was a far cry from the usual Hockey Canada press conference held during the reign of R. Alan Eagleson. No posters on the walls trumpeting another Team Canada foray into international hockey, no tables laden with hors-d'oeuvres and drinks, as was the custom. A couple of pitchers of water adorned a corner table.

Also absent was the Eagleson entourage, and the usual schmoozing that preceded such an event. Just a group of a dozen or so reporters and television crews, all waiting for the arrival of Ian Macdonald, the York University professor who is chairman of Hockey Canada, and Ron Robison, the current president of the group that has governed international hockey for the nation since 1969.

For Alan Eagleson was not the host of this gathering, but the subject. And most of those waiting were sure what the announcement was going to be: that Eagleson, once the most powerful man in hockey, had lost the last of his many hockey hats, this loss the most painful of all. For this hat was his crown in the hockey world, the source of most of his power and his riches, according

85

to his enemies. As Hockey Canada's chief international negotiator, Eagleson had extended his influence in hockey across the world, had become regarded as *The Czar* of the game.

Now, in the face of the federal U.S. grand jury and RCMP investigations, the directors of Hockey Canada were meeting at the Westin Harbour Castle to decide Eagleson's future with the organization he had dominated for more than two decades. Those waiting for the outcome believed the board — long cowed by Eagleson's aggressive manner and ability to bring in millions of dollars — had no choice but to ask for his resignation from the board and to announce that an independent agency had been asked to conduct a complete investigation of Hockey Canada's financial dealings involving Eagleson.

For years Eagleson had generously rewarded himself for his work in international hockey, particularly the Canada Cup tournaments, while at the same time insisting that his motivations were, for the most part, altruistic. In 1989, for example, he wrote a memo to his union membership, the NHLPA: "Neither I nor any member of my family nor any company with which I have been associated has ever received money directly or indirectly from any international hockey event."

This statement turned out to be untrue.

Hockey Canada financial records show that Eagleson and his good friend, Chris Lang, treasurer of Hockey Canada for many years and a board member since its inception in 1969, were both paid large consulting fees by the Canada Cup committee, which was run by Eagleson.

More than $1 million in administration costs was paid by Hockey Canada in 1991 out of its total operating costs of $3.5 million. In the same year, $941,000 of the Canada Cup's $8.5-million budget was spent on "management services." While financial statements from years prior to 1991 revealed both Eagleson and Lang had been paid for management services and consulting, the statements for 1991 did not specify who was paid for management services, although the notes to the financial statement for 1991 said "directors and other related parties" were paid for "consulting, management, secretarial and other office expenses." Both Ian Macdonald and a member of the board of directors who did not want to be named told *The Globe and Mail* they thought the directors receiving those payments for the 1991

Canada Cup were Eagleson and Lang.

Even the contract Eagleson signed with the players' association in 1986 brought him money from international hockey. It called for a $25,000 bonus, in U.S. funds, in every year the union earned more than $600,000 from international hockey. And Hockey Canada's financial statements show this level of earnings was attained in every year the Canada Cup was held, which meant Eagleson collected at least $125,000 in bonuses.

Chris Lang, who also received payments for services provided by his sports marketing company, Christopher Lang and Associates, argued that paying close to a million dollars in "management services" for a six-week hockey tournament actually represented a savings for Hockey Canada.

"That's the thing that floors me. I'm in the event management business. On the management of the Canada Cup, we'd charge a fee of 15 to 20 per cent, which is standard in the industry," Lang said. "The total administrative cost of the Canada Cup is 6 per cent; depending on what you include in that, I'm saying 6 to 7 per cent, certainly well under 10. I always give him hell and say, 'Get it up to market, because you're undercutting anybody who ever wanted to bid for it. But it's way under. The reason is, he (Eagleson) takes no salary."

Nevertheless, Lang didn't think it would be a good idea to put the Canada Cup's administration up for bids: "(There wouldn't be) the same continuity, being able to bring the sponsors in, being able to do the extra things you can't normally do with the arena, those kinds of things."

Lang's estimation of the percentage of the total Canada Cup budget that is paid in management services is a little off. At least it was for the 1991 tournament. The total budget for the event was $11.9 million, of which $941,000 was paid for management services. This represents 7.6 per cent of the total, but the financial statements of Hockey Canada show the Canada Cup fund, which operates the Canada Cup, paid an additional $297,000 in administration for the 1991 event, bringing the total to $1,211,000, which is 10.1 per cent of the total. This also doesn't take into account the $989,000 Hockey Canada spent on administration in 1991, which is 29.5 per cent of the organization's total costs and comes from its general fund, which is separate from the Canada Cup fund. It is not known how much overlap there was between the administration of both Hockey Canada and the Canada Cup.

Overlap is something Eagleson was quite familiar with during international events. Hiring out his own staff to Hockey Canada also proved lucrative. Eagleson made at least $160,000 by placing employees of his sports management company with Hockey Canada for international events. People such as his accountant, Marvin Goldblatt; and Bill Watters and Rick Curran, who worked for Sports Management Ltd., would continue their work for Eagleson's firms. But Eagleson would either deduct their salaries from the amount paid for their services by Hockey Canada and keep the difference, or have the employees sign their paycheques from Hockey Canada over to him.

Watters, now the Toronto Maple Leafs' assistant general manager, worked for Eagleson's Sports Management Ltd. from 1970 to 1980, and was paid a total of $105,000 to be general manager of Team Canada at the 1977, 1978 and 1979 world championships, plus $30,000 to be tournament co-ordinator for the 1977 world junior tournament. Working on a couple of other international events in that period brought Watters's total salary from Hockey Canada to about $150,000 from 1977 to 1980. At the time, Watters was being paid $50,000 a year by Eagleson to run Sports Management. However, Eagleson did not pay Watters in 1977, 1978 and 1979, saying his salary was covered by the payments from Hockey Canada. During this period, Watters continued to operate Sports Management for Eagleson.

Rick Curran, who also worked for Sports Management at that time, was paid nearly $60,000 by Hockey Canada from 1977 through 1979 for various duties at international events. He endorsed his Hockey Canada cheques over to Eagleson, and received only about $52,000 in salary from Sports Management over the same period.

Both Watters and Curran left Eagleson in 1980, partly because they felt they were not being treated fairly and partly because they disagreed with the way he conducted his business. They established their own company to represent players, Branada Sports, and worked together until the late 1980s when Watters decided to pursue a broadcasting career full-time before landing a job with the Leafs. Curran is still a player- agent, considered one of the heavyweights in the business.

Eagleson's family got into the act in 1991 when Hockey Canada paid his son, T. Allen Eagleson, $90,000 on a one-year contract to serve as assistant to the general manager of Team Canada and director of administration for the Canada Cup. During this period, the younger Eagleson said he continued in a reduced capacity as a lawyer for his father's law firm, Eagleson, Ungerman.

Eagleson also charged the Canada Cup during this period for secretaries and other office expenses incurred at his law office in downtown Toronto. In 1976, Eagleson billed Hockey Canada $83,281 for "office and general" expenses. At the same time, Eagleson was also being paid by the NHLPA for office expenses.

When *Sports Illustrated* brought this practice to light in 1984, Eagleson had a flip response: "The guy works for me, and if I can put him to work and make a million dollars, it's my million dollars, not his. If I pay my guy 30 (thousand) and rent him out for 50 (thousand), that makes me smart."

In 1991, when asked by *The Globe and Mail* about the practice, Eagleson put his own spin on it. "I keep reading stories about Watters and Curran and how underpaid they were, that they only got this or that from Hockey Canada. They don't understand there's something called overhead. It's pathetic, if nothing else. Bill did a great job for me but his telephone bills were two thousand, three thousand, four thousand dollars a month. And yet he always felt he was underpaid. I'll tell you one thing, he seemed to enjoy the work there. If he was underpaid, he was underpaid for 13 or 14 years." Watters actually worked for Eagleson for 10 years.

Watters will not comment on Eagleson publicly. Curran would only say that he quit working for Eagleson because of "philosophical differences in terms of how he conducted his business."

One man who never left Eagleson's side over the years was Arthur Harnett, a former news director for CFRB radio in Toronto. His long friendship with Eagleson proved to be extremely profitable, as several companies he operated handled the television and advertising rights for every major international series from 1972 to 1984.

Harnett and Eagleson go back to the early 1960s, when Harnett was a campaign worker for Eagleson during his career as a Progressive Conservative MPP and federal candidate. When Eagleson became president of the Ontario PCs, Harnett wound up as the executive director.

In 1972, after Eagleson formed Ballard-Orr Enterprises Ltd., and bought the television rights for $750,000 to the 1972 series, he transferred them to another company he incorporated, Team Canada Productions Ltd. Arthur Harnett was president of this company and acted as the sales agent for the television advertising time. Yet another company, Arthur Harnett Enterprises Ltd., was formed and it earned a share of the sales commissions in the sale of television and radio ads by acting as the agent for TC Productions. Russ Conway, in his first series for *The Eagle-Tribune* on Eagleson, discovered that of the $283,000 in commissions paid for advertising sales, $118,750 went to Arthur Harnett Enterprises Ltd.

The totals went up in subsequent years, Conway found out. Arthur Harnett Enterprises became Harcom Consultants Ltd., and it was a player in the advertising and television rights for the Canada Cups from 1976 to 1984, along with another company, Harcom Stadium Advertising Ltd., which also handled scoreboard ads at Exhibition Stadium when the Toronto Blue Jays and the Toronto Argonauts both took to the field there.

Over the years, Eagleson's accountant, Marvin Goldblatt, and his law partner, Howard Ungerman, both served as directors of Harcom Stadium Advertising Ltd.

Harcom Consultants acted for Hockey Canada in the sale of the television rights of the 1976 Canada Cup to Carling O'Keefe Breweries. An additional commission was earned when Carling hired Harcom as its agent in reselling some of the commercial time. *Sports Illustrated*, which had access to Hockey Canada financial records, could not find out how much Harcom made on the deal, but the records showed $1 million was spent on commissions for television ads. For the 1981 Canada Cup, Harcom paid $1.9 million to Hockey Canada for the advertising rights, but no records of its profits are available.

In addition to selling the television time, Harcom also held rights to rinkboard ads, which it then resold to companies such as Air Canada and the Westin Harbour Castle Hotel. No figures are available to show how much Harcom made on those ventures, although by the 1991 Canada Cup, those involved with the rinkboard ads said the rights were being resold to various companies for several hundred thousand dollars.

Eagleson has always maintained Harnett and his companies operate independently of him, but this is not the impression received by those doing business with Arthur Harnett. "As a radio-TV person, we slotted Harnett into a company to handle all communication aspects . . . so that when we go into a deal for international hockey or domestic hockey, we call Harnett; or when we go into the boxing business we work with Irv Ungerman. His company comes in and fills that role. But again, that's 100 per cent owned by him. I don't want any part of it," Eagleson told Deidra Clayton.

For the 1991 Canada Cup, all of the television, advertising and marketing rights were sold to Labatt Breweries of Canada for $4.2 million. Some of those rights were subsequently sold to other companies. One of those companies was All Canada Sports Promotions Ltd., which is owned by Irving Ungerman, a sometime business partner of Eagleson. All Canada received the rights to a couple of prime rinkboard positions, which it resold to Air Canada and Westin.

Despite Eagleson's protests to the contrary, people dealing with Arthur Harnett often assumed he was representing Eagleson. Evan Hayter, who was Carling's marketing director in 1976 when it bought the TV rights to the Canada Cup, told *Sports Illustrated* that any deal he made involving hockey was made directly with Eagleson. But, said Hayter, the payments were not made to Eagleson. "Well, no, not to Eagleson. He has a guy named Arthur Harnett. Harcom. He more or less does all the sales negotiations for Eagleson."

An insurance broker, Robert Bradshaw, said that he never dealt with Harnett when he was selling insurance to Harcom for an event. His deal was always made with Eagleson. "Then, at the end of the day, Harnett and I would go out and have a drink, and I'd say, 'Art, this is what (Eagleson and I) agreed to. This is the deal. I'm totally convinced that Eagleson controls Arthur Harnett and Arthur Harnett's business."

The treasurer of the International Ice Hockey Federation, Curt Berglund of Stockholm, was more succinct: "They say that before Harnett coughs in the morning, he must first call Eagle."

Eagleson's critics, among them Rich Winter, have long called for Hockey Canada and Eagleson to open the books to show the complete financial picture of deals such as those involving Harcom. However, Eagleson was quick to counter that all his deals were scrutinized by the board of Hockey Canada. "We have a meeting of what we call the legal, technical and banking committee every three weeks and we have anywhere from 10 to 15 people and we review what we've done in the previous three weeks and what we plan to do in the next three weeks. It's worked like that since 1976," Eagleson told *The Globe and Mail* in the summer of 1991. "They have questions. What about the board advertising, what about this, what about that?"

Eagleson has also said all the financial dealings of Hockey Canada are a matter of public record, that the records show he has never taken money he isn't entitled to. However, when *The Globe* obtained the financial records of Hockey Canada going back to 1969, they were no more complete than any company's annual statements. Most of the expenses, such as administration and management services, were listed as one-line items, with no breakdown as to what companies or individuals received payments. It was the same story when Winter, Ron Salcer and Ed Garvey pressed Eagleson to open the books of the NHL Players' Association.

"The auditors did a review of the books and basically confirmed the financial statements reflected the entries in the book," Winter said of the report done by Hamilton lawyer Bill Dermody on the NHLPA's finances in 1989. "That doesn't tell us if Alan Eagleson made 10 million dollars or 10 dollars from the Canada Cup, which is what we asked for. I have financial statements which indicate very clearly that Eagleson received reimbursement for office expenses. Were those the same office expenses he received reimbursement for from the players' association? I don't know. I would have liked to know."

Eagleson charged that Winter had no right to know the details of the deals he made for Hockey Canada. "Imagine if we sat down with Rich Winter and said 'Here's the deal I've got with Air Canada, here's the deal I've got with Westin Hotels.' First thing he's going to do is call a press conference or leak it and everybody's caught off-base. How would you feel if you're a big buyer and a guy named Eagleson's getting a better rate? Not too happy. And the first thing you do is pound the shit out of the guy at Air Canada. What right does anybody have to these documents? It would be different if it wasn't approved by Hockey Canada's board that's composed of 11 businessmen, including Sam Pollock, Ian Macdonald, Lorne Robertson, Bill Hay . . . that's what boards of directors are for."

But, in the summer of 1991, responding to rumours about hard cash moving from Canada to Switzerland, Eagleson said to his critics, "I don't have to tell them anything. Then they're suggesting that Ziegler and I have an international company and a Swiss bank account and we've made millions of dollars and kept it overseas. I mean, what the . . . ? If that's the case, why don't they go to the Mounties? Why don't they go to the police and lay charges?"

The reference to the international company was the acknowledgment of a rumour in hockey circles that Eagleson, his good friend John Ziegler, then president of the NHL, and Chicago Blackhawks' owner Bill Wirtz were partners in a European company that had bought some of the Canada Cup rinkboard advertising rights. No record of such a company has ever been found.

There is also the "rumour" of a hockey executive who was said to have seen an Eagleson employee flying out of Czechoslovakia once, carrying a briefcase full of cash to a supposed Swiss bank account. Again, there is no evidence to back up this tale, although it may have its impetus from the fact Eagleson did open a Swiss bank account in the late 1970s for Hockey Canada. It was there to hold funds in European currencies for Canadian teams and make a little money when the Swiss franc rose in value.

Aside from the brief statements gleaned from Hockey Canada, there are no detailed records about Eagleson's dealings with companies such as Harcom or All Canada Sports, as they are private companies.

Arthur Harnett dropped out of sight some time before the 1987 Canada Cup, when all the television, advertising and marketing rights were sold to Labatt for the first time. No one seems to know why Harnett and Harcom were not even subcontractors any longer, although one insider speculated "it was the heat from the *Sports Illustrated* story."

In any case, Harnett did not land on the unemployment line. An order from the Privy Council noted that Arthur Harnett of Toronto was appointed as a "full-time temporary member" of the Convention Refugee Determination Division of the Immigration and Refugee Board for a period of two years at a salary of up to $80,500 per year. In July 1992, Harnett was appointed for another two years. The job puts Harnett on a two-person panel in the board's Toronto office that determines whether or not prospective immigrants to Canada should be granted refugee status. Since the Conservatives came to power in Canada in 1984, the Immigration and Refugee Board has developed a reputation as a notorious Tory patronage trough.

Harnett is not the only Eagleson friend to enjoy special privileges at international hockey events. There was a large crowd of cronies and hangers-on who became fixtures at every international event that involved Eagleson, all of them decked out in their blue Team Canada blazers and other freebies the boss squeezed out of team sponsors, enjoying the European scene on the tab of Hockey Canada. They all ostensibly had duties with the team, although it was a mystery to many just what they were. The crowd of pals was there right from the start in 1972, when it was reported that the bill for all the players, officials and Eagleson's entourage was $1 million.

The rules were simple for the people in the entourage: do everything Al says. "If he has a difference of opinion with you, he'll almost treat you as being disloyal," Bill McMurtry said. McMurty is a former friend and law partner of Eagleson in the firm, now known as Blaney McMurtry Stapells, with which Eagleson had an acrimonious parting in 1975. "I get the feeling the only people who can really survive with Al definitely are sycophants . . . who will never criticize the emperor's clothing. It was my feeling the only way to please him was to keep agreeing with him."

The constants and the most prominent members of the entourage were Aggie Kukulowicz, Marvin Goldblatt, Jimmy Lipa, Ernie Lewis and, for a few years, Eagleson's nephew, Richard Daw. Eagleson ordered these men around and occasionally ridiculed them. He was, at once, a paternal figure and dictator who was both feared and revered by those who owed their jobs to him.

For years, Eagleson badgered Goldblatt, his accountant, to quit smoking, largely because Eagleson was allergic to cigarette smoke. When Goldblatt switched to chewing gum that, too, created problems.

During the 1987 world hockey championship in Vienna, Goldblatt, Richard Daw and Sam Simpson, Eagleson's assistant with the NHLPA, waited in the lobby of the Marriott Hotel for Eagleson to arrive before they went out for dinner. Goldblatt was chewing gum and Daw was carrying a trench coat.

Finally, Eagleson walked up to them in his usual quick pace. His first words were, loudly, "Marvin take that gum out of your mouth! I don't let my kids chew gum and I don't want you doing it either!" Goldblatt removed the gum.

Then Eagleson spotted Daw carrying his trench coat. "And, Richard, take that coat up to your room. If you bring it with you, you'll just lose it." Daw returned to his room to deposit the coat.

For his part, Goldblatt says you have to understand that when Eagleson snaps at someone, it isn't for keeps. "I laugh at this, being associated with Alan Eagleson for 31 years and not having an ulcer," he said. "I have to be a medical phenomenon. Al's the kind of person who blows his fuse and it lasts for maybe five minutes and he forgets about it. Unfortunately, a lot of us don't seem to have that characteristic where you can forget a little bit of verbal abuse."

For years, Kukulowicz functioned as Eagleson's Russian translator during international tournaments. As an executive of Air Canada, he took care of Team Canada's transportation needs. Aggie's relationship with Eagleson provided a significant boost to his career at the airline. "Aggie was Al's batman," said Derek Holmes.

Kukulowicz, described by Eagleson in his autobiography as a "tall, cheerful Winnipeger," has always been subservient toward Eagleson. When a friend asked Aggie about a ski chalet he had bought at Whistler Mountain in British Columbia, his immediate response was to say, "Now Al and John (Ziegler) will have a place to stay when they come to Whistler."

As the official team dentist, Ernie Lewis of Toronto accompanied Eagleson to the international tournaments. Although few can remember dental work being done, Lewis felt he was valuable by simply standing behind the bench with the coach and his assistants. Over the years, Lewis became known as "Coach Lewis."

Jimmy Lipa has been called everything from the Canadian team's mascot to its comedian. His official title is team photographer, but he is basically Eagleson's friend and occasional driver. Lipa has a thick European accent that is blurred by a speech impediment. Initially he was Bobby Orr's friend in Boston, but after Lipa ran into problems in Boston it was decided a more secure place for him to live was Toronto. Lipa attached himself to Eagleson and also became very close to Bill Watters and his family.

But when Orr and Watters made their split from Eagleson,

Lipa turned his back on both. Watters said it was difficult for his two young children to understand what had happened. Lipa had been virtually a member of the Watters family and the two children called him Uncle Jimmy.

Although Lipa is the official photographer of the Canadian team, his work is not good and eventually he was promoted to an executive position, in charge of photography.

Some of Lipa's income was earned from selling team pictures to players during the Canada Cup series. When *The Globe* reported during the 1984 tournament that Mike Bossy felt it was wrong that team members should have to pay for pictures when they were sacrificing their time and getting paid little to compete in the tournament, Lipa became furious with the reporter, calling him names and threatening him.

During tours in Europe, Lipa is usually to be found in the bars or at the gaming tables.

Terry O'Malley, an advertising man who is a friend of Eagleson, has never forgotten his first introduction to Jimmy Lipa. "He's got this photographer who goes everywhere with him. Jimmy Lipa. It's one of those bizarre things, your life recorded with Al Eagleson as photographed by Jimmy Lipa. Wherever you are and whatever you're doing.

"If there's an event, a couple of weeks later here comes a picture of you with whomever the celebrity was. Remember that movie, a Gary Cooper-Audrey Hepburn movie, *Love in the Afternoon*? They were followed everywhere by two violinists. I've got the same vision of Al. This is his own kind of music. It's perpetual publicity. He just fires them out. Thanks for coming, here's you with Frank Mahovlich or somebody. Just a thing he adds so the event has a memory."

Holmes remembers that "everyone was well dressed, well outfitted, well looked after because (Al) used to cut these terrific deals. If one brewery didn't like it, he'd walk down the road to someone else." Another insider was more blunt: "All I can tell you is this: when it came time for outfitting the team with all of the different things, the people that were first in line were always what we eventually called the suits. The guys that were first in line were the Goldblatts, the Ungermans, and all those people that wanted to get their jackets and pants and watches and luggage, and all that shit."

Aside from the regulars, Eagleson's circle at the tournaments included some of the top men in their fields. Often seen with him was John Sopinka, once Eagleson's lawyer and now a judge on the Supreme Court of Canada, a Hockey Canada director, Dr. Charles Bull and Dr. Simon McGrail. All of these successful and powerful men were quite happy to donate their services to Team Canada for a blazer and a chance to rub shoulders with the athletes.

"But look what they were able to get. They had a guy like Simon McGrail, a top eye, ear nose and throat guy in Canada, take off three and a half weeks," Derek Holmes said. "They'd get to go sit on the bench. That was the tradeoff: they'd get a blazer. They had the biggest team picture in hockey."

Eagleson bristled when anyone would ask why it was necessary to have a dentist or a nose and throat doctor on the team bench. "Here's a dentist who makes two hundred thousand dollars a year. Who else takes a week in Collingwood (at a Canada Cup training camp) and five to 10 nights during the Canada Cup?" Eagleson demanded. "It's just not my friends. I take people who are prepared to work and be as much a part of the team as any player. Ernie Lewis, Chuck Bull, Simon, they all earn hundreds of thousands of dollars and they give this country three to four weeks every year. The only guys who say thanks are me and the players.

"Then you read (Rich) Winter's comments. Why are these guys in the jackets all going over to Europe at our expense? All you have to have is one Joe Nieuwendyk injury (he suffered torn knee ligaments at the 1990 world championships) and you have Chuck Bull there and you realize you've done the right thing. What if we had the town doctor from Bern, Switzerland, operate on Joe Nieuwendyk? Yeah, there's good doctors in Switzerland. But maybe not in Bern that night."

In latter years, the entourage came to include Eagleson's son, Trevor Allen, who joined his father's law firm after graduating from law school. By 1991, young T. Allen had progressed to being the assistant general manager of Team Canada and director of administration for the Canada Cup, a job which paid him $95,000. The salary was the subject of controversy in the hockey community, considering the tournament lasted six weeks. But the Eaglesons protested that young Allen was working much longer than six weeks for the tournament, although he admitted he continued to work as a lawyer for his father in 1991, although in a "reduced capacity."

But some of his duties seemed to fall outside the bounds of the hockey team. For instance, there was his involvement with All Canada Sports Promotions Ltd., which held some of the rights to the rinkboard advertising. While Allen strenuously denied being in the employ of All Canada Sports, he did admit to dealing with advertisers like Air Canada and the Westin Harbour Castle Hotel on its behalf. But, he told *The Globe and Mail*, "I did that in my position as director of administration. I was co-ordinating the boards for everyone, all the board owners."

However, that isn't the way others involved in the rinkboard advertising remember it. Labatt, which owned all the advertising rights to the tournament, resold the rinkboard rights to three companies: All Canada Sports, the CTV and TSN television networks, which broadcast the event, and IFP, a Swedish company.

Geoff Moxley, a director of Rink Boards Inc., a London, Ont., company that actually manufactured the ads and saw that they were placed on the boards in the proper positions, said he dealt with Allen, Jr. only when he was handling positions held by All Canada. Executives of Air Canada and Westin, which bought the positions held by All Canada, also said they dealt with either Allen Jr., his father or Marvin Goldblatt. Irving Ungerman, the president of All Canada, was never mentioned.

Guy Bonnell, director of sports sales for CTV, said he handled all of the network's rinkboard advertising himself. He said he had no contact at all with Allen Eagleson.

But all of the off-ice intrigue still could not take the spotlight away from the real stars of the Canada Cup: the players. They were the true heroes of the tournament, playing for only a few thousand dollars (winning the Canada Cup meant about $5,000 in actual salaries for members of Team Canada in 1991) and for a long time under the mistaken belief they were improving their pension plan.

In fact, they were actually helping out the owners. The collective bargaining agreement between the players and management called for the NHL owners to pay 75 per cent of the annual pension contributions. The other 25 per cent comes from the players' share of international hockey proceeds. If the players did not make any money internationally, the owners had to make up the difference. By 1991, the annual pension contribution per player was $5,000. Since international hockey events have almost always turned a profit, the owners have never had to pony up the other 25 per cent.

Furthermore, Russ Conway discovered the owners got a double benefit from the players' generosity. In the 1988-89 season, the NHLPA carried a pension contribution of $693,811 on its books but that figure wasn't noted on the books of the NHL Pension Society, which administers the pension plans. Former NHL president John Ziegler told Conway that was because the actual pension payment is made by the owners, who are then reimbursed by the player's association. This allows each NHL team to deduct the full pension contribution from its taxes while paying just 75 per cent of it.

Eagleson, though, has always maintained that international hockey events up to 1991 have put more than $18 million into the players' hands. But this figure includes not only the pension money, but also the prize money paid to each player on each team in every tournament.

But even when the true state of the pension contributions was known in 1991, players still were anxious for a chance to play with and against the best players in the world.

Steve Thomas, a veteran NHL forward who was invited to Team Canada's 1991 training camp, epitomized the attitude that allowed Eagleson to remain in control of the players for so long. "I don't see where the money goes. I don't see the ledger sheets or anything like that. I get a track suit with Team Canada on it and I'm as happy as a pig in shit," he said. "I might be the wrong guy to ask. I'm sure the money does go back into the players' association, but I really don't know. To me, playing for my country is 99 and a half thousand times more important than where the money goes from the Canada Cup."

"We're hockey players, we're not businessmen," said Paul Cavallini, a defenceman with the St. Louis Blues. "We're here to represent our country and hopefully, the people who are taking care of us businesswise are representing us fairly."

But by 1991, not everyone was as trusting as Cavallini. With Eagleson gone from his post as head of the NHLPA, more and more players were declining invitations to play. Ray Bourque, arguably the best defenceman in the NHL, declined, as did fellow Boston Bruin Andy Moog. This was at least partly because of concerns about how Eagleson had handled Canada Cup finances.

Eagleson always seemed to have a cavalier attitude toward his members, and this was shown in 1991 in the matter of disability insurance. For the tournament, all players were guaranteed a total of $300,000 in disability insurance if they suffered a career-ending injury. This figure included both the NHL and NHLPA's disability coverage.

However, by 1991 player salaries were exploding, sparked by the $7.2-million, four-year contract signed a year earlier by Brett Hull of the St. Louis Blues. Even $300,000 in coverage was not nearly enough for a young player about to sign a multi-million-dollar contract.

This did not escape the attention of Rick Curran and several other player-agents, whose clients had been invited to play in the tournament. Curran was especially concerned about players who had played out their contracts and had yet to sign with a team. "Given the fact the player will have no additional salary income to rely on in the event of a disabling injury during his participation in the Canada Cup training camp and/or exhibition games and/or actual tournament games, do you really feel that $300,000 is sufficient coverage for these players?" Curran asked in a letter to Eagleson.

Eagleson's reply was curt. Enclosing a price list for optional insurance coverage with his letter, Eagleson wrote: "If you do not feel $300,000 is sufficient to protect your clients, you should purchase additional insurance, at your expense, for them."

Considering the amounts in question came to about $1,750 per player for $1 million in coverage, Curran was incensed. Considering that the league and the union was providing part of the coverage, Curran did some calculating and estimated Eagleson had budgeted about $525 per player in insurance premiums.

"The part that really pissed me off was that (Eagleson) was saying to me they can only afford to allocate 500 bucks per player for disability insurance," Curran said. "Although I had no idea specifically, generally I had a pretty good idea that (Eagleson's) expenses would be their usual horrendous totals, not to mention what he's paying half the fucking flunkies around there. And then I found out his own son was making somewhere around $90 thousand. My comment was forget about half the money he's paying for nothing, the priority should have been the players."

Still, several of Curran's clients paid for the extra coverage out of their own pockets, including Brendan Shanahan, who had signed a $4.4-million contract with the St. Louis Blues just before Team Canada's training camp opened. The decision cost him $3,500, which meant he played the six-week tournament for about $1,500. But this didn't matter to Shanahan, who was playing in the biggest hockey event of his young life.

"I probably would have paid my own hotel bill, too," Shanahan said. "I was 22 years old and I wasn't about to start making demands. The most important thing was the hockey. I probably would have paid my own expenses to participate in it."

Other players, like John Cullen, weren't as eager as Shanahan to foot the bill themselves. But when Cullen and Mark Recchi refused to play because of the insurance issue, they found their patriotism questioned by Eagleson, a familiar tactic when he was faced with reluctant players.

Now the Canada Cup no longer has the hold it once did on players. Even Wayne Gretzky has said he would prefer to see the NHL shut down for two or three weeks in February to let everyone play in the Olympics to another shortened summer for a six-week Canada Cup. The next Canada Cup is tentatively scheduled for 1995, but the only sure thing is that if it survives, the event will be moved around the world to make it a true World Cup. This idea was advanced by Eagleson, who emerged from a silence imposed on him by his lawyers (because of the various investigations) to say in early 1993 that he favoured such a format.

But Eagleson has little say in what happens next. After Bob Goodenow took over as executive director of the NHLPA, Eagleson was eased out of his position as the union's representative for international hockey. The next Canada Cup, or Dream Team tournament at the Olympics if the NHL decides to ape the NBA, will not bear the stamp of R. Alan Eagleson.

By February of 1993, Eagleson was out of the picture entirely in international hockey. When Hockey Canada's board of directors finally emerged from their meeting at the Westin Harbour Castle, it was left to chairman Ian Macdonald and president Ron Robison to announce that the position of international negotiator had been taken from Eagleson and given to Robison. The Eagle was finally a spent force. Robison also announced Hockey Canada would conduct an internal investigation of its finances and cooperate with the RCMP investigation.

But it was rightly criticized as a lame response. Not only did the directors allow Eagleson to retain his seat on the board, rather than step aside while the investigations continued, but they failed to call in an independent investigator to look at Hockey Canada's records. However, within a couple of weeks, stung by the criticism of the public and the media, the board let it be known an independent forensic accounting firm would conduct the investigation.

By then, even the future of Hockey Canada was uncertain. The Canadian Amateur Hockey Association, which had long fought the emergence of Hockey Canada as the boss of international hockey in the country, was again considering a coup by mid-1993. With Eagleson and his iron grip on the players a memory, the CAHA served notice it intended to seize control of such lucrative events like the world championships and even the Canada Cup.

First, the CAHA informed Hockey Canada that it would take back control of the Olympic team after the 1994 Games in Lillehammer, Norway. Hockey Canada was granted control of the Olympic team in 1981 as part of a settlement of a lawsuit brought against Hockey Canada by the CAHA. At issue was $1 million in Canada Cup revenue, which the CAHA had said rightfully belonged to it.

Hockey Canada was given a seven-year contract to operate the Olympic team, which was extended in 1988 until 1994. But the CAHA has said it will not renew the deal after the '94 Olympics.

It is suspected by some that Bob Goodenow will assist the CAHA in its fight, although he has not tipped his hand. But as international hockey in Canada heads into an uncertain future, this much is known: Alan Eagleson will have no part in the drama. In mid-July, 1993, it was announced by Hockey Canada that he had resigned his position on the board of directors of Hockey Canada.

The announcement came several months after Eagleson had actually resigned, and seemed timed to save face for him. He had actually resigned in March, not long after *The Eagle-Tribune, The Globe and Mail* and the CBC had each carried a series about the once-most-powerful man in hockey.

Chapter Seven

THE MORTGAGE MAN

THE SOURCES OF R. Alan Eagleson's wealth are as varied as the hats he wore during the height of his reign over hockey. But throughout his career as a lawyer, politician, union leader, player agent and international hockey czar, there has been one constant — one arena that Eagleson loved to play in as other activities waxed and waned — real estate.

Eagleson himself admits he has made a fortune in real estate. It is his pat answer to charges he has made his riches by taking advantage of his various positions in hockey for personal profit. In September, 1991, after the publication of Russ Conway's exposé of his financial and union dealings in *The Eagle-Tribune*, he smugly told *The Hockey News* that "I have not made my money off the backs of the NHL Players' Association. I have not made my money off the backs of professional hockey players. I have not made my money off the backs of international hockey competition. I have made my money mostly by fortuitous investments in real estate. There has not been one speck of impropriety."

Like many of the statements Alan Eagleson has made over the years, this one, too, does not stand up to careful scrutiny. Yes, Alan Eagleson has made fortuitous investments in real estate that have made him a great deal of money. But often his real estate dealings have involved close friends and clients of his law firm, Eagleson Ungerman, and were financed by money from the players' association and players he represented as an agent — but not the real estate kind.

Eagleson's name has appeared on dozens of mortgage documents over the years, as he moved money around from organizations he controlled such as the players' association, and from players he represented as an agent, to various residences owned by him, business associates, friends or clients of his law firm. The paper trail is dizzying, but one conclusion is inescapable: Alan Eagleson's favourite way of doing business, of moving money from one place to another, is via a mortgage.

Eagleson owes his expertise in mortgages to Blaney Pasternak, the law firm he and five other young lawyers had formed. In the first several years of his law career, Eagleson had been a generalist, handling criminal cases, real estate and wills. As noted in Chapter One, in 1960, he formed The Blue and White Group Ltd. with several Toronto Maple Leaf players he had met through his boyhood friend, Bob Pulford. Some prominent Toronto businessmen were also members, and the company invested its funds in mortgages. Eventually, Eagleson became head of Blaney Pasternak's real estate division, retaining the position even while his time was increasingly taken up with organizing the players' association.

In 1989, Eagleson's habit of granting mortgages from NHLPA escrow accounts first became public knowledge. Hamilton lawyer Bill Dermody was commissioned in 1989 to review loans made by Eagleson from the NHLPA's escrow accounts. Dermody was acting at the request of player agents Ron Salcer and Rich Winter, along with lawyer Ed Garvey, the former head of the National Football League Players' Association. Garvey had been asked by a group of more than 200 NHL players to investigate, with the assistance of Salcer and Winter, the operation of the NHLPA under Eagleson. Dermody discovered that in 1987 and 1988, Eagleson had loaned more than $2 million of NHLPA funds to several friends and associates, including a mortgage of $500,000 to his law partner, Howard Ungerman, who was acting in trust for a company headed by his father, Irving. When a lawyer acts in trust, it means he or she is representing an individual or company or a group of individuals and/or companies that may include himself/herself. Alan Eagleson and Irving Ungerman have been friends for decades and were involved in the same business deals many times. In 1982, the NHLPA gave Irving Ungerman and a partner, Martin Tauber, a $436,000 mortgage on an industrial building in the Toronto suburb of Scarborough.

Another audit of NHLPA finances, completed after the *Dermody Report*, by William Dovey of the Toronto office of the accounting firm Price Waterhouse, showed that Eagleson had a history of making mortgage loans to his friends with players' money. In the early 1980s, builder and developer Norman Donaldson, Eagleson's friend and tennis partner, received $775,000 in loans from the NHLPA for companies he either held interest in or owned. Despite Eagleson's claim that all the loans he made with players money were sound investments with solid companies, Donaldson's companies had a history of late and missed payments. On one occasion, in February, 1985, a Donaldson company failed to pay its taxes on a townhouse project and the players' association was forced to sell some of the lots through power of sale. Despite all the problems with the loans, the NHLPA, through Eagleson, continued to renew them. On all of the mortgage deals viewed by the authors, Eagleson's law firm handled the legal work, sometimes for both parties — work that was worth thousands of dollars in fees.

"I'm not Montreal Trust and the Bank of Commerce where strangers come in and borrow money," Eagleson told *The Globe and Mail* in the summer of 1991. "Clients of mine come to me and say, 'Hey, I need a mortgage on my house.' Well, who's the first person I'm going to talk to? Another client.

"Just as Irv Ungerman in one of those deals was the mortgagor (the person borrowing the money), in many deals it's his money and he's the mortgagee. With any law firm, when people come to you and want advice on a mortgage, the first guy they go to is their lawyer."

Eagleson and his associates, such as NHLPA director of operations Sam Simpson (whose name appears on many documents as the person making the loans in trust) argued strenuously that all of the loans were solid investments made to stable companies that commanded better rates than other financial institutions were offering. This was disputed just as strongly by people like Dermody, who made the first audit, and by several mortgage experts contacted by Russ Conway for his background research.

There is also the matter of disclosure to the people whose money was being loaned out. While Eagleson, Simpson *et al.* always maintained the executive committee of the NHLPA was kept informed of the mortgages, Conway could find only one player who said he knew about them. That was Bryan Trottier, who served as NHLPA president during the period the loans were made. At the June, 1989 NHLPA meeting in Florida when Dermody gave his report revealing the mortgages, there were about 80 players present, including some on the executive committee, and only Trottier appeared to have had some knowledge of the loans.

Trottier was rather vague on the subject, telling Conway and later *The Globe and Mail* that he was informed of them in telephone calls from Simpson. He seemed to have no idea who was receiving the mortgages. "My understanding is that Sam (Simpson) had full authority to move funds around as he saw he needed to (carry out) the operations of the players' association until our annual meeting," Trottier said. "All he had to do was notify someone from the executive (committee) what he was doing, whether it was the executive director or one or two players on the executive board.

"I can just remember one or two times Sam would call me up and say 'These things came due, I'm just letting you know we're going to roll them over,' and I said, 'Fine.'"

As for who was receiving the mortgages and how secure they were, Trottier said: "Some of the (players) at the time knew, like Darryl Sittler I think was involved at the time, and he knew where the property was.

"Some of these guys knew some of the people that were involved in some of these mortgages and said they're like Triple A-type companies. It wasn't like we were going into junk bonds or something like that. These people are not nobodies. When you're taking the word of some of your peers, who know these guys, that's a pretty good recommendation for a lot of guys in the players' association."

Eagleson was much more certain: "There was never any risk involved. The players knew that. We were a little outfit trying to create additional revenue for the purposes of the association."

However, the experts contacted by Conway, as well as a lot of the players, held a different opinion, especially when it was learned how much trouble there was collecting on some of the Donaldson loans, and the fact that most of them were interest-only mortgages,* and that one of them was a second mortgage, a far less secure investment.

"It's no contest that as far as the loans were concerned, that they were for clients," Jim Peplinski, at the time of the June, 1989 meeting a player representative for Calgary, told Conway. "It's no contest they were in conflict, that they were unauthorized. But he defended them by saying they were good."

Eagleson has always claimed, possibly under the theory that if you repeat something often enough other people will believe it's true, that Dermody's report on the mortgages vindicated him. This opinion is not shared by Dermody, whose report recommended several changes as to how the players' money should be handled: only allow the executive committee to grant loans, fully disclose all conflicts of interest by union officials and put your money affairs in the hands of an investment manager. Dermody pointed out that his report was based only on what financial statements Eagleson allowed him to see. Eagleson was allowed to negotiate a deal where Dermody only had access to the NHLPA's financial statements from 1987 and 1988, and Eagleson had control over just how much of the statements Dermody saw. Dermody was given no information on the mortgages the NHLPA made from 1981 to 1986 to Donaldson and others.

"The players (Mr. Eagleson and Mr. Donaldson) knew one another, had business back and forth. There is a connection of friendship, characterized again later in the '87-'88 loans by Eagleson," Dermody told Russ Conway after the earlier loans became known. "These files clearly show why private mortgage investments with escrow funds are unsatisfactory and undesirable. The funds — players' money invested in these loans — were put at a real risk. After reviewing the latest information (about the Donaldson loans), one thing is perfectly clear: when it is other people's money you are responsible for managing, you have to use a higher standard of care in handling those funds."

Conway also spoke to a number of mortgage and pension experts in the Toronto area about the 1987 mortgages as well as

---

*When an interest-only mortgage is taken out, the borrower pays only the interest on the loan. None of the principal is paid off. The principal balance becomes due at the expiration of an agreed-upon term of years.

the earlier ones made to Donaldson's and Ungerman's companies. All agreed to speak to Conway as long as the companies they worked for were not identified.

Of the 1987 loans, several of the experts did not like the fact they were interest-only. "What that does is minimize the investor's outlay while increasing the mortgagee's risk," said John Leeson, who has more than 40 years of experience in the mortgage business. "If anything happens to the real estate, or mortgagor, the principal balance is right where it started."

Of the loans from 1981 to 1986 to Donaldson's companies, Leeson and others were even more critical. "I still do not see in any of these loans how any rational lender could hit serious delinquency, power of sale even, and then not only renew (and increase the loan) but also reduce the rate and create unfavourable terms, such as agreeing to allow a new first (mortgage) to be registered ... without repayment of your existing mortgage. Talk about giving the shop away," Leeson said. "The loans appear to have been made as if they were his own money. When loaning your own funds out you do not have to consider the decisions you are making. The funds are your own and it is no one else's business what you do, and the losses, if any, are yours alone. However, when you are a solicitor, or mortgage company, et cetera, loaning on behalf of some other person or group, then it is incumbent upon you to take precautions to ensure the funds are invested wisely. He should know these things. This is Alan Eagleson we're talking about, Alan Eagleson, Q.C., Queen's Counsel. We're not talking about Mary from Milwaukee."

Leaving most of the NHLPA loans for a moment, there are two separate series of mortgage transactions involving Eagleson that stand out in particular. The first has to do with Eagleson's former home, a Rosedale mansion, and involves his friend and tennis partner, Norman Donaldson, and Harcom Consultants Ltd., owned by Arthur Harnett. Harcom received millions of dollars in television rights and advertising sales work through contracts awarded by Eagleson. Those doing business with Arthur Harnett and Harcom have said they believed that company and others that listed Harnett as president were actually controlled by Eagleson.

The latter concerns land sales and mortgages revolving around a $500,000 mortgage granted by the NHLPA to Howard

Ungerman, in trust for one of his father's companies, in financing the purchase of 50 acres near Collingwood.

The series of mortgages and transfer of ownership, as well as their timing, of the Rosedale mansion are intriguing. Located on a tree-lined street in one of Toronto's wealthiest neighbourhoods, the home at 30 Rosedale Road was a stunning showcase, the very epitome of a poor-boy-makes-good status symbol. Eagleson bought the house on November 29, 1976 from his next-door neighbour, Dr. Charles Best of insulin fame. Once he had sold his house next door, at 2 Cluny Drive, Eagleson moved into 30 Rosedale in early 1977. Writer Ron Base described the house this way, not long after Eagleson had taken possession: "The mansion is huge. Eagleson bought it last January for $350,000, when he heard it was going to be turned into apartments. Inside are wide expanses of highly polished hardwood flooring, presided over by marble fireplaces, with old period furniture pushed back against the walls as if in preparation for a magnificent ball — or a game of floor hockey. Eagleson led the group to the back of the house, past dark pictures of thin-lipped Presbyterian gentlemen who stared down unpleasantly from atop the mantlepieces. They entered a family room with a dove-grey carpet and dark wood shelves full of expensive art books. To the left, french doors opened on to a patio. The windows at the rear of the room overlooked a magnificent ravine, and at the right a corner of the swimming pool peeked into view."

The complicated transactions began on May 6, 1982 when Eagleson transferred the title of this house to Norman Donaldson Construction Ltd. for $2 (two dollars). Eagleson also took back a mortgage for $1,250,000 that had a few unusual conditions. First, it was interest-free, with $350,000 of the principal due in about 10 weeks, July 31, 1982, and the balance in another four months, on November 30, 1982. Eagleson also granted Donaldson's company the right to build on the land and agreed to postpone his mortgage if Donaldson received a construction mortgage for no more than $1,150,000.

It seems Eagleson, the man who once saved the home from being turned into apartments, was participating in a scheme to turn it into five condominiums. On the same day Eagleson granted his friend the $1,250,000 mortgage, Harcom Consultants also gave Norman Donaldson Construction Ltd. a mortgage, this one for $1,150,000 at 3 per cent above the prime interest rate. It was also an interest-only loan (Donaldson only had to make interest payments), with the principal to be advanced in portions as construction proceeded. If construction stopped for more than 21 consecutive days for any reason that was not out of Donaldson's control, the mortgage would become due. Eagleson also postponed his mortgage, so that Harcom's loan became the first mortgage on the property, with his the second.

The transactions came about eight months after the 1981 Canada Cup, an event which was very lucrative for Harcom Consultants. Alan Eagleson sold the television advertising rights to Harcom, and thus to his good friend Arthur Harnett, for $1.9 million, according to Russ Conway, although it isn't known what the company's profit was. It was the second consecutive time Harcom had a hand in television rights for the Canada Cup. In 1976, Harcom acted as Hockey Canada's agent in selling the rights to Carling O'Keefe. The brewery then hired Harcom as its agent in selling some of the television time to other advertisers. As a private company, Harcom's profits are not made public, although Conway noted that Hockey Canada's records show it paid more than $1 million in commissions for television advertising. Harnett's first involvement in international hockey came in the 1972 Canada-Soviet series when Team Canada Productions Ltd., of which he was president, handled the television and radio rights, which made a profit of $2.4 million. The commissions paid to sales agencies were $283,000, of which Arthur Harnett Enterprises Ltd. (a separate company which listed Harnett as president) made $118,750. It has already been noted that Evan Hayter, Carling's marketing director in 1976, said the company's deals were always made "directly with Eagleson."

There was a quick turnaround on the mortgage given to Norman Donaldson Construction Ltd. by Harcom. Three and a half months later, on August 17, 1982, Harcom Consultants discharged its $1,150,000 mortgage to Donaldson. The mortgage discharge documents do not indicate if the money was paid, only that Harcom was satisfied the terms of the deal had been met.

Two months later, there were two more mortgage transactions on consecutive days. First, on October 27, Eagleson noted that Donaldson had failed to pay $350,000 of the prinicpal on the mortgage he had issued the company, but forgave that in favour of new terms, also interest-free. Now, Donaldson had to pay $500,000 of the principal by November 1, 1982, with the balance of $750,000 due November 1, 1984. Donaldson also agreed to pay Eagleson $50,000 plus interest for each of the five condos as they were sold. The next day, October 27, Marvin Goldblatt entered the picture. He gave Donaldson a mortgage in trust for $800,000 on the house at 16 per cent interest, due November 1, 1984. Donaldson had to pay Goldblatt $200,000 plus interest for each condo as it was built. Eagleson agreed to again postpone his mortgage in favour of the new one. The house now had $2,050,000 in mortgages on it. One year later, almost to the day, on October 18, 1983, Norman Donaldson Construction Ltd. sold the mansion to a company called Projector Holdings (Canada) Inc. for $1,090,000 in cash. No more mortgages.

Thirteen days later, on November 3, Marvin Goldblatt discharged the $800,000 mortgage against Donaldson, and one day after that Eagleson discharged his $1,250,000 mortgage.

There is no public record as to whether Donaldson Construction ever turned the house into five condos. In the last public mention of the house, it was still a single-family residence. *The Globe and Mail*'s former society columnist, Rosemary Sexton, who happens to be married to Eagleson's lawyer, Edgar Sexton, wrote on July 11, 1992 that the house had been languishing on the shell-shocked Toronto real estate market for more than three years despite having "11-foot-high ceilings, eight bedrooms, nine fireplaces and rich panelling." The owner had listed it in March, 1989 for $4.9 million and had turned down an offer for $4.3 million. Sexton said the house was now listed for less than $4 million.

Equally intriguing is a series of deals surrounding a 50-acre tract of land near Collingwood, Ont., Eagleson's favourite vacation retreat and, before the bottom fell out of the real estate market in 1990, a popular place to buy real estate. Eagleson's connection to Collingwood begins with his wife, Nancy, a native of the town. After more than 30 years of business and play in Collingwood, Eagleson has developed a large circle of friends in the area, including John Kadwell, a builder and president of Monterra Properties Ltd., and Ernie Rawley, another builder who was an original partner in the Orr-Walton Sports Camp. Other friends include George Weider, the chief executive officer and chairman of Blue Mountain Resorts Ltd., which operates the famous ski resort, and Gordon Canning, president of Blue Mountain. Weider and Canning are also on the board of directors of Monterra Properties. He also has a number of land holdings in the area, some of which started out as buys in partnership with Norman Donaldson. Those included five acres of waterfront in Thornbury, just north of Collingwood, bought in 1979 for $176,000 by Donaldson, Eagleson and a third party. In 1986, Eagleson built a three-bedroom house on the lot, which serves as his weekend getaway. Not far away is a lot owned by the Eagleson children, Jill and Allen, purchased for $98,000 with Eagleson providing interest-free mortgages of $45,000 to each. Nancy owns a farm not far from their vacation home.

The 50 acres in question was bought on November 25, 1987 by Irving Investments Ltd., a company owned by Eagleson's long-time friend Irving Ungerman, for $1,070,000. Part of the financing was an $800,000 mortgage at 12 per cent taken out by Irving's son, Howard, in trust. The NHLPA provided $500,000 of that money via a six-month mortgage granted in trust by the association's director of operations, Sam Simpson. Another $100,000 came from Jill Eagleson. When Bill Dermody, who audited the loans and other NHLPA financial dealings in 1989 for a dissident group of players, asked Simpson who the other lenders were, Simpson said he was not in a position to name them.

On July 4, 1988, after the NHLPA loan had been renewed, the players' association suddenly needed to get $100,000 of its mortgage back, which it did. Eagleson later told Dermody a substitute investor was found, but he didn't identify the lender. It was during this period that a mortgage for $100,000 appeared on the books of Hockey Canada, which operated international hockey for Canada under Eagleson's direction. It was the only time in Hockey Canada's 24-year history that a mortgage ever appeared on its financial statements.

Almost five months later, on November 30, the players' association mortgage came due and $200,000 of it was repaid, with the balance of $200,000 renewed until August 31, 1989. At the same time, Jill Eagleson's $100,000 loan was repaid. Howard Ungerman renewed his whole $800,000 loan for one year at 13 per cent. The lenders' identities were not disclosed.

Over the next several months, Dermody began his inquiry for the players and the subject of the Collingwood land and the

NHLPA mortgages was raised. In a letter dated June 22, 1989, Eagleson told Dermody that he had personally visited the land with the developer and was assured by him that the property was now worth $2.2 million. By August 30, 1989, the value of the land had dropped to $1,918,000, for that was the sale price Irving Ungerman received from Monterra Properties — 21 months after he had bought it from that company — for a profit of $848,000. By September 7, most of the mortgages on the property had been discharged, including the one from the NHLPA. One month later, on September 26, Monterra turned around and sold a series of lots from the property to a group of individuals and companies connected with Eagleson or his law firm for a total of $1,520,000. Eagleson Ungerman handled the legal work on almost all of the transactions.

1. Robert Fung, Jr. bought a lot for $135,000 (on March 16, 1990, he transferred it to Robert A. Fung and Jialson Holdings Ltd., an Eagleson company for $150,000).

2. Sam Simpson, director of operations for the NHLPA, and his wife Marianne bought one lot for $135,000.

3. Jialson Holdings bought one for $140,000.

4. Kadwell himself bought a lot for $125,000 with Monterra taking back a mortgage for the full purchase price (he transferred this lot to his wife Sherry Lee Kadwell on January 26, 1993 for "natural love and affection").

5. Marvin Goldblatt and his wife Marian bought a lot for $125,000 (one half-interest was transferred on December 7, 1992 to Rae-Con Consultants Ltd., a company owned by Goldblatt and Nancy Eagleson, for $62,500).

6. Another Eagleson firm, Kingsmar Holdings Ltd., paid $115,000 for a lot with Goldblatt signing for it and Monterra taking back a mortgage of $115,000 at 13 per cent.

7. Kingsmar bought a second lot for $125,000 and took another mortgage from Monterra for $125,000 at 13 per cent.

8. Claude Builders Ltd., whose president is John Kadwell, bought a lot for $125,000 with yet another mortgage from Monterra and on January

26, 1993, Sherry Lee Kadwell gave Claude Builders a $125,000 mortgage at 8 per cent.

9. HUD Holdings Ltd., an Ungerman company, bought a lot for $135,000.

10. James Bull, brother of long-time Team Canada doctor Charles Bull, bought a lot for $125,000.

11. T&C Bianchi Ltd., whose principal is Teresa Bianchi, bought a lot for $115,000.

12. Manorhampton Investments Ltd., whose principal is Maria Rietta, bought a lot for $120,000.

The connection of the latter two companies with Eagleson is not known, but his law firm handled the legal work for both purchases.

Then, one year later, on February 21, 1991, Monterra obtained a mortgage on the same property for $750,000 from Toronto mortgage broker Monty Beber. The mortgage was guaranteed by Alan Eagleson. Almost one year after that, Eagleson was added to the board of directors of Monterra Properties on January 15, 1992.

All of which leaves a few questions: Why would Monterra buy back its own land to create a profit of $848,000 for someone else? Why would Alan Eagleson guarantee a mortgage on property owned by Monterra? Did this have anything to do with getting a position on the board?

Eagleson has been questioned a few times about the original loan to Ungerman for $500,000. He has usually employed his tactic of throwing up a smokescreen and then leaving the question unanswered. In this case, more than once, Eagleson has zeroed in on his daughter's participation in the Collingwood deal. He proclaimed to *The Globe and Mail* that Ed Garvey had falsely accused him of lending NHLPA funds to his daughter, although there was no solid evidence of this. "Aggie Kukulowicz called me from the (NHLPA) golf tournament to say that one of the players told him that Garvey had given out some material which said that I had loaned Jill money from the players' association fund. Whether he gave that document out, I don't know, but he certainly told the players at the golf day that we loaned money to my daughter."

Eagleson said his daughter put her $100,000 in the mortgage because "it was a good mortgage, land that was worth $3 million to $4 million. She's not an investor. She likes the monthly interest payments to help her offset her financial burden."

Left unanswered was why players' money was being loaned to a friend in the first place, and how a 23-year-old student could produce $100,000. Or how land described as being worth $2.2 million in 1989 had grown to "$3 million to $4 million" by 1991, when Collingwood real estate values had taken a deep plunge.

The real estate connection with Norman Donaldson began in Collingwood when he and Eagleson bought the property on which they built their vacation homes and grew into a company called Doneagle Investments Inc. Eagleson was listed as president and Donaldson as secretary. The company was in existence from 1980 to 1984, and according to corporation papers examined by Conway, both men were authorized to borrow money and mortgage "any currently owned or subsequently acquired property."

In 1981, the trouble between Donaldson and the players' association began with a plan to build some townhouses in Cabbagetown, a neighbourhood just east of downtown Toronto, one of the first working-class areas of the city to see an invasion of yuppie renovators which began in the late 1960s. A company called New Leaf Florists, which listed Donaldson's wife, Marie, as president, borrowed $275,000 from the NHLPA with Norman Donaldson listed as guarantor, and planned to build the townhouses.

In October of 1981, the NHLPA gave Tesson Developments a $300,000 loan to buy five house lots in Scarborough, a city on the east side of Toronto. The president of this company was William Wilson, but Norman Donaldson was the secretary-treasurer. Both loans were trouble free until early 1983 when New Leaf and Tesson started falling behind in the payments on the mortgages which, as per Eagleson custom with his pals, were interest-only. There was also no penalty specified for late payments, according to documents read by Conway. Despite the problems, Conway found that the New Leaf loan was "restructured" in April, 1983, "despite the fact no interest had been paid since the previous August. The loan was 'extended' in January, 1984 with a reminder to Donaldson to pay back taxes." New Leaf owed about $22,000 in taxes to the city of Toronto, a debt which took priority over delinquent mortgage payments. By August, 1985, nine months after it became due a third time, the New Leaf loan was still outstanding, this time with $10,000 in late interest payments. But it was forgiven again, with Donaldson getting a further extension, this one to November, 1986.

During this period, Conway discovered that Sam Simpson, the NHLPA's director of operations who had been granting the mortgages with the approval of Eagleson, had given Donaldson a separate $80,000 loan on his Collingwood property. Simpson acted as a trustee for the loan, which was granted in 1985, but the source of the funds was not revealed, although Conway was able to conclude it didn't involve NHLPA money.

Tesson was an even bigger headache; the NHLPA finally had to take action in February, 1985 and sell two of the Scarborough lots under power of sale because Tesson still owed it $290,000. The lots were sold for $250,000, but the NHLPA had to take back a $230,000 mortgage on the deal. The same purchaser saved the association a month later by buying the other three lots, which let the NHLPA get its money back. But this didn't help an unnamed party who held a second mortgage on the property. Conway reported that NHLPA documents show this mortgagee lost "a significant sum." The New Leaf debacle was finally resolved in 1986, when a Toronto lawyer who had guaranteed the original mortgage was forced to pay it off. As Conway noted, this misadventure had lasted more than five years on mortgages that were supposed to last just one year, and that "a total of $395,000 was loaned to Tesson and $380,000 to New Leaf."

Howard Ungerman handled a lot of the paperwork on the loans. One letter from Ungerman to Donaldson in January, 1985 was obtained by Conway and showed that Eagleson had stepped in personally to give his friend more time to come up with the money: "Mr. Eagleson has indicated that you may need some extra time in this regard, so Mr. Simpson is prepared to give you a few months if necessary to rearrange funds."

An interesting sidelight is a memo from Simpson to Eagleson in March, 1983 that was given to Conway. Simpson writes to Eagleson that "in response to your request about refinancing the (Tesson) mortgage, I have now spoken to the investment committee, who has agreed to redo the mortgage." This goes to the whole issue of disclosure, as many players have said they had no idea their money was being loaned out to Eagleson's friends and clients. Conway interviewed a number of NHL players, including some on the association's executive committee, which was supposed to approve all NHLPA moves. All said they had heard of neither the mortgages nor the investment committee.

"Investment committee? We didn't have any investment committee," said Mike Milbury, a player rep for the Boston Bruins who tried to have Eagleson brought to heel in 1979. "If I had known about loans or any of that stuff, an investment committee or Eagle using our money to loan to his friends, you know darn well I would have raised the topic and asked questions."

Bill Dermody, who is often cited by Eagleson as clearing him of any conflicts of interest or improper conduct in his 1989 report that looked into a group of loans to Eagleson friends in 1987, was convinced the players were kept in the dark. The players "didn't know a thing about the mortgages made using their money," he told Conway. "They had never been informed."

Unchastened by his experiences with Donaldson from 1981 to 1986, Eagleson made some more loans of the players' money in 1987, although this collection performed a little better.

Aside from the $500,000 mortgage issued to the Ungerman company for the Collingwood purchase, Eagleson loaned $320,000 to his friend David Baker, a car dealer from Richmond Hill, Ont., north of Toronto. Baker was granted the interest-only loan to buy a property in Richmond Hill for $370,000. Also lining up at the mortgage wicket was Marvin Teperman, whose family operates the well-known wrecking firm. He landed a whopping $1.2-million interest-only mortgage from the NHLPA for Teperman Family Holdings Inc., which used it to finance a small shopping plaza in Burlington, Ontario.

Not all of the funds loaned out by Eagleson were for business deals with clients. Sometimes he seemed to just want to help out a close friend. Like Carol Patterson and her husband, Malcolm Gray, a former reporter for *The Globe and Mail*, whose last posting was as correspondent for the Maritime provinces. In 1983, Eagleson gave Patterson and Gray a mortgage for $87,000 on a house in the west end of Toronto. Conway discovered that $27,000 of that money came from the NHL Players' Association. Now the bureau chief in Moscow for *Maclean's* magazine, Gray told Russ Conway that he had become friendly with Eagleson while working on "big sports stories," although records at *The Globe* show Patterson wrote only one sports story for the newspaper, and it did not involve Eagleson. Gray left *The Globe* in the fall of 1979. Gray said he had no idea that some of the money came from the players' association, although he indicated that Eagleson "mentioned there were monies, investment monies available . . . money that active and formerly active NHL players had put up."

Gray also told Conway that Eagleson was an acquaintance of his father-in-law, Arnold Patterson, a Halifax businessman who once served as Prime Minister Pierre Trudeau's press secretary. However, others have said Eagleson seemed to be a close friend of Carol Patterson, who was living in Moscow in the late 1970s when Eagleson spent a lot of time there taking care of business surrounding the 1979 world championships.

Luckily for the players, all of these loans were repaid, the last one to go being the Teperman mortgage, which was retired early in 1993. However, the mortgage experts who spoke to Conway were not impressed with these loans either, chiefly because they were interest-only and no credible checks seemed to have been done either the properties or the borrowers. All that Conway found in the NHLPA files were letters from Baker to Eagleson saying the property in question was valued by his real estate agent at $750,000, and Eagleson said Baker had given him a statement saying his net worth was $2.5 million.

"That appraisal is worth nothing," said Erv Brewda, who has been in the mortgage business for more than 20 years. "It's from a sales person. An appraisal from a sales rep — that blows me away."

A senior official with a mortgage company, Paul Morris, wasn't impressed with Eagleson's claim about Baker's net worth. "Net worth and 60 cents might get you a cup of coffee. I wouldn't have made the loan on an 86 per cent — 320 versus 370 — no way."

The experts were less critical of the Teperman deal, which involved a more solid property. But John Leeson questioned the interest rate, which was 11 per cent, despite the fact Teperman had said he could have received a lower rate elsewhere. "That's an absurd statement — they could make better loans elsewhere. Why didn't they?" Leeson also noted that the Baker, Ungerman and Teperman loans all had the legal work done by Eagleson Ungerman and that "the solicitors appear to be acting for mortgagee and mortgagor. One thing is clear. Any normal commercial mortgage transaction should be backed by a competent full appraisal of value — not 'I visited the site and it was worth, etc.,'" Leeson wrote in a statement to Conway.

Mortgages in which Eagleson had a personal stake seem to have done a bit better, such as the one he held on the Orr-Walton Hockey Camp in the late 1970s. In 1974, Eagleson, acting in trust, gave a $230,000 mortgage to Owaissa Hockey Camp Ltd. (the camp's corporate name) that was guaranteed by Orr. On January 20, 1977, Eagleson (acting as Orr's financial adviser and lawyer) transferred ownership of the property to Bobby Orr Enterprises, the parent company of Owaissa. The camp ceased operations in 1978, after Orr signed with the Chicago Blackhawks and moved to the Windy City.

Then, on March 27, 1980, after Orr and Eagleson had their famous split, Orr sold the property to Eagleson for $330,000 and then paid Eagleson off for the mortgage a few days later, along with a $300,000 operating loan on the camp, leaving him with a huge loss on the deal. Eagleson held onto the property (considered to have good potential for development as a site for cottages) for almost a year and a half, then sold it to some investors headed by Mike Walton and his cousin, Dan Casey, for $500,000 on September 8, 1981. Eagleson took back a $475,000 mortgage from the buyers, then granted two more mortgages a week later for $350,000 and $127,000, bringing the total mortgage amount on the property to $952,000.

When Walton, Casey and the other investors defaulted on the mortgages, Eagleson foreclosed in 1988. He sold the 180 acres to a developer for $900,000, which more than covered the shortfall in the mortgages, less Walton's down payment of $25,000. Just another "fortuitous" real estate investment.

Alas, things did not go so well for Robert Arpenif, the developer who bought the property. Arpenif told Wayne Parrish of the *Toronto Sun* that he had turned down an offer of $9.8 million for it. But Arpenif couldn't make his mortgage payments on the property (which he planned to turn into a subdivision) and the bank foreclosed. Today, the property is still vacant and is for sale.

By 1991, with Eagleson out as head of the players' association, and the NHLPA extricating itself from the mortgage business, suddenly it almost became his idea to get out of the mortgage game (and not anything to do with Dermody's report).

"I don't remember exactly what all (Dermody's recommenda-
tions) were, but what we decided to do because of the concerns —
it was my suggestions (sic) — I'm proposing that from now on we
only have deposit receipts, bank deposits and guaranteed investment certificates, and whatever less money we earn, too bad,"
Eagleson said, the summer after he was replaced by Bob
Goodenow as executive director of the NHLPA. "We don't need
the money that bad."

Eagleson still maintains Dermody's report cleared him of any
improper conduct, but Dermody told Conway that isn't the case.
"He read the text of my report before it was even issued. I did that
as a courtesy. What he read and agreed to in that report was that
there was a perception of his benefiting by position. He could call
that whatever he wants, but that point was explicitly clear. That
was certainly not condoning or clearing him of his past involvement with allowing escrow funds to be issued to his personal
friends or clients."

By the summer of 1993, Eagleson himself was trying to cut
back on his real estate holdings. This could have been because the
Collingwood real estate market, among the hottest in the country
in the late 1980s, had collapsed with the recession that struck
early in 1990. Eagleson put his lakefront home up for sale in 1991
for $750,000, he said, because he and Nancy wanted to move to
the farm they had bought a few years previously. "We'll take
another year at least before we move (to the farm), so we're in no
hurry to sell this," Eagleson said in the summer of 1991. By the
summer of 1993, Eagleson had changed his tune. The price of the
property was reduced to $575,000, and a real estate agent who
had spoken to Eagleson about the house said he was "anxious" to
sell. Also on the market was a lot Eagleson owned, not far from
the house, for $250,000.

Chapter Eight

THE UNION BOSS

BY THE LATE 1980s, R. Alan Eagleson appeared to have achieved all of his goals. He was rich, famous, powerful; he circulated at the highest levels of Canadian society. Eagleson, who had grown up in poverty in West Toronto, now counted among his friends some of the most important and influential people in Canadian business and politics.

They included Brian Mulroney, the prime minister of Canada, for whom he had worked as a money raiser; Iona Campagnolo, who had been the Liberal minister of Sport in the 1970s; Liberal senator Keith Davey, a long-time sports fan; Paul Godfrey, the *Toronto Sun* publisher, a Tory and former Metropolitan Toronto chairman; Supreme Court justices Willard "Bud" Estey and John Sopinka; and financiers Ross Johnson and Paul Desmarais.

Ross Johnson is a former RJR Nabisco president who was immortalized in the book *Barbarians at the Gate*, a best-selling account of Wall Street greed in the 1980s. Described by *Barbarians* co-author Bryan Burrough as "a Canadian-born accountant who transformed himself into an outsize captain of industry, a backslapping, Chivas-swilling country-club pal of politicians, entertainers and sports stars," Johnson has been a friend of Eagleson and a drinking pal since the late 1950s when both men were beginning their respective careers in Toronto. Over the years, Johnson, the former CEO and chairman of Standard Brands

121

Inc., which was eventually swallowed up by RJR Nabisco, hired several of Eagleson's clients, most notably Bobby Orr, to endorse Standard Brands products.

In Eagleson's National Hockey League Players' Association office, a painting by Jean-Paul Lemieux, a Quebec artist, was displayed prominently. Eagleson would tell people that it was a keepsake from the time he spent with Lemieux "down at Paul Desmarais' house." He often spoke about the night he and Johnson celebrated Canada's triumph at the 1976 Canada Cup in Montreal, when, about 3 a.m., Ross said to Al, "Let's get Paul Desmarais out of bed and over here." Eagleson savours the memory. "Half an hour later," he wrote in his memoirs, "Paul Desmarais, a financier not known for 3:30 a.m. strolls, was walking through the lobby with a top coat over his pyjamas."

In the late 1960s, Eagleson's name started appearing in the society columns. The annual Premier's Luncheon, which Eagleson first organized in 1969, became a significant social event and important item in the social pages. In 1988, *The Globe and Mail*'s social columnist wrote approvingly: "Lawyer Alan Eagleson sure knows how to throw a party, and he did it again this week at the reception at Windows, the glass-surrounded top floor of the Four Seasons Hotel in Toronto. The reception was in honour of the premier of Ontario, David Peterson, and the co-hosts were William Bremner and Terrence O'Malley, chairman and president respectively of Vickers and Benson Co. Ltd., which numbers among its advertising clients the Liberal government of Ontario. Mr. Eagleson is such a well-known Tory that he thought he'd better get help from some prominent Liberals or the premier might not come."

When Premier David Peterson fêted Princess Anne at the Royal York Hotel in 1986, Al and Nancy were among the invited guests. Nancy sometimes made the social pages through her interest in art and interior design; Al would appear in connection with political functions.

Eagleson had a reputation for being a generous host, but he also underwrote his generosity with National Hockey League Players' Association funds amassed from players' membership dues. In 1988, he billed the NHLPA $4,928 for a large dinner party at the Sutton Place Hotel for John Sopinka. When Eagleson attended Wimbledon in 1987 with Tory friends Roy McMurtry, the Canadian government's high commissioner in London, and Tom

Wells, the agent general for the province of Ontario in the United Kingdom, the NHLPA picked up the tab.

Just what these social occasions had to do with union business or how such expenditures furthered the aspirations of the NHL players is not on record. What did become clear as the years went by was the players' growing unease with Eagleson as executive director of the NHLPA. They bridled at his autocratic style, detested his arrogance and were concerned about his conflicts of interest.

In addition to being a union leader, Eagleson was a corporate lawyer with a lineup of gilt-edged clients, a player-agent, Canada's chief international hockey negotiator, a tournament organizer and a businessman. But the NHL players were Eagleson's power base. Without them, he could not have organized his hockey tournaments or used the collective bargaining agreements with the NHL owners as leverage to get the league's approval for these tournaments. Without the players, Eagleson would never have become Canada's international hockey czar. And he would never have achieved the wealth and fame that went with his hockey dealings.

But where did the players' interests rank in priority with Eagleson's? Were their needs his principal concern? And could a man, who needed the support of the NHL establishment for his international events and who counted among his close friends the NHL's most important executives, properly represent the players in labour negotiations?

Eagleson argued that he served the membership well and that he was not breaching any moral or ethical code because he did not attempt to hide his conflicts of interest. "A conflict of interest becomes a problem when it is concealed," he told *The Globe and Mail* in 1991.

Furthermore, Eagleson's personal contract with the players allowed him to work on outside interests. It was stipulated in his contract that he needed to devote only 60 per cent of his time to union business. He argued that the NHLPA could not afford to hire him on a full-time basis because it would have to compensate him for the loss of his lucrative interests outside the union. Still, the players' association was the source from which all control and power flowed for Eagleson. Little could develop in hockey without Eagleson's approval or direct participation.

Rival agents argued that Eagleson's position as NHLPA executive director gave him an advantage in recruiting clients. During the 1970s, for example, Eagleson, wearing his hat as Hockey Canada's controlling director, ensured the Canadian junior hockey team's training camp was held at the Orr-Walton Sports Camp. This presented one big advantage, Herb Pinder, a Saskatoon-based player-agent, said. "It just happened that the guys working with him, Bill Watters and Rick Curran, would drop in on the kids in the evening and talk about why they should be represented by Alan Eagleson. There was a endless litany of not only being in a conflict position but using it and abusing it terribly."

When Eagleson was working for the players' association, he ran it with an iron fist. The membership did not elect the NHLPA's important executive committee, to which Eagleson was directly accountable. Instead, the members of the executive committee were hand-picked by Eagleson, and over the years they were consistently supportive of him. When players asked questions, they risked the wrath of the executive director, who would use a combination of profanities, insults and legalese to make his point.

Basil McRae, an NHL enforcer who would have no trouble handling Eagleson in a physical confrontation, was pointedly rebuked when he asked a question of Eagleson at a meeting. He told journalists David Cruise and Alison Griffiths in 1990, "As soon as I questioned him, it was like he jumped right on me. I started stuttering. He actually did intimidate me in front of my teammates and in front of his colleagues.

"Guys are scared, and they don't want to sound stupid. He talks at such a high level, he's almost got to communicate to hockey players at the hockey players' level. I'm not saying hockey players are stupid, but we definitely cannot talk or communicate at a lawyer's level, his lingo. So we are paying him to represent us. He's actually working for us, but he makes it feel like we are his labourers and he's the president of some big company. It's like we are scared of him."

During Eagleson's term as union boss, the membership dues rose from $1,000 per player in the 1970s to more than $2,000 per player in the 1980s, but the flow of information was kept to a minimum. In September, during training camp, Eagleson visited each NHL team's dressing room, sometimes with an insurance representative in tow, and deliver a quick speech outlining what would be taking place during the season. Then he was gone and virtually out of sight to the full membership until training camp the following year. "There was no flow of information," Jim Korn recalls. "He was supposedly there to answer any questions. The problem was if you had a number of questions, he would say, 'I've got a flight booked out of town.' He wouldn't respond or he'd put you off. He'd say, 'I'll look into it,' but you'd never hear back from him."

Except for Sam Simpson, the NHLPA's director of operations under Eagleson, who would jot down notes, official minutes of NHLPA meetings were not recorded. The meetings were kept short and sweet, which was how the majority of the players liked it. Each June, the NHLPA team representatives and the executive committee met for the annual meetings in Palm Beach, Fla., usually at the Breakers, a palatial hotel of European architecture and imperial mien that reeks of old money. After a quick run-through of union issues in the morning, it was off to the golf course. "If there was something you wanted to say and it cut into the afternoon golfing, you got in trouble from everybody," Mark Johnson, a former player, says. "It was like hurry up and get this thing over because at one o'clock I'm teeing off."

If the players had access to or understanding of a limited amount of information, government regulatory bodies had less. The NHLPA was not fully answerable to labour authorities in Canada or the United States. Unlike the unions representing professional baseball, football and basketball players, the NHLPA was not registered with the Office of the U.S. Labor Management Standards. The NHLPA did file reports with Labour Canada as a voluntary union, but the reports listed only the players on Canadian teams, about one-third of the membership.

Korn says: "If you're not registered you don't have to comply with anything. As soon as the government recognizes a union, it has authority over the union. Eagleson's attitude was 'Screw you. We're a private organization. Go mind your own business.' Al didn't want disclosure of anything. Why would he want anybody in his little world? People would have access to information only he had access to."

What frustrated the players at a more basic level was the inability of Eagleson's union to negotiate a more liberal free agency — in other words, to lift the restrictions on players who wanted to move from one team to another and put more money in their pockets. While salaries in other sports skyrocketed in the

1980s, NHL player salaries stagnated following the 1979 merger between the NHL and its rival the World Hockey Association. At the same time, the players were growing uncomfortable over Eagleson's close relationship with the owners. Eagleson owned a residence in the Palm Beach area close to homes belonging to influential NHL executives such as Bill Wirtz and Bob Pulford; Lou Nanne, the general manager of the Minnesota North Stars; and Cliff Fletcher, then general manager of the Calgary Flames.

Eagleson socialized with the executives and was often seen on Bill Wirtz's yacht. Players can remember seeing Eagleson arrive at a players-owners meeting in the 1970s aboard the Wirtz yacht. "After a while, you start wondering," Mark Johnson said. "Is he working for us? Or is he working for them?"

In a confidential memo to businessman Peter Karmanos in 1988, Eagleson briefly outlined his relationship with another influential owner, John O. Pickett of the New York Islanders. "He is a very wealthy man. He is married to Robin, his second wife. They are a great couple. Their home in Palm Beach is 3 miles (and 5 million dollars) north of our villa in Manalapan, Florida. We see them socially each time we are in Palm Beach."

Although Eagleson cultivated and cherished his friendships among the owners, the players did not appear to benefit from these relationships. For example, in public Eagleson complained about NHL's reserve clause, which bound a player to a team for life, but the NHLPA did not challenge the clause in court as other sports unions had successfully done. It was left to the World Hockey Association which began operation in 1972 in direct competition to the NHL to fight the reserve clause. This occurred when the WHA began signing players whose contracts had expired with their NHL teams. The NHL clubs argued that these players were still their property, because of the reserve clause, even if they wanted to play in another league. A protracted court battle followed, the result of which was a victory by the WHA and payment of $1.7 million in restraint-of-trade damages to the WHA by the NHL. Terrified by the Sherman Anti-Trust Act which had the power to wipe out the NHL's reserve clause totally and free the players from any restrictions of movement whatsoever, the NHL voluntarily eliminated the reserve clause, but at the same time replaced it with a clause almost as restrictive — the compensation clause.

Compensation, or equalization, was a system in which a team

losing a free agent to another team was awarded a player or players off the roster of the free agent's new team. If the two teams could not agree on compensation, each submitted a proposal for compensation to an arbitrator and the arbitrator decided in favour of one or the other. This was a dubious venture for a team interested in signing a free agent because that team risked losing its best player, or one of its best. So punitive was the compensation formula that only one star player, goaltender Rogatien Vachon, was able to move from one team to another, through free agency, between 1976 and 1980 — and that transaction caused a furor.

The compensation clause existed because the players' association agreed to it in its 1976 collective bargaining agreement. In return the players received an increase in the players' pension plan and the owners' approval for the 1976 Canada Cup. But the pension increase was to be funded by profits from international hockey; in other words, the players' own hard work.

In 1978, Eagleson was given another opportunity to fight the compensation clause when a dispute arose between the league and Dale McCourt, a highly rated young player with the Detroit Red Wings who had been awarded to the Los Angeles Kings as compensation for the Wings' signing of free agent Rogatien Vachon of the Kings.

McCourt's lawyer, Brian Smith of Detroit, filed suit and obtained a U.S. federal court order blocking McCourt's move to Los Angeles. For the 1978-79 season, McCourt remained in Detroit while Smith and the NHL disputed the legality of the option clause in court. The NHL won, but when Smith threatened to appeal the case under the U.S. anti-trust laws, the NHL decided not to press its luck and instead arranged a trade between the Kings and Wings that kept McCourt in Detroit. A clear-cut victory by McCourt would have helped free players from the restrictive compensation clause, but Smith said he received no support from Eagleson.

"I couldn't believe it," Smith said. "The union, instead of supporting the players and trying to make headway like every other sport — baseball, football and basketball — took an adversarial position. They said it needed this restriction in the agreement and that it had been bargained in good faith, because it got all of those wonderful benefits like international hockey."

In 1979, Eagleson's real motives were under scrutiny again as the NHL and WHA approached an agreement to end their seven-year war. The two leagues decided on a merger, with the NHL absorbing four WHA teams: Quebec, Hartford, Winnipeg and Edmonton. But for the merger to take place, the NHL needed the approval of the players. However, folding the WHA was of no benefit to the players. During the war between the two leagues, salaries had escalated like never before in the NHL's history. Competition for the players' services had been a positive development, and it was hard to think of a reason why the players would want to return to the old monopolistic system of one league — unless there was a trade-off.

The players were in an excellent position to demand a move toward a more liberal free agency. Moreover, there was a precedent for such leverage, set in 1976, when the National Basketball Association Players' Association successfully took the NBA to court to ensure that the merger between the NBA and American Basketball Association was consummated on terms agreeable to the players. Those terms included limited free agency and higher salaries.

In June, 1979, the NHLPA met in Nassau for meetings and to vote on the proposed merger. On the day before the vote, Phil Esposito, who was then the NHLPA president, says Eagleson came to him and pleaded with him to approve the merger. Esposito described Eagleson's pitch as an "impassioned plea," during which he said "search your soul" and "do the right thing for all the players."

Eagleson told him that the owners were in financial trouble because of the seven years' war with the WHA, but, regardless, were offering the increased benefits and an improved pension package. In addition, Eagleson said the owners were willing to give the players international hockey and they were offering their assurance that no player's job would be lost through the merger. There was no mention of liberalizing free agency.

"I remember that as clear as a bell because I took a long jog on the beach that night thinking about it," Esposito said. By the next morning, Esposito had made up his mind. For the good of the game, he recommended to the player representatives and executive council approval of the merger, or expansion, as the NHL preferred to call it.

The NHL did very well by the agreement. Not only did it eliminate the competition, but it received $24 million in expansion fees from the four WHA teams it was absorbing. And it gave up little in terms of concessions to the NHLPA. So certain was the NHL of the players' approval, that the two leagues cut the deal months before the players' association gave its approval in Nassau, according to several executives.

Bill Putnam, former assistant chairman to WHA commissioner Ben Hatskin said, "The Nassau meeting was only a formality. It had no bearing on the merger. Benny told me it was a foregone conclusion . . . a done deal. It was one of the technicalities that had to be approved, but there was never any doubt in anybody's mind that I talked to — on both sides — that it was anything more than a formality."

Another WHA official, Larry Gordon, told Russ Conway: "Everything had been agreed to by the Nassau meeting. That meeting was more of a formality. I don't know that the NHL players had a say in the merger."

Two years later, Esposito met Glen Sather, the president, general manager and coach of the Edmonton Oilers, one of the four WHA teams absorbed by the NHL, and mentioned to him how difficult a decision it had been to approve the merger.

According to Esposito, Sather said: "Did you guys think you had anything to do with the merger?"

"Yeah," replied Esposito. "Without the players, you guys wouldn't have had a merger."

"Jesus Christ, Phil. Don't be so naive," said Sather. "It was already done (before the Nassau meetings). It was already done."

"Are you kidding me? Can I say this to anyone?"

"I'll deny every word of it," said Sather.

Sather later confirmed the meeting with Esposito, but told *Sports Illustrated* that Esposito read too much into it. "I was saying that in principle the deal was set, it was going to be made either way. Essentially I was saying that whatever the players wanted they could have gotten. They would have gotten some concessions (if they had held out for them)."

The players, of course, did not hold out and received little, but Eagleson denies he was involved in a secret merger deal with the NHL and WHA. For his part, Esposito said he regretted not standing up to Eagleson. "I was like his puppet. I admit that."

Although some players were beginning to doubt Eagleson, NHL management was not. After the 1982 collective bargaining agreement which, arguably, tightened restrictions on free agency by factoring in high draft choices as well as players in the compensation formula, Toronto agent Gus Badali, who represented Wayne Gretzky, said two general managers told him it was the best deal yet for management. "They certainly don't hide their faces," Badali said. Leaf owner Harold Ballard didn't attempt to hide his approval of Eagleson. "How do the owners feel about Eagleson?" he said. "We like him. Wouldn't you rather have him negotiating against you than Marvin Miller (the former Major League Baseball executive director)? Sure it's a great contract — for us." Bill Wirtz told *Sports Illustrated* that Eagleson was a "brilliant negotiator."

In the 1980s, Eagleson's business activities became more closely tied to international hockey, especially the three Canada Cups in 1981, 1984 and 1987, which had been sanctioned by the NHL in collective bargaining agreements. The Canada Cups of the 1980s produced revenue of $24 million: $13.6 million in gate receipts, $7.2 million from television rights, $1.5 million for additional advertising rights, $1.2 million in prize money and interest of $452,861.

A whopping three-quarters of Canada Cup profits went to expenses. Of these expenses, $1.5 million was designated as "management services." According to directors on the board of Hockey Canada, the management services were provided almost entirely by companies tied to Eagleson and Hockey Canada accountant Christopher Lang.

Chapter Nine

THE HAT TRICKS

THE FACT that R. Alan Eagleson was the most commanding figure in world hockey was less important to the rank and file of the National Hockey League Players' Association than his performance as their executive director. His conflicts of interest were not a secret, but was disclosure enough? Hockey agent Herb Pinder thought not. "Eagleson told the media, 'Sure, I wear all these hats, but I declare them.' That seemed to justify it. It was like saying, 'I'm going to run over you with a bus, but I'm going to declare it.' Does that mean it's going to hurt less?"

One key issue affecting the players was the role of the NHL president as the sole arbitrator in disputes between players and management over contracts. The players' association had agreed to this arrangement in collective bargaining agreements, but lawyers and agents found this — in varying degrees — strange, outrageous and appalling. The NHL president, after all, was an employee of the owners. How, then, could the players expect to get an unbiased hearing?

Blair Chapman learned what a Ziegler ruling meant in 1984 during a contract dispute with the St. Louis Blues. Chapman had been playing with back problems for several years when suddenly in September, 1983, the Blues told him they were releasing him and paying him one-third of his $135,000 contract, even though the deadline for buying out players had passed two months earlier on July 1. When Pinder, who represented Chapman, called the NHLPA he said Eagleson's attitude was, "Go away, don't come back. I can't help you."

Pinder says that Eagleson told him that Chapman's only recourse was to have John Ziegler, the NHL president, arbitrate the dispute. Pinder says Eagleson assured him Chapman would get an "impartial hearing."

Chapman notified the Blues he was taking them to arbitration and then waited for more than nine months, during which time he received none of his player's salary, for Ziegler to hear the case. In the fall of 1984, Ziegler announced his decision. It seemed a curious mixture of twisted logic, flim-flammery and doublespeak. He ruled that, yes, the Blues were late in notifying Chapman of his buyout and as a result they owed him his $135,000 salary. However, Ziegler decided that because Chapman had notified the Blues he was taking them to arbitration, he had breached his contract. Just how this could be construed as grounds for a breached contract, given that the Blues, themselves, had decided to end the contract, wasn't made clear. Nevertheless, Chapman ended up receiving about the same amount of money originally offered by the Blues — slightly more than one-third of his salary. Pinder was outraged. "What Ziegler was saying was, 'If you lose, you lose. If you win, you lose.'"

Pinder says his complaints to Eagleson fell on deaf ears. "It was, 'I'm Alan Eagleson, so shut your mouth.' I sensed that he was glad. I had problems and we were competitors (as agents) so tough on you."

Michael Flynn, a St. Louis lawyer who represented Chapman at the arbitration hearing, wrote a letter to Pinder in 1985 stating that the Ziegler ruling "thoroughly disgusted" him.

At about the time of Chapman's problems with the Blues, Carl Brewer returned to the NHL. And after a long absence, he met up with his old friend Eagleson. During the 1970s, Brewer had played hockey in Finland and had become something of a national figure there for helping develop the Finnish hockey program. Suddenly, in December, 1979, Brewer was back in the NHL, playing for the Leafs at age 41.

Brewer's return had been arranged by Punch Imlach, who had been hired that summer to manage of the Leafs. Imlach had become a hero in the 1960s when, as Toronto's outspoken coach and general manager, he had led the team to four Stanley Cups. But the team fell on hard times after the 1967 championship and Imlach was fired in 1969. A year later, he resurfaced as coach and general manager of the Buffalo Sabres and quickly built that team into a contender before losing his job there because of clashes with the ownership and the players.

The Leaf players, led by their captain Darryl Sittler, wanted nothing to do with Imlach, a renowned disciplinarian, and the 1979-80 season quickly deteriorated into a series of feuds and crises. Imlach was hoping Brewer's playing experience would upgrade a weak defence and that he might have a friend in the dressing room. The players, including Sittler, an Eagleson client, were immediately suspicious of Brewer. They suspected he was a spy planted by Imlach and took to calling him "007." Brewer was many things, but not a management snitch. History had demonstrated that Brewer was more inclined to confront management, particularly Imlach, with whom he feuded in the 1960s.

Brewer signed a one-year $125,000 contract with the Leafs, but at the conclusion of the 1979-80 season the club failed to give him his notice of termination. This failure, according to the standard player's contract, meant he was still under contract for the following season. After his requests to join the team were ignored, Brewer, accompanied by his lawyer Donald Fiske, met Eagleson at his NHLPA office to find out what his rights were.

Brewer says Eagleson told him that his contract was still valid and he should wait a year and then sue the Leafs for the full value, $125,000. According to Brewer, as he and Fiske were leaving Eagleson's office, Eagleson called Fiske back and said, "Don't waste your time with Brewer. In a few weeks, he'll be back in Finland playing hockey and he'll forget all about this."

It's worth noting that Fiske does not remember this conversation taking place. Fiske recalls Brewer and Eagleson carrying on as if they were old friends. He says that if Eagleson did make such a remark, it wasn't with any intended malice.

Brewer rejected Eagleson's advice of waiting to file suit, and instead filed an immediate grievance. When he discovered Ziegler would be the arbitrator, Brewer wrote a letter to the president asking, "How can you, as a paid employee of the owners, be an impartial arbitrator?" Ziegler wrote back saying he was empowered to do so through the collective bargaining agreement.

Brewer attempted to get the court of Ontario to assume jurisdiction of his case. But the court rejected Brewer's motion, upholding the NHL's arbitration procedure since it was part of the collective bargaining agreement. Brewer went through a total of 22 lawyers in an attempt to fight the arbitration system, but all to no avail. One lawyer told him that Ziegler as arbitrator violated "the law of natural justice," but nothing could be done to change it because it had been formally agreed by both the players and owners.

Finally, Brewer accepted arbitration through Ziegler, who ruled in his favour. But, as with Chapman, there was a catch. Instead of awarding Brewer the amount of his contract, $125,000, Ziegler ruled that Brewer was owed the minimum wage in the NHL during that period, about $46,000. Brewer's settlement covered his legal bills.

Jim Harrison was another player who lost in arbitration, but his circumstances were quite different. For starters, he was an Eagleson client, retaining Sports Management Ltd. as his agent. Harrison had played in Boston and Toronto, and also in the WHA before joining the Chicago Blackhawks in 1976. He was a big, hard-driving player who had a history of back problems. Harrison had undergone surgery in 1967 and 1974. After yet another operation to treat a ruptured disc in 1978, Harrison was commandeered into action at the insistence of coach Bob Pulford. Pulford questioned the seriousness of Harrison's ailment and punished him for missing games.

"He called me a phoney," Harrison says. "One day in practice, he skated me for two hours straight because he thought I was faking it. I took painkillers and muscle relaxers, but I couldn't play because I couldn't walk."

In December, 1978, the Blackhawks told Harrison they were demoting him to their farm team in Moncton. Harrison didn't want to make the move because it would mean leaving the care of his doctor in Chicago. Furthermore, he thought NHL rules prohibited a team from demoting an injured player. When Harrison balked at the demotion, the Blackhawks suspended him. Harrison subsequently filed a grievance and a hearing was scheduled, again with Ziegler as arbitrator.

Eagleson was on friendly terms with everyone in attendance at the December 28, 1978 hearing. At the meeting was Ziegler, the arbitrator; Pulford, Eagleson's long-time pal and client; Bobby Orr, Eagleson's star client and the Blackhawks' assistant coach; and Harrison, also Eagleson's client.

After Ziegler heard the evidence, he asked Harrison to leave the room. A few minutes later, Eagleson came out and told Harrison and his wife Liz that he had been demoted.

"Al said to me, 'Ziegler ruled you have to go to the minors.' Tears came to my eyes. I was in constant pain and I didn't know what kind of medical attention I would get in the minors. Al said, 'That's the way it is.'"

Liz Harrison says, "I remember it like it was yesterday. When Eagleson told Jim that Ziegler had ruled in favour of Chicago, my heart dropped. I thought there was a rule against demoting injured players."

Almost 10 years later, Harrison learned through a lawyer whom he had retained that Ziegler had not actually made a ruling. Instead, he had told Pulford and Orr that it was in their best interests to work out a deal with Eagleson. Ziegler says he then told Eagleson, "I think you've got one on them, but you and I know that next week they can do the same thing, and what have you accomplished?"

Orr confirmed that there had been no ruling by Ziegler and no demotion. "I left figuring (Harrison) was still with the team," Orr said.

Harrison describes the months that followed as a nightmare. He agreed to join Chicago's farm team and attempted to play, but he could not. "I dressed for a couple of games, but (coach) Eddie Johnston wouldn't put me on the ice. He said, 'Jim, I'm not taking responsibility for you on the ice because you can barely walk.'"

Trevor Johansen, who roomed with Harrison in the minors, said, "There were days he couldn't get out of bed because of his back. The guy was on painkillers, hunched over. He'd have to lay down every hour it seemed."

Harrison made one last attempt to continue his career the following season. Although still under contract to the Chicago Blackhawks, he was given the club's approval to try a comeback with the Edmonton Oilers. He played only three games before he and the Oilers mutually agreed that he should not continue. Harrison says that Eagleson called him shortly after that to inform him that the Blackhawks wanted his signature on a waiver releasing them from future medical claims against the club. Harrison refused. He and Eagleson clashed, and they soon parted company.

When Harrison tried to collect the $175,000 disability insurance carried by the NHL and the NHLPA, he was refused by claims adjusters because he had a "pre-existing back condition" prior to 1978. But he thought that because he had passed a medical examination arranged by the Chicago club in October, 1977, he no longer had a "pre-existing condition."

After years of litigation in an attempt to get his insurance money, Harrison ended up collecting only $10,000. All of this amount went to pay legal bills. He says he gave up the fight because he was broke. Eagleson, he says, in his capacity as either a friend, a former agent, or NHLPA executive director did not offer to help him collect and, in fact, would not even return his phone calls.

Today Harrison is in constant pain, has trouble walking and has no feeling in his right leg or foot. "I put all of my trust in Eagleson," Harrison says. "I took his son fishing in the summers. . . . I wasn't an angel. I was outspoken. But I came to play every night and I played hurt."

Brewer says: "How Jimmy Harrison got screwed is absolutely incredible. The man is virtually a cripple. And Pulford and Eagleson and Wirtz just laughed at him. They used him when they could. They used him to fight all their battles (on the ice) for them. But Eagleson never knew what hat he was wearing. His best friend was Wirtz, his best friend was Pulford and then there was the punk kid, Harrison. Obviously, Harrison came out on the short end of that deal."

Disability insurance and Eagleson's role as NHLPA executive director was a strange mix. For years, the responsibility of choosing the administrator and insurance plans that were purchased by the NHL and the NHLPA was left to Eagleson. From 1986 to 1990, the association received $8.1 million from the league to buy players' insurance plans that included medical, dental and disability coverage. Before his forced retirement in 1992, John Ziegler told Russ Conway, "We've usually said, 'Alan, pick your coverages, they're your players.'"

Eagleson placed the disability insurance, which in the 1970s amounted to $175,000 ($100,000 from the league, $75,000 from the NHLPA), through Robert Bradshaw, who was living in Toronto at the time. Then, in 1981, he switched to William Sutton, a former employee of Bradshaw. Bradshaw told Conway that Eagleson's involvement in disability insurance went beyond selecting and paying for the policies.

"He wanted to dictate whether benefits should be paid in full or in part," Bradshaw said. "He'd always use it as a negotiating tool. . . . He would say, 'Well, we can work out a deal on this guy. Maybe it shouldn't be the whole thing. But we need to get a better price on the group plan.' There was always an angle."

To file for a disability claim, players submitted a notice to the NHLPA. The claim was then either accepted or rejected by a Boston claims adjuster for Lloyds of London, the syndicate that wrote separate NHL and NHLPA policies. When Conway investigated disability insurance, he discovered that disability claims were usually denied, forcing the claimant to hire a lawyer and fight for the insurance benefit he felt he was due.

Conway learned that in 40 cases of players whose careers had ended because of injury, 35 filed disability claims. In 11 cases, players said they received the full benefits with little difficulty. Six of those players were Eagleson clients.

The other 24 were compelled to retain lawyers in order to fight for the disability insurance that they felt they were due. Two players ended up receiving no benefits, even after hiring lawyers, and the remainder received settlements. Brian Smith, a Detroit lawyer who represented several Red Wings in disability disputes, says, "If I went back in my files, I'd probably find 12 or 13 guys who had career-ending injuries and couldn't get to first base collecting their money. We were always told, 'Well, you don't have a claim.' Then we'd call the union and they'd say, 'Forget it. There's no point going after this.'"

When Trevor Johansen attempted to collect his disability insurance benefit, he says the players' association was no help at all. He said: "Nobody jumped up from the players' association and said, 'Let me handle that for you. This is how you go about it. This is what you need to do. These are your rights.'" Johansen got his disability insurance money, but it cost him $75,000 in legal fees to do it.

Several players were denied their insurance because of a 20-game exclusionary clause in the policy. If a player participated in 20 or more games after an injury, he would no longer qualify for the insurance. Norm Schmidt of the Pittsburgh Penguins was initially denied his insurance claim because of the 20-game clause, but threatened a court fight and then collected.

Mike Healy, a Minneapolis lawyer who acted for several Minnesota North Star players in disability insurance claims, blames Eagleson for allowing exclusionary clauses in the policies.

"They even had exclusions in the policy in which a disability due in any part to osteoarthritis or degenerative disc disease meant you couldn't collect. Well, you can't sustain an injury to a joint that doesn't eventually involve some form of arthritis."

Blair Chapman discovered the consequences of the exclusionary clauses. Today, he can barely walk, can't work and has financial problems. In November, 1981, he injured his back while playing for the Blues and underwent surgery a month later to repair a ruptured disc. Ten weeks later he was told by club doctors he could play. He dressed for one game and then hurt his back again. He missed the rest of the regular season, but played parts of the 1982-83 season before the Blues bought out his contract.

Chapman retained lawyer Michael Flynn to collect his disability insurance, but the claim was turned down. In a letter dated April 18, 1985, Flynn was informed by a Lloyd's claims adjuster that no benefit was payable "unless the disablement sustained by the insured person shall be continuously and totally disabling for a period of 12 months."

That eliminated Chapman who, 10 weeks after the initial injury, was back on the ice. He says he was unaware of the exclusionary clause in the policy. The team cleared him to play, so he went out and played.

In 1990, Chapman was still trying to collect on his insurance. In a letter dated March 22, 1990, Sam Simpson informed a Pittsburgh law firm retained by Chapman that a copy of the 1981-82 disability insurance policy with Lloyd's of London was in the mail. Chapman finally got a look at the policy, but he received no money.

"I got nothing except a headache," Chapman said. "I've seen three neurosurgeons and a couple of orthopedics and they basically told me I'm history and I'm not going to get much better. I don't leave the house much, because it really gets painful if I get out and try to walk. If I stay in the house, I can lay down or sit down when it gets sore. Basically, I'm going kind of nuts."

There may be no better example of a player paying the price

for not knowing the basics of the NHLPA insurance plan than Ed Kea, who is brain damaged, suffers from severe depression and is incapable of working.

Kea had played almost 10 full NHL seasons in Atlanta and St. Louis when he was asked by Blues' general manager, Emile Francis, to join the club's minor league team in Salt Lake City for conditioning purposes. Kea agreed and played so well that the Blues planned to bring him back up on March 8, 1983. Kea's last game for Salt Lake was March 7, and it turned out to be the final game of his career. A body check sent him flying into the boards where his head smashed against the dasher, the top edge of the board. He almost died during six hours of surgery to remove blood clots from his brain.

"He was a big strong guy," Francis said. "That's the only thing that saved him."

Kea suffered a permanent brain injury and had to learn how to walk and talk. Unable to work or speak clearly, Kea was admitted to hospital three times in 1992 suffering from severe depression.

Ed's wife, Jennifer, expected to collect the NHL's $100,000 disability insurance until she was told that Kea didn't qualify because the policy had been changed several months earlier to read that players who passed waivers to go to the minors were not covered. Kea hadn't been told this, nor had anyone else.

"Nobody knew," said Francis. "I guess the league and the players had been negotiating with the insurance company, and usually the association came around and visited the players and advised them, but we hadn't got anything."

Jennifer Kea went from being a stay-at-home mother with four children aged 1, 3, 6 and 9, to handling everything, including searching for a job. When she asked the players' association for help in collecting the full $100,000 from the league, she says she received none, although the association did pay the Keas its $75,000 insurance payout.

"Alan Eagleson felt that I should be very gratified that one year, almost to the day, after Ed's accident, I received the $75,000. He felt that was very hasty action on his part and that they had been very expedient in handling the matter. It had been a year in which finances had been very tight. It did not seem all that expedient to me."

Jennifer Kea says she also received a sharply worded letter from Eagleson in which he expressed his displeasure over hearing rumours that she had criticized the NHLPA for not doing enough to help her husband claim the $100,000 from the league.

"He said that I should not have said derogatory things about the association. But the only thing I'd said was I thought the association was supposed to help the players. I think I said that to the player representative on the Blues. I hadn't talked to other players. I certainly hadn't gone to the press. I was just trying to survive at the time. It seemed like an adversarial relationship with Mr. Eagleson."

Glen Sharpley's relationship with Eagleson also became adversarial, although initially they were friends. Sharpley, who was from Toronto, was a high NHL draft choice, had a bright future and held the potential of perhaps succeeding Bobby Orr as Eagleson's No. 1 client.

In Sharpley's final junior season, 1975-76, he was solicited by player-agents in both Canada and the United States. He opted for Eagleson's Sports Management Ltd., even though Eagleson had not called him and did not know who he was. "I was in Toronto, Al was in Toronto, and he was the best there was, so I called him," he says.

Sharpley considered Eagleson a friend. When he was married in Aylmer, Quebec, Eagleson spoke at his wedding. Eagleson handled all of his money and set aside a monthly allowance for him. As payment, Eagleson took 7 per cent of Sharpley's earnings. It was an agreement, Sharpley says, bound only by a handshake.

On December 19, 1981, while playing for the Blackhawks, Sharpley was hit in the eye with a stick during a game against the Washington Capitals. He suffered internal bleeding and pupil damage, and there was a long-term prognosis of a traumatic cataract. Because of the injury, Sharpley's eye would not adjust to light, making playing under the bright television lights in the arenas difficult and painful.

Sharpley's career-ending accident produced a disability insurance benefit of $340,000 because, on Eagleson's advice, he had purchased additional coverage. But Sharpley says before Eagleson would assist him in obtaining his insurance benefit he demanded a written contract and extra money. "That's what really upset me," Sharpley said. "Our agreement through my whole career was a handshake. All of a sudden, I got injured and I get a contract in the mail. I chucked it in the garbage, but Marvin

(Goldblatt) sent me another one, and I had to sign it or I wouldn't have gotten my insurance. It was as simple as that. I was furious, but I had no job to go to, and when I sold my house in Chicago I lost money on it."

Even though Eagleson was executive director of the players' association, and as Sharpley's agent had been collecting a percentage of his income for about six years, he charged Sharpley an additional $14,000 to process the disability insurance claim. Later, Eagleson told the NHLPA in a memo, that Sharpley's case had been "difficult" and that a lawyer had been retained.

Eagleson also told Sharpley that some of the $14,000 had to be used to pay the costs of a business trip by Bernard James Warren, the president of Crawley Warren, the British insurance brokerage company that handled the NHLPA's disability insurance. Eagleson told Sharpley that Warren would need to see Sharpley to talk to him about his injury.

In January, 1983, Bernard James Warren and his wife took a flight on a Concorde to the United States. While visiting, they attended some NHL-Soviet Union exhibition games organized by Eagleson. Sharpley had breakfast with Warren, his wife and Eagleson. He told Warren that his vision prohibited him from playing. Looking back, he viewed the meeting as a waste of time. "The doctors had all examined me. The insurance company knew that. Al knew that. I think the man and his wife had a nice vacation."

Sharpley's understanding was that some of the money he paid to Eagleson was being used to finance Warren's trip to the United States. But Warren told Russ Conway that Eagleson did not pick up the tab. "I can confirm Mr. Eagleson has never, ever paid for my flights, particularly my Concorde flights. The hockey people don't pay for my flights. I pay my own expenses."

On another front, Robert Bradshaw, the Toronto insurance agent, had been working closely with Eagleson. But their relationship eventually ended, after some setbacks for Bradshaw. In 1981 he was fined in Pennsylvania for selling disability insurance to NHL players without a licence. There was also a problem with Bradshaw's handling of a separate health insurance policy with Boston Mutual Insurance Company. Bradshaw, according to John Ziegler, was late in sending the premiums to Boston Mutual.

Bradshaw's ties to Eagleson started in 1966, when he arranged an insurance policy for Bobby Orr. Later, he started handling the

NHLPA insurance contracts and by the 1970s, he was the biggest sports insurance broker in North America. Initially, Bradshaw says, "I liked Eagleson very much. I was swept up by his charm and his enthusiasm and his exciting approach to life and his bright ideas."

But as time went on, Eagleson's "ego and greed" came into play, Bradshaw said. "His demands on us became unbusinesslike."

Bradshaw told *Sports Illustrated*, "It started when we would be told right out of the blue what our company's contribution to Toronto Big Brothers (of which Eagleson was a director) was going to be. That went on for a couple of years. Then he started to use our assets. We kept a car and driver in Toronto. He'd phone up and tell us when he was using them. Then he would advise me when he was staying at my flat in New York and when his wife was. We sort of put up with that stuff. . . . Over the years, if you get hit on the head enough, you learn to live with the headache."

Bradshaw told Russ Conway that he gave work to Eagleson's law firm "to stay on the right side of him," and also provided insurance coverage for Eagleson, his family and even his accountant at no charge to Eagleson.

"With him, it was never straightforward. He wanted good insurance in place under proper circumstances, but then he always had to get something extra that nobody else got."

Bradshaw said when he complained to Eagleson, "his answer was always, 'If you don't like it, I'll do business elsewhere.'"

Eagleson eventually did take his business elsewhere, and Bradshaw, like a growing number of others, became a former Eagleson friend and business associate. Eagleson, of course, continued to prosper and did particularly well through the NHLPA.

Eagleson's NHLPA perks included expensive suits from Marty's Custom Clothiers in Toronto through free vouchers purchased by the NHLPA or Hockey Canada or Eagleson's law firm. Marty's customers have included Prime Minister Pierre Trudeau, Ross Johnson and William Davis, a former premier of Ontario. A former employee of Eagleson says the gift vouchers used by Eagleson, visiting hockey people and Eagleson friends were inscribed with the name of the NHLPA.

Eagleson's law practice, Eagleson Ungerman, did well through the players' association. From 1987 to 1991, the NHLPA paid the law firm $918,000 in legal fees. The players' union also paid

Nancy Eagleson $15,000 to redecorate its headquarters situated in a building in Toronto owned, unbeknownst to the membership, by the Eagleson family.

For the fiscal years 1987, 1988 and 1989, the players' association was billed $19,274 for golf and tennis club dues and expenses, and $2,130 for YMCA memberships for Eagleson and Sam Simpson. In 1987 and 1988, the NHLPA also paid $24,000 for a London apartment for Eagleson. When Eagleson spent Christmas in London in 1988, the players were billed $2,835. The reason for the trip was recorded somewhat cryptically as S.M., or special meetings.

Eagleson lived well, but the number of his enemies and the ranks of the disenchanted continued to grow. Next to Bobby Orr, his most determined adversary became Carl Brewer. In 1982, as Brewer pursued his grievance against the Leafs and petitioned to have the case heard by Ontario provincial court rather than John Ziegler, he received a letter from Eagleson. Dated August 3, 1982, it read:

> Dear Carl:
> After a great deal of thought, Nancy and I have decided to change the godparents of our daughter Jill.
> We consider godparents to be important and our daughter Jill in her 17 years has not heard from you and your wife.
> For that reason, Nancy and I do not wish to impose on you further as godparents. We will ask another couple to replace you. Thank you for your co-operation.
> Yours truly,
> (signed) Alan

Brewer viewed the timing of the letter as more pertinent than the content. It was, he thought, a rebuff and retaliation for his fight against the Ziegler arbitration policy. But this was trivial stuff. The important battle, the one that would be waged over the retired players' pension fund, was several years down the road.

Chapter Ten

THE PENSIONERS

ON A FRIGID DAY in early February, 1993, a group of middle-aged men trickled into the Montreal Forum, the shrine of hockey as it's known to many fans. Most of the men walking into two small dressing rooms off a narrow corridor were instantly recognizable, some of the greatest athletes to play in the National Hockey League.

Many of them, such as Doug Risebrough and Serge Savard, both now NHL general managers, in Calgary and Montreal respectively, showed the extra pounds that the years and a stressful job can bring. Others, such as the elegant Frank Mahovlich and Jacques Laperrière, looked (aside from some grey hair in Laperrière's case) as if they could still play in the NHL.

This group of slightly more than 40 men was there to play in the Heroes of Hockey Game, a preliminary act to the NHL's annual All-Star Game, when former stars are brought back to play a gentle facsimile of what they used to contest so fiercely. But it was not an oldtimers' game in itself that brought them to Montreal for about $800 in cash each plus airfare, a hotel room, meals and a few parties for each of them and a guest. Rather it was the *game*, the chance to see some old friends, have a few laughs and some drinks, and bask in the sheer joy of a locker-room atmosphere. This, more than anything, was what many retired athletes said they missed most about their sport, the

144

Early success: Eagleson on the campaign trail in the mid-1960s. He was elected to the Ontario Legislature as the Conservative member for Toronto Lakeshore.

Eagleson's successful intervention in the Springfield Indians players' strike was was essential in the eventual formation of the NHLPA.

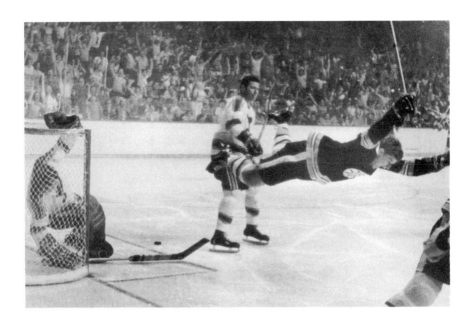

Above: Bobby Orr, hockey's greatest defenseman, scores the winning goal in the 1969-70 Stanley Cup Final against St. Louis.

Right: Orr with Eagleson. Their relationship disintegrated in 1980.

Alan Eagleson and former NHL President John Ziegler.
Their close relationship was disturbing to a number of
players and their agents.

Eagleson's role as the Czar of international hockey was cemented by his creation of the Canada Cup tournament, which pits the NHL's top Canadian players against the best players from the United States and Europe.

Team Canada celebrates its winning goal against the USSR in the 1972 Canada-Russia hockey series.

What does the FBI want with this man? Alan Eagleson began to face his adversaries in 1989. By 1993 he was being investigated by the FBI, the RCMP, a Boston Grand Jury, the Law Society of Upper Canada, and the Board of Hockey Canada.

Lawyer Ed Garvey, a former executive director of the National Football League Players' Association, was retained by Eagleson adversaries to investigate the NHLPA.

Left: Player agent Ron Salcer joined Ed Garvey and fellow agent Rich Winter in leading the opposition to Eagleson.

Below: Carl Brewer in action with the Toronto Maple Leafs in the middle 1960s. Brewer's ground-breaking request to include an agent (Eagleson) in contract negotiations infuriated Leafs' GM Punch Imlach.

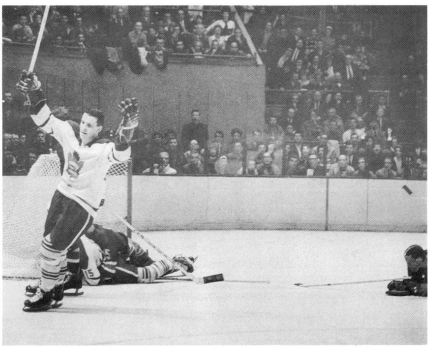

Down time: Relegated to the sidelines of the NHLPA and international hockey, Eagleson awaits the results of the various investigations.

carefree exchange of profane insults and one-liners that accompany any gathering of young men.

"I played the game for 18 years and I recognized what a privilege it was," said Paul Henderson, a man who became a hockey icon by scoring the series-winning goal in the historic confrontation with the Soviet Union's national team in 1972. "Sometimes when you're there you don't realize what a privilege it is. Sometimes you forget about the mystique of the game in Canada.

"I think as we get farther removed, we appreciate it more. I know I appreciate the game more. I appreciate my career, I appreciate Team Canada so much more today. You know, when you're young you're trying to raise a family, you're trying to make a buck. Now, you look back and think, 'Goodness, gracious, it really was terrific.'"

This was the third year for the Heroes of Hockey Game, but the first under the league's new management. NHL president John Ziegler was gone, resigning his post in June, 1992 when it became obvious he was about to be fired. Also out was Bill Wirtz, the owner of the Chicago Blackhawks who served for years as the chairman of the NHL's board of governors, a post which made him the most powerful owner in the league. Los Angeles Kings' owner Bruce McNall, representative of a supposed younger, more progressive group of league owners, has supplanted Wirtz as league chairman. And Ziegler's replacement is Gary Bettman, a New York lawyer whose post as third-in-command at the National Basketball Association went a long way towards getting him the renamed job of NHL commissioner. The hope is that the patina of the wildly successful NBA will buff the NHL's sometimes scruffy image.

It was the hope of the NHL that the 1993 Heroes Game would be seen as an attempt at rapprochement by the league toward its retired players, who were often treated shabbily by the owners. The shoddy treatment was epitomized in the NHL's pension plan, which left such legends as Gordie Howe, who played 26 seasons in the NHL, with an embarrassing pension of about $13,000 a year at age 45. Brad Park played 17 seasons and gets the same amount as Howe because he retired in 1985 (five years after Howe) and so receives additional benefits from international hockey proceeds. These are kings' ransoms compared to the pension left the widow of the late George Hayes, an NHL lines-man who died in 1984 at the age of 73. Despite the fact Hayes worked for the NHL for 19 years, appearing in 1,704 games, Judy Hayes was left with a pension of $16.98 per month when he died. Reggie Fleming, one of the toughest players in the league for 12 years beginning in the late 1950s, collects $7,700 annually.

R. Alan Eagleson, who negotiated many of the collective agreements surrounding the pension, did not have any pension worries. In 1986, he negotiated a contract for himself with the NHLPA that provides him with a pension of U.S.$50,000 per year at the age of 65. The majority of the players' pensions are paid in Canadian dollars.

Less than four months before the Heroes of Hockey Game in Montreal, an Ontario judge agreed with the retired players that the NHL owners had mishandled their pension plan. Mr. Justice George Adams of the Ontario Court, General Division, ruled that the owners had misappropriated more than $21 million in surpluses from the pension plan in 1983 and 1986. The ruling was the result of a lawsuit launched in 1990 by a group of retired players. Andy Bathgate, Carl Brewer, Gordie Howe, Bobby Hull, Allan Stanley, Eddie Shack and Leo Reise had their names on the court papers on behalf of themselves and all players who retired before 1982.

Most of the pension surplus was earned in the 1980 s, when annuities were bought from Manufacturers Life Assurance Company to finance the pension plan. Thanks to the record high interest rates of the 1980s, the annuities earned far more money than had been projected by actuaries as needed to fund the pension plan. In 1982, there was a $2.9-million surplus, of which almost $1 million was used to improve the pension plan, while the rest was divided among all NHL clubs. In 1986, there was a surplus of $23.7 million, of which $4.5 million went back into the pension while about $9.4 million was used to finance a benefit that was part of a new collective agreement between the NHL and the NHL Players' Association. The new benefit paid a $250,000 lump sum at age 55 to all players retiring after 1986 who had played a minimum of 400 NHL games. This excluded all players who retired earlier, including those who launched the lawsuit, and whose contributions had provided the surplus. The remaining sum, about $9.8 million, was distributed to club owners, which they used to make current pension contributions.

The NHL's lawyers argued that the players had given up their rights to the pension surplus as a result of the 1986 collective agreement and an earlier one in 1969 that dropped the players from the board of the NHL Pension Society (the group that administered the pension) after the owners took over making all the payments to the plan. When a subsequent agreement in the early 1970s called for the players to contribute 25 per cent of their pension contributions, they still weren't allowed representation in the NHL Pension Society. However, Justice Adams said in his decision, "When the NHLPA negotiated with the NHL in 1986, it was representing only active or present players, and the NHL and NHLPA had no power to extend the NHLPA's authority to former players without their consent. . . . Yet, monies to which they were exclusively entitled were used by the NHL and NHLPA to fund a benefit of little or no value to these former players."

The judge also had strong words for Alan Eagleson as the former executive director of the NHLPA who had negotiated the 1986 agreement with the NHL, and had co-operated with the NHL in taking the surplus away from the players. Eagleson also co-authored a letter, with his good friend John Ziegler, just before Christmas, 1988, which informed the retired players that the $4.5 million the owners granted the plan from the surplus, represented an impressive improvement in their pension. Since the $4.5 million was spread over hundreds of players, this was laughable.

"Had the NHLPA been representing the Applicants and had it been a trade union subject to the duty of fair representation under the Ontario Labour Relations Act, I fail to see how it would have honoured its duty in the circumstances. However, the apparent moral shortcoming in the NHLPA's conduct captured by its executive director's participation in the Nov. 21, 1988 'Merry Christmas' letter to former players, should not be confused with the association's then limited mandate. Moreover, the NHLPA was not a party to these proceedings and, accordingly, it is not appropriate to say more," Justice Adams wrote.

The phrase "moral shortcoming" gave some of the retired players as much satisfaction as winning the lawsuit, for it was a direct slap at the man most of them saw as giving away their pension benefits and rights without telling them. Eagleson had angered many retired players by echoing the view of the NHL owners that the surplus belonged to them. Dozens of former and current players interviewed by Russ Conway said that they had no idea they were not represented on the Pension Society. Conway also couldn't find any players who were aware Eagleson wrote a letter on August 1, 1989, at the request of the NHL to the Ontario cabinet minister in charge of pensions. Eagleson said in the letter that he represented both active and retired players, and requested the government allow the NHL Pension Society to keep the players off its board. On several other occasions, Eagleson said he did not represent retired players. The letter, an enormous favour to NHL management, was written at a time when Eagleson knew his job as executive director of the NHLPA was in jeopardy.

And most of the active players were not aware their $250,000 pension bonus was funded by money that properly belonged to players who had retired before 1986. They found this out at the June, 1989 meeting in Palm Beach, Fla., in the report delivered by Ed Garvey.

The pensioners' lawsuit was an acrimonious affair, even without the scene of three of the NHL's greatest players — Howe, Hull and Bobby Orr — actively involved in suing the league. When the retired players publicized their plight, Ziegler reacted by threatening to sue Howe and Orr, along with Carl Brewer, the driving force behind the lawsuit, and former players Dave Forbes and Billy Harris. Ziegler, a diminutive corporate lawyer whose critics accused him of having no feel for the tradition of the sport, went so far as to serve an official notice of libel.

The action subsequently was allowed to lapse with no further action being taken, but not before drawing this response from a group of the ex-players, including Brewer, in a letter to Ziegler:

> It is regrettable the NHL and its member clubs would resort to such treatment of one of our game's greatest icons, Bobby Orr. Perhaps your recent tactics of filing this notice and distributing it widely to all hockey players is seen by you as a worthwhile intimidation and scare tactic. We believe that you will find this effort on your part to discredit the two players in question (Howe and Orr) will succeed instead in rallying tremendous support for the players being maligned by you.

The same day Judge Adams released his ruling in the pension case, the NHL, through interim president Gil Stein, announced it would appeal the decision to the Ontario Court of Appeal. However, when Bettman took over as NHL commissioner on February 1, 1993, he sounded conciliatory toward the players, showing little stomach for continuing a court battle against some of hockey's greatest stars. He dropped a few hints that the league would like to reach a settlement. "The heroes of the NHL are not a group I want a dispute with," Bettman said at the All-Star break in Montreal at his first press conference as commissioner.

It was not seen as a coincidence that a few of the players involved in the lawsuit were invited to Montreal, including Howe and Bobby Hull. Hull did not play because of a bad shoulder, but he was introduced to an appreciative crowd. Just before the Heroes Game, Howe was presented with a large birthday cake to mark his 65th birthday, which was a little more than a month off. On March 31, when Howe's birthday was official, he was in Hartford to mark it with the Whalers, his last NHL team. And Bettman sent him another cake, which was seen as a smart public relations gesture, one that was unlikely to have been made by Ziegler. "John would have sent over a writ," said one member of the Whalers' front office.

The retired players, many of whom had discussed a boycott of the first game three years earlier, were happy to accept invitations to the game, although the man who sparked the lawsuit was not there. Carl Brewer still felt strongly that the old players were not paid enough for taking part. He said that the league, based on gate receipts and sponsorship deals, would take in at least $1.5 million in revenue from the All-Star weekend. Brewer, who termed the eagerness of players to participate "pathetic," felt strongly that the players deserved to be paid much more. He pointed out that, in exchange for sending business to airlines and hotels, the NHL probably paid a minimal amount for tickets and rooms for the players, and that $500 of the players' $800 stipend was covered by Upper Deck, a card company that had a sponsorship deal with the league.

Brewer also said there was only a token number of invitees from the group of players publicly identified as being supporters of the lawsuit. "Look at the rosters and see how many of the players work for NHL teams," Brewer said. Indeed, of 44 players invited to the game, 19 of them were employed by NHL teams, most in management positions.

Nevertheless, a visitor to the dressing rooms couldn't blame any of the retired players for participating. The pleasure of play-

ing the game and being in the company of others who feel the
same way is something that seems to be disappearing from many
NHL dressing rooms as salaries, and the attendant pressure to
produce, climb. The league may, once again, be paying them a
pittance while making a tremendous profit, but no one in Montreal seemed to mind.

"Carl's entitled to his opinion," said Paul Henderson. "I'm
here to have a good time. If they ask me to come next year, I'll be
here. The money's incidental. Who cares about the money? I
could care less about the money. I don't even care if they give me
expense money. To me, it's just a great thrill to come back and
have a sense of camaraderie with the guys.

"Sometimes when you're (playing), you don't realize what a
privilege it was and you get sidetracked by all the garbage. Like
Ballard drove me nuts for a while. I think when you come back to
a do like this you forget about all the garbage and it's the good
times that come to you. I sat down and talked to Rocket Richard
last night and some of the other heroes I had when I was a kid. I
mean Maurice Richard . . . we were in that room last night and
there were five generations of hockey players. It was wonderful."

But the players' feelings about their game, the feelings that
allowed them to be exploited for so long by Eagleson and the
owners, are more complicated now. Even for Henderson, who
said he, too, contributed money for legal fees for the pension
lawsuit. Almost to a man, the older players who were interviewed at the All-Star weekend felt they had been cheated by the
NHL, but were optimistic things were going to get better now
that the league was under new management. As always, thoughts
of Eagleson, the man who had given away the players' seats on
the board of the NHL Pension Society but still maintains NHL
pensions as the best in sport, were never far away.

"We relied so much on one man, and now we have to go back
and go over everything," said Frank Mahovlich. "We have to,
through (the pension matter) with a fine-toothed comb."

Henderson, once an Eagleson client and booster, admits the
union leader could have done a much better job on pension
matters. But so could the players. "I guess if you ask any player if
he had any regrets, it's that we didn't do more with (the pension).
Obviously, I think Eagleson did a lot for hockey. Without Eagleson,
there would not have been an association. In hindsight, there
probably was a little conflict (of interest). (Eagleson) was trying to

make a good deal for the owners and a good deal for us. I think we could have done a lot better pension-wise, there's no doubt about that. I wish I could have been smart enough to take care of that a little better, but that's the only regret I have. I should have been better informed. That's my fault, it's all of our players' fault," Henderson said.

There is a group of ex-players, though, that feels others are equally at fault — such as the NHL owners and the union leader who left those who retired before the 1986 bonanza with tiny pensions. And this after a decade spent trumpeting how wonderful the NHL pension was, especially with its infusion of cash from international hockey.

One of these people is Carl Brewer, who has been suspicious of the pension plan (and Eagleson, for that matter) for years. Angered by the $6,200 annual pension he was due after 12 seasons in the NHL (it was upgraded to $7,800 when the owners gave the ex-players $4.5 million of the $23.7-million surplus), Brewer began writing letters and asking questions. When both John Ziegler and Ken Sawyer, the NHL vice-president in charge of the NHL Pension Society, declined to answer his questions in detail, Brewer refused to back off.

By 1990, he had teamed up with Rich Winter, another Eagleson gadfly. Eagleson tried to brush them off, too, but by the end of the year they had rallied more retirees to their side. An attempt to provoke a similar investigation in the early 1980s, led by former Maple Leaf great Bob Baun who spent thousands of dollars of his own money in legal and consulting fees, had fizzled. This time Brewer was able to rally enough players to the cause and keep them there. In the United States another group of players, led by former Boston Bruin Dave Forbes, was also beginning to ask questions.

Forbes, now an investment counsellor in Southern California, had also been angry for a number of years about his pension. His anger began in 1981, a year after he retired, when Ken Sawyer gave him some answers he didn't like about his pension.

"I had read the pension documents, and I saw in there an option for me, as a member of the plan, to take my money out for whatever reason," Forbes said. "So I got in touch with Ken Sawyer and said I'd like to find out more about this, because if what I'm reading is true, I'd like to execute that option.

"He got back to me, and he was surprised. He said, 'You're the first guy who's ever called. I wasn't even aware that was in there.' Then he said, 'To answer your question, it's no, you can't do it.' I asked why not, and he said, 'Because no one's ever done it before.' I said, 'Ken, that doesn't sound like a very good reason. It's written right in the document. I don't care if anyone's never done it before. If it's there, I'd like to take advantage of it.'"

Forbes said he was never able to get his money back, because "they rewrote the document and (Sawyer) said that (the previous) document no longer applies. It was kiboshed."

Sawyer has shown a similar reluctance to answer reporters' questions. *The Globe and Mail*, for example, has tried to interview Sawyer about the pension on at least two occasions and he either did not respond to the request or declined through the NHL's public relations department.

Up until then, Forbes had only a mild interest in his pension plan. His experience with Sawyer made him take a more active interest, enough that he exchanged some correspondence with Eagleson about "ways I thought (the pension plan) could be enhanced and so on. Of course, nothing ever happened with any of it."

Then, in 1989, Ed Garvey made his report to the NHL Players' Association membership that raised a number of questions about Eagleson's leadership. The huge pension surplus was mentioned, along with the fact that all of the pension contributions the players had raised by playing in international hockey events over the years had merely gone to ease the owners' 75 per cent share of the annual $5,000 pension contribution per player, rather than fund any improvements. This really caught Forbes's attention, and by the end of 1990 he had joined forces with more ex-players in the United States and combined with Brewer and the other players in Canada.

Garvey shot holes in Eagleson's and Ziegler's boasts that the NHL had the best pension in sports. He pointed out that his investigation found there was only $28 million in the plan, compared to $440 million in baseball's plan, and $240 million in football's. Basketball and NFL football players can't start drawing their pensions until the ages of 50 and 55, respectively, which makes comparisons with hockey a bit tricky. But baseball players can start collecting at 45, and Mark Belanger of the Major League Baseball Players' Association told *The Eagle-Tribune* that a player who lasted 26 seasons like Gordie Howe would be eligible for a pension of $48,156 (U.S.) a year at the age of 63. At 63, Howe was collecting $13,000 (Cdn.). John Havlicek, who played 16 seasons for the NBA's Boston Celtics, is eligible for a pension of $38,400 (U.S.) beginning at the age of 50.

While Garvey was challenging Eagleson on the pension issue, Brewer, Stanley and Shack put up their own money, a total of $25,000, to hire Mark Zigler, a Toronto lawyer who specializes in pensions, to investigate their suspicions. On December 11, 1990, a group of 93 former NHL players, their wives and girlfriends, met in Toronto to hear the results of Zigler's look at their pension plan.

After Zigler was finished his report, the players and their spouses were shocked. By the end of the evening, there was enough support (although some players faded in and out) to proceed with a lawsuit, which was launched in April, 1991.

The pension plan was started in 1947, and was first administered by NHL president Clarence Campbell. Each player could contribute $900 per year to the plan, which was a large amount, considering that players' salaries at the time were not much higher than $5,000 or $6,000 annually. The owners contributed $600, which was actually taken from revenue from the annual All-Star Game, in which the players participated for nothing. As the authors of *Net Worth* stated, "The owners donated the players' own wages to fund their pension plan." There was also a special levy on playoff tickets of 25 cents to help pay the owners' share.

This cozy arrangement continued until 1957, when a surplus of more than $1.5 million had collected in the plan. When the owners sought a lawyer's opinion on what to do with the money, they were told the plan called for all surplus funds to go to its participants. Thus the players were awarded $315 more in their pension for each season they played. However, in 1964 the owners rewrote the plan's rules to allow a surplus to be used to fund new contributions. In 1967, the rules were changed again, this time calling for any surplus to be shared by the players every five years.

The next major change came in 1969, when the owners decided they would pay all of the pension contributions themselves and deny the players representation on the board of the NHL Pension Society. At least one person, Bill Putnam, part-owner of the Philadelphia Flyers, was surprised Eagleson did not fight the move. "The league could do whatever they wanted with the pension fund. I doubt the players really understood the ramifications of it," he told *The Eagle-Tribune*. "At the time, as owner of a financially struggling franchise, I was in favour of it. But it really was not a fair situation for the players."

The players resumed contributing to the pension in 1972, as part of Eagleson's trade-off with the owners to let them play international hockey. Eagleson agreed to have the players put up 25 per cent of the annual contribution. The money came from their share of the proceeds of international series. Eagleson was heard over and over again during the 1970s and 1980s emphasizing that international hockey money was making the NHL players' pension the best in sports.

For the 1976 Canada Cup, the players lost significant ground again when it came to their pension. In the spring of 1976, they agreed to a five-year collective bargaining agreement in which they were granted a 50 per cent increase in annual pension benefits (the amount a player could collect in pension for each year's service). The total benefit was now $750 per year per player. In exchange, the owners allowed Eagleson, who negotiated contract for the players, to avail himself of the players' services for international events.

However, the players paid a stiff price to participate in the Canada Cup, Alan Eagleson's dream. The new collective agreement called for them to give the NHL owners an equal share in the profits of international hockey (all the poor owners got from the 1972 series were the pension contributions), plus half the cost of the pension increase would come out of the players' share of the profits. The players also agreed to play for free in the annual All-Star Game, whose profits went to the owners. In exchange for all this, aside from getting to play in international events for next to nothing, the players could expect an annual pension of $14,000 a year at the age of 55. But that would be only for those who managed to survive 10 years in the NHL. Moreover, it seems neither Eagleson nor the players stopped to consider just when the $14,000 would be paid and what long-term inflation would do to its value. It was the same sort of thinking which 10 years later would lead the players, under Eagleson's direction, to give up free agency for a $250,000 lump-sum pension bonus.

Now that the players were once again contributing money to the pension plan, it did not mean they were back on the board of the NHL Pension Society. Eagleson apparently never saw the need. When asked by Russ Conway why the players did not regain their representation on the board, former NHL president John Ziegler primly replied, "They never asked for it." Conway subsequently discovered, after interviewing dozens of current and former players, that none of them knew they had lost their membership in the board in the first place, now that they had no say in how their pension was administered. "I was a vice-president (of the NHLPA) for 12 years and I never knew we weren't represented," said Brad Park, a former Boston Bruin and old foe of Eagleson.

Eagleson defended his failure to ensure the players had representation on the Pension Society. "What is forgotten in all of this is that in the negotiations of 1969, with one sweep of a pen, it ended the contributions of every NHL player. There were 12 teams and 300 players and they were paying $1,500 per person as their cost in the pension plan. In that year, that was a lot of money, and it meant no payments by the players. If every player on (the current) list of retired players had put away $1,500 (starting in 1969) for the next 10 years, by 1979, with compound interest, they would probably have $25,000. They'd be sitting with $100,000 probably right now," Eagleson said.

Actually, there was one former player listed as a member of the Pension Society from 1982-86. Only he said he knew nothing about it. Gordie Howe was notified by the NHL that "I had been elected to a position with the Pension Society," he said in an affidavit filed with the pension lawsuit. "I further recall subsequently telephoning the office of the National Hockey League and indicating I did not wish to accept any position with the NHL Pension Society." But the Pension Society continued to list him as a member of its board, even though Howe said he was never informed of this or about any meetings. Ken Sawyer said in an affidavit that material concerning the board had been sent to Howe through the Hartford Whalers, who employed him after he retired as a player. "Whether or not it didn't get from the club to him, I don't know," Sawyer said. Sawyer also testified he thought Howe did attend a meeting, "but I am not sure."

Gil Stein, who was NHL president from June, 1992 until June, 1993, said he thought that former league president John Ziegler was responsible for putting together the slate of Pension Society officers each year.

As for international hockey providing every NHL player with

a comfortable retirement, by 1982 some prominent NHLers were asking questions about that. It had become obvious that profits from such series were high enough to cover more than the 25 per cent of the players' contribution to the plan. People were starting to wonder where the rest of the money was, and Eagleson wasn't providing any answers, even after Phil Esposito, a former NHLPA president, went public in 1982.

Esposito, sounding a lot like Carl Brewer would almost 10 years later, in the late summer of 1982 say that he estimated the NHLPA's share from the 1972 series, the Canada Cups in 1976 and 1981, and the Challenge Cup in 1979 (a series between the Russians and the NHL All-Stars) to be about $4 million. He said that more than covered the pension contributions and should have produced an increase in pension payments.

"But that hasn't happened," Esposito said. "I've asked Eagleson as recently as June (1982) about it, but he told me there was a legal problem and the lawyers were working on it. It seems an awful long time for them to be trying to solve it.

"I'd like to know — and I think many other players would, too — why it hasn't been done. When I was a player, I didn't pay enough attention to things like pensions. Now that I'm retired, I do and I wish I could get some answers."

Eagleson admitted there was an excess and called it a "bonus pension pool." He said this money was the subject of a tax dispute between the NHLPA, Revenue Canada and the Internal Revenue Service. "When (the governments' tax departments) agree within our tax counsel's position, a distribution will be made. Until then, the money is held by the NHL Players' Association. Until the collective bargaining agreement expired in 1982, we were not permitted legally to create a bonus pension," Eagleson said.

By the 1990s, the "bonus pension pool" was still not officially registered with the Ontario government. If it had been, the money would have been subject to strict regulations governing pension funds and how they are handled. The money in question sat in an NHLPA escrow account and was referred to in the NHLPA's 1988 financial statement as "the employee benefit plan." The statement also said that until December 31, 1990, "all income and capital gains earned by the plan shall be reinvested to form additional contributions to the plan. The balance remaining at that date will be distributed to eligible players over the following three years."

It was from this escrow account that Eagleson granted mortgages to his friends, business associates and clients of his law firm. The NHLPA statements show that of the $5.5 million in escrow, $2,020,000 had funded mortgages in 1988. Eagleson also collected legal fees from clients and friends for lending them the players' money, out of a fund he controlled.

By early 1993, the Ontario Pension Commission had been asked by some former NHL players to rule whether the escrow account should legally be considered a pension plan. No ruling had been made by midsummer, but Lynda Ellis, assistant superintendent of the Pension Commission from 1983 to 1987, said "I cannot see how they could not deem it as a pension plan."

Eagleson countered the critics by saying international profits were used for more than just offsetting the NHL owners' contributions to the pension plan. "What (the critics) are saying is that international hockey is not that good a deal because you take part of the profits and give it to help fund your own pension. Therefore it's not that good," he said. "What they fail to mention is that between 1975 and 1991, international hockey has earned a surplus for pension, bonus and employee benefit purposes of $12 million. Of that, $5.2 million was used to fund our pension obligation to the NHL in accordance with the collective bargaining agreement, which means the surplus for players, over and above any expense for our pension, was $7 million, and it's $7 million more than any other players' association in any other sport has earned from international events.

"During the period 1976 to 1991, a sum of $18 million has (been paid) to the benefit of players: $12 million in the pension plan, of which $5 million goes to the pension plan and $7 million was for the bonus pension, and another $6 million in all those tournaments in expenses and salary to all the players."

What Eagleson didn't say was that given the number of international events (at least 20), the $7-million surplus seems low. And it has to be divided among hundreds of players who played in the NHL after 1976. Those who retired before 1976, such as Andy Bathgate, Leo Reise, Allan Stanley and others in the pension lawsuit, don't receive any of that money. Even considering the $7 million is a nice surplus, people like former Boston Bruin

Dave Forbes are not impressed by Eagleson's arguments that international hockey has raised $12 million for the players' pensions.

"Well, how much has it raised for Alan Eagleson?" Forbes said. "I submit to you that it has raised millions of dollars for him. When he says that, then you need to ask him, 'What was the gross?' How much has international hockey grossed over all these years? There's just so much incomplete information."

There was another arrangement by Eagleson in the owners' favour that cost the players money. Instead of the NHLPA making the 25-per-cent pension contribution directly from its cut of the international hockey money, the NHL owners were allowed to make full contributions themselves, and then be reimbursed by the NHLPA. This meant the owners could claim an income tax deduction for the full pension contribution.

In 1983, the owners made a change to the pension plan that would eventually lead to the lawsuit from the retired players as well as the grand jury investigation in Boston. The owners rewrote the rules, retroactively to January 1, 1982, to say the Pension Society could distribute any surplus funds among the NHL teams and the players in proportion to their contributions to the fund. The regulations also said the clubs' share of the surplus was to be used to "reduce member club contributions to the Club Pension Plan," according to a plan filed with the Ontario Pension Commission on December 9, 1983. Immediately, the owners used $900,435 of the surplus to cut their pension bill almost in half for the 1982-83 hockey season. In almost every year throughout the 1980s, the owners used the surplus to help pay their share of the pension plan, while they granted the players only 25 per cent of the surplus funds. The owners claimed this was all the players deserved, since they were responsible for just 25 per cent of the contributions. In many years, the cash grab allowed the owners to take what they liked to call a "contribution holiday." In other words, the surplus was large enough to preclude the owners from making *any* pension contribution. In 1987-88, for example, the Montreal Canadiens owed $165,320 in pension payments, but their share of the surplus covered the entire amount.

In his series on Eagleson, Russ Conway searched for players who knew the pension rules had been changed in 1983. He couldn't find anyone who did.

When Dave Forbes was looking to Eagleson for answers about the pension plan, he discovered the union leader had taken a curious position in regard to the surplus. In a letter to Carl Brewer, Forbes recounted a meeting he had with Eagleson on December 13, 1990, shortly after the retired players had decided to pursue the matter vigorously:

> (Eagleson) then said, "I understand Mark Zigler (the players' lawyer) was saying at your meeting the other night that this surplus belongs to the players. Well it doesn't. It's the owners'. I've retained counsel to look into this and they have assured me that this money is the owners'. However, if someone wants to file a lawsuit, maybe they could get it." I then asked him if he would file a lawsuit on behalf of the players and he said no. It appeared clear that he had aligned himself with the owners.
>
> I mentioned the language in the 1967 plan document that specifically addressed surpluses and that it said any surplus was to be solely for the benefit of the players. He said he hadn't heard about that, nor did he ask me further about it. This in itself I found surprising. I mean, here I was informing the executive director of the NHLPA about language in the document itself that said surpluses were the players' and he didn't even so much as say, "Could you get me a copy of that document? I'd like to look into that." He couldn't care less.

By 1986, thanks to soaring interest rates, the surplus had grown to $23.7 million. This time, the owners granted the players about $4.5 million in additional pension benefits, or about 25 per cent of the total. Players did see an improvement to their pensions that year. For example, Woody Dumart, a Hall-of-Famer who played 16 seasons from 1935-36 to 1953-54 for the Boston Bruins, saw his pension go from $2,500 a year to $5,500. He has a quick answer when asked if he depends on his pension to survive: "Hell no."

Of the remainder, the owners kept $9.2 million for more "contribution holidays." And they were regular vacationers. In 1987-88, the owners were committed to paying $3.3 million, but they used $2.6 million of the surplus to offset that, paying a total of just $729,000. Of the 21 NHL teams, 14 did not have to make a payment at all. In 1988-89, $2.3 million of the surplus was used to take a bite out of the owners' $3.8-million obligation.

The year 1986 marked another significant change in the pension plan. This time Alan Eagleson played an active role in convincing the players to give up their demands for freedom of movement between teams for a pension bonus that was another bargain for the NHL owners.

Looking at their colleagues in other sports, hockey players saw that they had fallen behind in salaries and free agency. Baseball players could sell their services to the highest bidder after six years in the major leagues, while National Football League players were in a fight for free agency that would result in a strike followed by a long court battle. Technically, there was free agency in the NHL, but the compensation system effectively kept players from moving.

When bargaining began between Eagleson and the owners in 1986, the union leader made the appropriate noises about a possible strike over free agency. This drew the usual response from the owners, who moaned about free agency meaning the death of hockey, the same sort of rhetoric put out by the baseball owners 10 years earlier during their union struggles. But Alan Eagleson was no Marvin Miller. Miller had gained undying love and respect in union circles for leading the baseball players' union in its fight for many of the same freedoms enjoyed by most workers in North America.

It wasn't long before Eagleson was telling the players he had just pulled off a stunning negotiating coup. Forget free agency, he said, this is better. This was a lump-sum pension bonus of $250,000 that every NHL player who appeared in 400 games would collect at the age of 55. This fabulous "security package," as Eagleson called it, would cost the NHL owners $15 million by his (and the owners') estimation. If the players would give up their demands to be unrestricted free agents, the owners would give them this bonus.

To a group of people in their 20s who, despite the fact they were earning less than players in other sports, were still making six-figure incomes, this sounded like a great deal. One that might even be worth giving up free agency for, as Eagleson recommended. One player who said he wasn't fooled was Jim Korn.

"What Al said was . . . 'Hey guys, I've got a great deal for you. Free agency is going to ruin hockey. St. Louis is going to fold, Minnesota might fold, Winnipeg will be gone for sure. We're going to lose jobs. So here's what I've done. I've had a stroke of genius. We're going to give up free agency, but I've got you guys 250 grand guaranteed.'

"And all these players are sitting down saying, 'Geez, that's a lot of money. That's a good house, plus a car, that's great money.'"

Eagleson, according to the players, did not back up his contention with any figures or projections from pension experts. There were no figures to refute the owners' claims they would go broke if the players became free agents, and there were no figures to spell out how the $250,000 bonus worked. Korn decided not to take Eagleson's word on the deal and went to see an insurance expert. His suspicions were confirmed, and he told this to his teammates on the Buffalo Sabres.

"I said, 'Hey guys, do you know what $250,000 at age 55 is?' I made a call to an insurance agent and he told me it would cost about $20,000 (per player). I said, 'You just gave up free agency for $20,000. Think about it.' Nobody wanted to hear it. They just said, 'No, no, it's $250,000.' Well, it was $250,000 30 years from now."

Like their colleagues had 10 done years earlier, the players were thinking of their bonus in present-day money. This was something else of which they weren't aware. This great pension gain was being paid for out of the surplus, so it didn't cost the owners anything. Of the surplus, about $9.4 million was committed to pay for the bonus. This was far less than the "$15-million" benefit that had been advertised by Eagleson and the owners, and eventually Eagleson had to admit as much even though he remained adamant that it was a great deal for the players.

Even today, many of the players may not be aware that the $250,000 is not necessarily guaranteed. Eagleson said as much in a 1991 interview: "We run the pension plan in two separate areas, one a security package, or senior player benefit and we aim to do 10 per cent on that (as an annual return on invested contributions), so that will give the guy $250,000 in a lump sum." By "aiming" for 10 per cent returns each year does not guarantee that $250,000 will ever be realized. Especially now that the interest rates of the 1990s seem to be staying well below 10 per cent, with the prime rate headed for 20- and 30-year lows at less than 6 per cent.

Something else the players failed to consider thoroughly was just how many of them will play 400 games. When the agreement was struck, 400 games represented five 80-game NHL seasons (the playoffs don't count). There are no official figures available, and calculating whether a majority of players who have retired since 1986 played 400 games is difficult because of the variables involved. Any figure would be subjective, since you could include every player who appeared in even one NHL game. However, Ed Garvey said that when his 1989 report was prepared, he worked under the assumption most players didn't reach 400 games. Jim Korn, who saw the effects of the bonus first-hand, agreed. For every Charlie Simmer (14 seasons, 712 games), there are several Mark Taylors (five seasons, 209 games). "Very few (play 400 games)," Korn said. "But everybody thinks they're going to. Sure as shooting, you'd get guys on the bubble, with 350, 360 games. These guys were hanging on for a couple of years or more, trying to get those 400 games, and for what? For those guys (older players near retirement in 1986), it might have cost (the owners) $30,000 (to fund the benefit). But look what's happened to salaries now. With free agency, those players could have made $30,000 in three games. To say that was a good deal is mind boggling."

In 1992, under Eagleson's successor NHLPA executive director, Bob Goodenow, a change was made to the lump-sum scheme. Now players can begin to qualify for the payment once they have played 160 games. At that point, payments are started to fund the benefit, although a player still does not qualify for the full $250,000 until he hits 400 games. But players who have made 160 games will get a bonus, pro-rated to how many games they have played. The $250,000 is still not guaranteed, and is dependent on the success of the investment.

This benefit was restricted to players who retired after 1986, and most of those men were not aware it had been funded from a surplus generated by players who had already retired. Jim Fox, a player rep for the Los Angeles Kings at the time, told Russ Conway that the player representatives at meetings concerning collective bargaining were aware of this. But the word did not filter back to the rank-and-file membership. Many of them learned the surplus was the source of the funds at the famous 1989 meeting when Ed Garvey delivered his report on the union.

The subject of notification played a large role in the lawsuit launched against the league by the players. The suit filed in U.S. federal court in Camden, N.J., charges that by changing the pension rules in 1983 without notifying the players and by using the surplus for themselves, the NHL and its owners have committed violations of the U.S. Employee Retirement Income Security Act (ERISA). An affidavit with the lawsuit filed in the provincial court of Ontario supports this claim. Paul Saunders, a Canadian insurance expert, said in his affidavit that "the consequences of these actions, in my opinion, represent a gain to the benefit of the NHL clubs and the current and future players at the expense of retired players, whose pensions continue to lose their value due to inflation." Those who have been before the grand jury in Boston say a lot of questions concerning the pension plan and ERISA were asked by its members.

Eagleson maintained he was not at fault for any problems with the pension. "Notice they didn't sue me. Notice they didn't sue the players' association," he said.

While the retired players were seeking answers to their questions about the pension from Ziegler and Sawyer, Eagleson did nothing to help them. Indeed, he even seemed eager to put distance between them and himself. "The dispute is between the retired players and the NHL," he said in the summer of 1991. Several weeks later, Eagleson told Bruce Dowbiggin of the CBC that his duty as executive director of the NHLPA was "*not* to look after retired players."

This was interesting, for just two years before that, Eagleson wrote a letter to Murray Elston, then the Ontario minister of financial institutions. Elston's ministry was in charge of pensions registered in the province. In the letter, Eagleson said he represented "all hockey players who participate in the National Hockey League Club Pension Plan." Presumably this would include the retired players, since they were participants in the plan, too.

In his letter, Eagleson asked Elston to continue to exempt the NHL Pension Society from a law in the Pension Benefits Act that requires equal representation for employees in all multi-employer pension plans. Eagleson wrote the letter at the request of Ken Sawyer. Eagleson told Elston that the letter "will confirm the NHLPA's support of the application to have the National Hockey League Pension Society exempted (from the law)."

While it isn't known why the head of a players' union would go to bat for management to the detriment of his members, the timing of the letter is intriguing. It was written on August 1, 1989, two months after Eagleson had narrowly survived a vote by the players to fire him. But he had agreed to begin a search for a deputy director who would be designated his eventual successor, and a follow-up meeting in July to discuss the terms of the succession had been re-scheduled for later in August. On August 1, 1989, when he wrote the letter to Elston, time was running out on Eagleson's tenure as NHLPA executive director was in doubt for the first time.

Once again, no players could be found who had been informed about the letter. "I never saw that letter, was never aware of it until now and I was a players' association team representative for the Bruins when it was written," said Andy Moog. Pat Verbeek of the Hartford Whalers said, "It was just business as usual, Eagle going along with whatever the league wanted. I never knew about any pension exemption supported by the players' association."

When Elston learned that many players had not been informed of the letter, he said if he had known that at the time, the exemption would not have been allowed. He also said he made the assumption, based on Eagleson's letter, that he represented the retired players as well. "Absent of the approval of the players — knowing what is being represented now — I think it was a drastic misrepresentation of the facts," Elston said.

The matter of representation on the pension board did not come up again until the spring of 1993, by which time the retired players had won their lawsuit against the NHL. Judge George Adams ruled the surplus was improperly taken from them, and his decision said an officer of the court should be appointed to decide just how much the $21 million in surpluses were worth in 1993 and how they should be distributed. Mark Zigler, the lawyer who successfully argued the case for the players, said, with the accumulation of interest, the amount due the players could now be worth more than $40 million.

The NHL, under interim president Gil Stein, immediately announced plans for an appeal to the Ontario Court of Appeal. When Gary Bettman took over as NHL commissioner on February 1, 1993, he hinted about reaching a settlement with the players. Obviously the NHL owners had other ideas. By the late summer of 1993, the appeal was still going ahead and was expected to be heard in late September.

The U.S. version of the lawsuit has not fared so well. In the spring of 1993, it was thrown out of federal court, but not because the case lacked merit. Rather, the judge ruled, the lawsuit was out of the jurisdiction of the U.S. federal court, as the union head-quarters was in Canada. The players have sought leave to appeal that decision to the U.S. Supreme Court. And they have an ally in the appeal — the NHL Players' Association. Under Bob Goodenow, the NHLPA has intervened in the case, arguing to the Supreme Court that the lawsuit should be heard in both Cana-dian and U.S. jurisdictions because NHLPA members reside in both countries.

Around the NHL Pension Society, things have changed, too. Sawyer, no doubt encouraged by the Bettman regime, resigned as an NHL vice-president in the late spring of 1993. He is still secretary-treasurer of the Pension Society, but that will probably change when his successor as vice-president, finance and treas-urer of the NHL is found.

And the players are back on the Pension Society's board. Floyd Laughren, Ontario's finance minister, notified the NHL that if it could not produce documented evidence by April 30, 1993 that a majority of pension plan participants did not want representation on the board, he would revoke the exemption. The NHL did send an eight-page letter through a lawyer asking that the exemption be retained but could offer no proof that was what the players wanted. Laughren also received notice from the NHLPA that it wanted back on the board, as well as a petition opposing the exemption that was signed by 118 retired players. Within a week, Laughren notified the NHL it was losing the exemption. For the first time in 24 years, the players would again have a voice in the operation of their pension plan.

Chapter Eleven

THE WATCHERS

OVER THE YEARS, sports writers have followed the career of R. Alan Eagleson with a mixture of interest, curiosity and caution. One is Trent Frayne, who worked both as a magazine writer and columnist for publications that included *The Globe and Mail*, *Maclean's* and the *Toronto Sun*.

In 1972, at the time of the Canada-Soviet Union Summit Series, Frayne was writing for *The Toronto Star*. He had missed the first four games of the series played in Canada because he had been on assignment in Munich covering the Olympic Games. From West Germany, he went directly to Moscow for the last half of the series. The day after the fifth game, which the Soviet Union had won 3-1, Frayne was waiting for an elevator on the sixth floor of the Intourist Hotel in Moscow. An elevator arrived and out stepped Eagleson.

"What'd yuh think?" asked Eagleson.

Frayne told him he had been knocked out by the puck control of the Soviets and noted that he had never seen a team pass the puck that well.

"Jesus," said Eagleson, "you must be a communist."

Frayne could see that Eagleson wasn't joking. His lips were a thin line and his eyed burned behind his glasses.

"All I said was their passing knocked me out," replied Frayne.

"We lost, you know," said Eagleson.

"Yeah, I know we lost."

"We lost, and you're telling me you like their passing."

"Well, yeah, I certainly liked their passing."

"Anybody who thinks like you do has to be a bloody communist," said Eagleson.

"What is this? I tell you I like their passing and you give me this ideological gobbledegook. What the hell has . . ."

"Are you calling what I have to say gobbledegook?"

"Well," said Frayne, "friendship ought to be worth more than that."

At that point, Frayne grabbed an elevator and escaped.

A few years later, Frayne happened to profile Eagleson in a *Maclean's* magazine article which he felt, as a balanced piece, exposed a few of Eagleson's warts and made note of a few of his halos.

Just as the issue hit the newsstands, *Toronto Star* sports columnist Jim Proudfoot, one of Eagleson's oldest friends in the newspaper business, ran a note at the bottom of his column stating, "Alan Eagleson is hot over an article in *Maclean's*. Says it's a hatchet job."

In his memoirs, Frayne wrote, "I didn't have that in mind, putting the piece together. I figured the Eagle was a reasonable enough guy to recognize that not every move he made drew universal favour. But as I discovered in nearly half a century in the toy department, when you're an athletic supporter you meet all kinds."

Over the years, other sports journalists would occasionally find themselves on the wrong side of an argument with Eagleson. It could be a singularly unpleasant experience, as a hockey writer for *The Globe and Mail* learned during the 1987 Canada Cup.

In June, just a few months prior to the tournament, the hockey writer reported on the reluctance of some players to participate. Anonymous sources were quoted as saying several members of the Stanley Cup champion Edmonton Oilers, including coach and general manager Glen Sather and its star player Wayne Gretzky, weren't enthusiastic about playing.

The Oilers had just finished a long regular season and a gruelling seven-week playoff. They were tired and the last thing they wanted to do was jump back on the ice in early August and work at defending Canada's honour in the most demanding hockey competition in the world. Besides, the Oilers — Sather, Gretzky, Glenn Anderson, Grant Fuhr and others — had led

Canada into the 1981 and 1984 Canada Cup tournaments. Wasn't that enough?

Sather did not get involved in the tournament, but Gretzky and his teammates did. It turned out to be a spectacular sporting event capped by a best-of-three final between the Soviet Union and Canada which veteran hockey writers today describe as the highest level of hockey they have ever seen played.

The Globe and Mail gave the tournament excellent coverage, as did the other two Toronto newspapers and some of the other major Canadian dailies. Despite the front-page reports and the hype, ticket sales for some of the marginal games in the smaller markets had not gone as well as Eagleson had hoped.

Before the last game of the tournament at Copps Coliseum in Hamilton, Ontario, reporters, some of whom had worked long hours every day for most of two months, and tournament officials, were tired and of ill disposition. In the press box that night, Eagleson was interviewed by a radio reporter, just before the game, in an open area where the media mingled.

Eagleson was asked if he was satisfied with ticket sales. Yes, he said, but quickly added that *The Globe and Mail* was to blame for slow sales in smaller markets. He went on to explain why he thought *The Globe*'s "irresponsible reporting" on the Oiler situation had hurt the tournament.

Eagleson was speaking loudly, almost as if he wanted to be sure *The Globe* reporter who had written the Oiler stories overheard his remarks. Surprised and angered by Eagleson's remarks, the reporter approached him and asked curtly what he was talking about.

"Those stories you wrote were lies," Eagleson said. "Gretzky played, Fuhr played. Your newspaper hurt our ticket sales and it was because of the bullshit you were writing."

"There isn't a newspaper in the country that's given your tournament better coverage than we have," the reporter shot back. "For you to say that is ridiculous."

The argument became more heated.

"Just who the hell do you think you are to talk to me like that?" Eagleson snarled. "You're just a midget compared to great sports writers in this country. The guys like Red Fisher, Milt Dunnell and Jim Proudfoot. You couldn't carry their fucking bags."

"I'm a midget?" said the reporter. "What the hell do you think you are? Take a look in the mirror. . . ."

At that point, the reporter saw Eagleson's eyes changing, blazing angrily but also losing focus. Given the Eagle's reputation, this, the reporter knew, was a worrisome turn of events. The argument, however, ended seconds later when several reporters intervened. With the game about to start, *The Globe* reporter took his seat but then heard somebody behind him. It was Eagleson, and in his hand he was carrying a large pretzel. He smiled, held it out, and said, "A peace offering." It was accepted and the two shook hands.

To incur the wrath of Eagleson is not a pleasant experience, as Frayne, *The Globe* reporter and any number of people can attest. But confrontations were the exception rather than the rule. The media has enjoyed a generally warm and mutually supportive relationship with Eagleson.

Over the years, Eagleson has carefully avoided making enemies of reporters. In the press box at Copps Coliseum after his argument with *The Globe* writer, he knew it made no sense for a feud to fester, especially since their relationship had been cordial up 'til then. Eagleson may have disliked Frayne for some of the things he had written or said, but he would never have cut him off or refused to speak to him. To the media, Eagleson was accessible, approachable, friendly; and also unpretentious, which was a welcome change for hockey writers who dealt with general managers and owners, most of whom could variously be described as smug, pompous, arrogant and self-important.

The majority of reporters covering hockey are lucky if they get more that a perfunctory nod from high-level hockey people whether they are players or in management. But Eagleson remembered names, would say hello and was one of the guys. During the 1987 Canada Cup, a prominent columnist working for a Western Canadian newspaper arrived in the East to cover the tournament. When Eagleson saw the man at a team practice, he immediately went over to him, shook his hand, called him by his first name and asked him about his family. The veteran writer was thrilled. His face glowed. An important man had taken time to stop and say a few words and that made the writer feel important. If Eagleson received a telephone call from a reporter, he would either take the call or return it quickly, always the same day — a courtesy that wasn't always accorded members of the NHLPA or even Eagleson's own clients.

So, for all of these reasons, Eagleson was liked by the people reporting on hockey. Not that the journalists were blind to Eagleson's methods of operation and character. One well-known Toronto hockey writer called him "Hitler's Kid." The reporters knew he could be a bully, was dictatorial and sometimes abusive. But he wasn't that way with them. The reporters shared a symbiosis with Eagleson that served both sides well for more than 20 years. In the closed, tight-lipped culture of pro hockey in the 1970s and 1980s, Eagleson's candour was refreshing and useful. He provided information quickly, and if the right question was asked, his answer could give a reporter an exclusive story. Eagleson in turn received excellent coverage and hardly ever had to field a tough question.

Glen Sharpley, a former Sports Management Ltd. client, says Eagleson used to boast to him that he could get a story on the front page of any one of the three Toronto newspapers any time he wanted, and that he virtually controlled the city's top sports writers. Eagleson's agreeable relationship with the Toronto sports media gave him a critical advantage in a fight, several of which he had with the Toronto Maple Leafs' management. There were Carl Brewer's contract hassles with the Leafs in the 1960s. Later, in the late 1970s and early 1980s, Eagleson found himself in the middle of a feud between his then star client Darryl Sittler and the Leaf management.

In 1979, Sittler, the team's captain, opposed the idea of Punch Imlach coming back to manage the team. Their relationship started deteriorating almost from the first day of training camp. The team's inept and capricious owner Harold Ballard first supported Imlach and then Sittler. At one point, Sittler ripped the C off his jersey in a rage after Imlach had traded his close friend Lanny McDonald; several months later he agreed to take the C back. Imlach couldn't trade Sittler because Eagleson had negotiated a no-trade clause in his contract, but after Imlach was fired, Sittler demanded a trade and then walked off the team to force the Leafs to move him.

It could be argued that Sittler, as the team's captain, had behaved selfishly, and that Eagleson, by representing seven players on the Leaf team, had more control in the Leaf dressing room than either the team's coaches or manager. But Sittler received almost uniformly positive press during his "ordeal" and rarely was Eagleson criticized for his role in the standoff. The villains of the piece were consistently portrayed as Imlach and Ballard.

One sports writer who found himself on the spot during the Sittler-Leaf battle was the *Toronto Sun*'s sports editor, George Gross, who was one of Eagleson's closest and oldest friends in the Toronto media. But Gross had covered Imlach's teams in the 1960s when they had won four championships. And George did not simply like Imlach; he worshipped him. At the *Sun*'s sports department during Gross's years, reporters joked that the sports editor's friends were accorded special privileges, but there were only two sacred cows — Imlach and Eagleson. The lone dissenter was the *Sun*'s hockey writer of the 1970s, John Iaboni, who would occasionally get away with a criticism of Eagleson.

Eagleson, in his biography, listed the reporters he respected the most. He wrote, "Then and later, the media people I met whom I found I could trust completely never changed — Jim Taylor and Jim Kearney in Vancouver, George Gross, then of the *Telegram* and later with the *Toronto Sun*, Red Burnett, Jim Proudfoot and Milt Dunnell of *The Toronto Star*, Beddoes, Red Fisher and Tim Burke in Montreal, Claude Bedard in Quebec. And there were others along the way. As well, some I never could share a confidence with without seeing it published the next day, half wrong. In time I would answer their questions, wouldn't lie to them, but I wouldn't *offer* any information."

Red Fisher, the *Montreal Gazette* sports editor, has enjoyed a particularly warm relationship with Eagleson. They first met in the mid-1960s when Eagleson, on the advice of *Globe* sports columnist Dick Beddoes, gave Fisher a call while in Montreal. Fisher was then with the *Montreal Star*, and they met for a coffee in the newspaper's cafeteria. The next day, a column by Fisher appeared in the *Star* reporting on Eagleson's aspirations to establish a union. Fisher at one point in his column referred to Eagleson as "the Eagle," a nickname that Eagleson had attached to himself in childhood. It fit for obvious reasons — his name and the fact that Al had a significant proboscis. But Fisher said he called him the Eagle, "because of his unswerving gall."

Most of these men got to know Eagleson in the 1960s, made the trip to Moscow for the 1972 Summit Series, and subsequently had helped create the cult of Eaglemania, the great Canadian story of the tough, young patriot who had led the Canadians to Moscow and beaten the reviled communists. They not only became loyal friends of Eagleson, but they were also his first line of defence when unfavourable reports were published.

They would not only jump to his defence, but also work to discredit the heretic responsible for the untruths. A former Eagleson employee, said in 1991, "The thing that has really saved him (Eagleson) is that he owns the key guys in the media. He has owned them. As a result, he's been very sheltered, very well protected, because he's provided them with meaningful stories along the way. There's been, in my humble estimation, sometimes a lack of objectivity when it comes to criticizing Al and I was a part of it when I worked for him. I know it worked to my advantage as well. But that exists."

Curiously, when critical stories initially came out, women reporters were often the source of Eagleson's grief, and he theirs, which might in part speak to the fact Eagleson was a product of the male-dominated sports environment that viewed women as intrusive. But just how Eagleson related to women in a general sense is question worth considering. In *Net Worth*, the authors reported on his "legendary Christmas parties, where he behaved like a reincarnated Lenny Bruce," humiliating the wives of employees, players and friends.

"Hey you, where the fuck are yuh going," Eagleson would shout as a woman got up to go to the bathroom.

"Yuh going to take a piss? A crap? Hey, can I come with you?"

When they returned, Eagleson would say, "Hey, did you wash you hands? Wipe yourself?"

The *Net Worth* authors wrote, "The women loathed it and over the years more and more of them refused to attend."

Christie Blatchford, who wrote a sports column for *The Globe* in the 1970s, was probably the first woman journalist to delve into Eagleson's world of international hockey intrigue. She was convinced he was wearing too many hats and that his pals were getting the top jobs in the hockey deals. Eagleson was furious over her reports, although she discovered nothing illegal, and after she left *The Globe*, he boasted: "I got her off that paper."

In fact, Blatchford quit because she objected to her columns being edited by Bob Walker, who at the time was called a "writing coach." Blatchford went on to cover news and write columns at *The Toronto Star* and today is a columnist with the *Toronto Sun*.

Deidra Clayton investigated Eagleson in a 1982 unauthorized biography titled *Eagle: The Life and Times of R. Alan Eagleson*, which was well researched and, although not an attack, showed him for what he was — brilliant, manipulative and a hustler, juggling a mass of overlapping interests. Eagleson initially gave Clayton access to information and agreed to a series of interviews. But before the book came out, he threatened to sue if he wasn't shown the manuscript before publication. Clayton refused and Lester & Orpen Dennys proceeded with the book's publication.

What followed was a compelling example of Eagleson's power in the sports media. Eagleson didn't sue, but Clayton was vilified in the sports pages and in reviews written by sports writers. Columnists wrote long pieces pointing out mistakes she had made in the book. Most of them were relatively unimportant background errors — misspelled names and some factual errors about the game (Clayton was not a hockey writer). Nevertheless, the book was thoroughly denounced and Clayton discredited and quickly forgotten.

A few years later, Ellie Tesher of *The Toronto Star* enraged Eagleson when she used Bobby Orr and his Windsor, Ontario, lawyer, Harvey Strosberg, as sources for an article titled, "Bobby Orr speaks out at last," which laid out Orr's side of the Eagleson-Orr feud. Eagleson, in his biography, went on at great length about Tesher and, in fact, mentions her name on six pages, which puts her ahead of his oldest media cronies such as Proudfoot, Dunnell, Red Fisher and even Gross, although Gross, Eagleson's tennis partner during world hockey championships in Europe and companion at Wimbledon, comes in a close second, getting his name on five pages. Eagleson said he found Tesher "very obnoxious — that is the least offending word I can use," and then spent several pages presenting his rebuttal to assertions made in her story.

In the late 1980s, Alison Griffiths began researching Eagleson and the NHLPA for *Net Worth*, which was co-authored by her husband David Cruise. Griffiths interviewed Eagleson and apparently it went well, but when she called back with the tough questions, Cruise says Eagleson was rude and abusive to his wife and of no further help. *Net Worth* was a fine piece of investigative journalism, by far the most realistic look at the NHL's history vis-à-vis player relations. The Eagleson loyalists either ignored the book or pointed out its failures. Like the book *Eagle*, *Net Worth* was criticized by Eagleson's friends for its factual errors, such as

Red Kelly's wife Andra being referred to as Andrea. Red Fisher, in conversation with a *Globe* reporter, dismissed the book as jumble of inaccuracies. He noted that when he looked his name up in the index it wasn't there (the index was off by about two pages).

So, given Eagleson's enormous influence on Canadian sports journalists, it should not have been a surprise that the revelations in the Russ Conway's 1991 investigative articles for *The Eagle-Tribune* and the subsequent federal grand jury investigation into Eagleson's conduct were greeted by the Canadian media with a deafening silence. The lone exception was Bruce Dowbiggin of CBC television in Toronto, who did a follow-up to Conway's first series in September, 1991, and then assisted Conway in his second set of articles in February, 1993.

At *The Globe*, a reporter in the sports department heard about Conway's investigation in June, 1991, a few months before the articles appeared. The reporter passed on the information to the *Globe*'s sports editor, David Langford, with the suggestion that the newspaper buy Conway's series. When Langford pitched the idea to Tim Pritchard, who was then the managing editor, Pritchard instead decided to commission a *Globe* investigation of Eagleson. Two reporters were assigned to the story and were given about three weeks, during which time one of them was given other assignments. They managed to scratch the surface, but what finally ran was a generally uncritical profile of Eagleson with little new information on his business and union activities.

Conway, on the other hand, worked for more than a year on the story and examined, in depth, at least half a dozen critical areas of Eagleson's career: the pension fund issue, his real estate dealings, the Bobby Orr controversy, the conflicts of interest, the insurance situation with the players and the NHLPA and the financial activities of Hockey Canada. The five-part series was a brilliant work of journalism and was a runner-up for a 1991 Pulitzer Prize in the category of newsbeat reporting.

The Canadian media, subsequently but not immediately, were accused of missing a story that had been developing under their noses for more than 20 years. Roy MacGregor, a columnist for *The Ottawa Citizen* who joined that sports department in 1992 to cover the Senators, strongly voiced his opinion on CBC radio in early 1993 when he said that sports writers had not been doing their job properly, had missed an important story and should be ashamed of themselves.

Why did the Canadian media miss the Eagleson story? Good sports writers are a versatile lot, having knowledge of peripheral issues such as labour negotiations, contracts, television, medicine and business. But most, as a matter of fact the majority of working journalists, are not skilled investigative reporters. It is a specialized area for which considerable time, expertise and resources are needed. That the Canadian media missed the Eagleson story can, in part, be attributed to the fact that even the most informed hockey reporters didn't know a fraction of what Eagleson was up to, and even if they did, few newspapers, if any, would have committed the time and resources Conway used to investigate him.

What is inexcusable is the paralysis that overcame the Canadian media when Conway's first series finally did appear. Except for CBC in Toronto, no news organization followed the story. None of Eagleson's friends in the media commented on the series because, presumably, there was nothing to discredit The stories were strong, compelling and apparently accurate.

In the months that followed, the U.S. grand jury investigation was announced, Conway started work on his second series, the FBI began interviewing witnesses in Canada and the United States, and the media, except for Conway and Dowbiggin who worked together, looked the other way. Many veteran reporters, both Canadian and American, who had been covering hockey for years hadn't yet read Conway's first series one year after it had appeared. But as 1992 drew to a close and another Conway series loomed in early 1993, the Eagleson story had become too big to ignore. In January, *The Globe and Mail* became the first newspaper in Canada to conduct a thorough investigation. It lasted two months, involved three reporters, with help from two others, plus full-time assistance from one editor.

In February, *The Toronto Star* and *Sun* both threw together quick reports updating the readers on what was happening. *The Globe* then came out with its series, as did *The Eagle-Tribune* and the CBC in Toronto. Reaction to the articles from Eagleson's friends was predictable. Bill Stephenson, the sports director of Canada's largest A.M. station, CFRB in Toronto, and a veteran broadcaster who thought himself a close friend of Eagleson, denounced the *Globe* and *Eagle-Tribune* articles as "rumour and innuendo." It didn't matter to Stephenson that all the quotes and allegations in both the *Globe* and *Eagle-Tribune* series were made on the record, and in most cases the anecdotal material was supported by documentation.

Of the news organizations in Toronto, the *Sun* was most supportive of Eagleson, although earlier the newspaper had done some good reporting on the Eagleson case. Sports editor Scott Morrison, for example, had broken the pension scandal story in 1991. But in 1993, *Sun* sports reporters and columnists were ready and willing to wave the flag, sound the bugle and go to war for their friend Al Eagleson. And, if moral support were required, they didn't need to look any further than the company's president, Paul Godfrey.

Godfrey, a prominent Tory and would-be sportsman who helped bring a major league baseball franchise to Toronto, has never attempted to conceal his deep affection and admiration for Eagleson. He once told Deidra Clayton, "He's a social as well as a political friend. I cherish Al's and Nancy's company. . . . I also value his political advice: he's the type of person who makes things happen — closest thing to a human bombshell that God could create, vibrant, daring — God only makes an Al Eagleson once in every thousand years."

In the July, 1993 issue of *Toronto Life* magazine, Godfrey was profiled in an article that, at one point, questioned the *Sun*'s weak coverage of Eagleson's difficulties. Godfrey noted that he had organized a stag for Eagleson in 1992 to lift his spirits during the FBI investigation. He said he was going to stay loyal to his friend. "On election night, I would never go to the party of a winner. They don't need you there. The losers — they're the ones who need you." He described Eagleson as "a dear friend — as far as I'm concerned he's innocent. . . . I have a philosophy: you stick with your friends."

The Sun's defence of Eagleson had started several weeks before *The Globe*, CBC and *Eagle-Tribune* articles appeared. Both Scott Morrison and television columnist Rob Longley had tossed darts at Dowbiggin, charging that he had been smugly patting his own back over the fact he was the only Canadian journalist working on the Eagleson story.

That was followed by a column written by Douglas Fisher, the newspaper's long-time Ottawa columnist, an Eagleson friend and a former director of Hockey Canada. Under the headline "In defence of Alan Eagleson," Fisher wrote, "I believe the nasty imputations about Eagleson, vis-à-vis Hockey Canada are haywire. . . . Although Eagleson was hardly the A to Z in all such competitions and their deals, I know he was the crucial catalyst for the international series as enterprises. I believe he seized such a role to give his NHLPA leverage with the NHL owners which they could not evade."

That some of the younger sports reporters, those who presumably might be more skeptical of Eagleson and more inclined to question what he had been doing, rallied to Eagleson's defence was seen as surprising. Columnist Steve Simmons, for example, wrote a heart-felt piece about how much Al had meant to him as a young reporter on the beat and how sorry he was for what was happening.

It was perhaps understandable that Godfrey would stay loyal to his friend Eagleson. Godfrey, after all, is not a journalist. But when a writer, whose job it is to report on matters that may involve somebody the writer knows, takes the same position as Godfrey, the obvious question is what comes first? A reporter's responsibility to his reader? Or his loyalty to a friend?

Jim Taylor of the *Vancouver Province* made his position clear in a cloying column written February 23, 1993, three days after *The Globe* articles on Eagleson started appearing. With a simplistic and rather naive perspective of the NHL and Eagleson, Taylor wrote, "Defending himself may cost him every dollar he possesses. If he is charged and found guilty he could be ruined. If he is exonerated he has no recourse to get that money back. The players he made rich by forming the players' association, wrestling the salary whip from the owners and handing it to the athletes, will get him either way. In court of law or public opinion, Alan Eagleson may be guilty or innocent or a little bit of both. When it's over, he will still be my friend."

It can be argued that Eagleson helped organize the most important sporting event in Canada's history, the 1972 Summit Series, which was covered extensively, and then he became the biggest hockey story of the 1990s, which was not covered well at all. The observation could be made that the two most prominent sports figures in Toronto over the past 30 years have been Harold

Ballard, the late Maple Leafs' owner, and Eagleson. Like Eagleson, Ballard had a symbiotic relationship with the media and until very late in life was rarely criticized, even though he was a destructive man whose team languished under his control in the 1970s and 1980s. It was perhaps because of Ballard that the sports media came to admire and support Eagleson and gravitate toward him. He represented a sharp contrast to the atavistic Ballard. He was bright and dynamic, he said the right things and the media believed in what he was doing and they supported him. But when the Eagleson story took a turn for the worse, and Al, the friend, became Eagleson, the news story, his friends in the media found themselves caught in the middle. And some forgot what their job was all about.

Chapter Twelve

THE SIEGE

IF THERE EVER WAS A TIME when R. Alan Eagleson's true feelings surfaced about the players who financed his way to the top of the hockey world, it came on a June day in 1986. The 21 player representatives from each NHL team, plus the seven-man executive committee, had gathered in Toronto to prepare for negotiations for a new collective bargaining agreement. The talks with the club's owners were scheduled to begin in just a few hours when Larry Latto, an attorney from Washington, D.C., walked into the room where the players were meeting. Latto, a corporate lawyer from the firm of Shea Gardner, the NHLPA's counsel in the United States.

Latto came bearing a bombshell from Eagleson who was demanding a new contract: a six-year, no-cut deal with an escalating salary starting in 1987 at $170,000 per year and topping off at $300,000 in 1993, along with a pension for life of $50,000 a year starting at the age of 65. There were also some generous bonuses, such as $25,000 for every year the players' share of the profits from international hockey was $600,000 or more, $23,000 a year for a car, $10,000 a year for office expenses plus $30,000 a year for secretaries (he was also getting paid by Hockey Canada for office expenses and work done by his employees for Canada Cup tournaments), and $49,000 a year for office rent. The rent was paid to an Eagleson family holding company which owned the building near Maple Leaf Gardens that housed the NHLPA and Eagleson's law firm. The contract also called for Eagleson to devote only "60 to 65 per cent" of his time to the NHLPA. The rest of the time he was free to operate international hockey tournaments, act as an agent for players, work as a lawyer and dabble in real estate and other business ventures. Moreover, his contract was to be paid in U.S. funds, despite the fact he lived in Toronto, and that most NHL players who worked in Canada were paid in Canadian dollars, which have been valued 15 to 30 per cent below U.S. currency during the 1980s. The first (and least expensive) year of the contract called for Eagleson to receive the equivalent of $410,000 in Canadian funds from the players for his part-time job.

Eagleson sent word that if the players did not approve his contract he would quit on the spot. "(Latto) said, 'This is what he wants and he won't come back unless this is what he gets,'" said Pat Verbeek, then a 22-year-old player representative for the New Jersey Devils.

At the time, the periodic rumours that Eagleson was being courted by the owners to take over as president of the NHL from the hapless John Ziegler had surfaced again. The players, far from skilled in the art of negotiation, panicked. They quickly formed a committee to approve the contract, and agreed to every one of Eagleson's demands. There were no cries of outrage that someone would use the timing of collective bargaining to his advantage in squeezing the very people who made him rich. There was no call to approach the owners to request a delay in the bargaining process while the contract was sorted out. There wasn't even a question directed to Latto about his role as messenger boy for Eagleson, considering that he was being paid by the association. (To this day, Latto is still under retainer to the NHLPA. He declined a request from the authors to discuss his role in the affair).

"We couldn't tell him to stuff it," Pat Verbeek said. "There was talk of Alan Eagleson going to represent the owners. Had things been like they are now, we would have asked for a delay. But at that particular time, I don't think the players were particularly well informed. I don't think the players were knowledgeable about the affairs of the association."

Jim Fox, a Kings player representative, admitted the players should have stalled the owners. "It was the surprise and the fear. You're going into a meeting with the owners and you have no leader. I will take part of the blame. We had the whole summer. We should have gone for a postponement."

Eagleson, new contract safely in hand, assured one and all that he was committed to the players. "Now they don't have to worry about getting a new deal on September 1, then getting up on October 1 and finding me as president of the NHL," he said. Looking back at the tight friendship between Eagleson, Ziegler and Bill Wirtz, the chairman of the NHL's board of governors, the idea that Eagleson would shove his buddy aside in a mutually rewarding relationship seems implausible. But it wasn't at the time when a group of athletes believed that Eagleson was the only man who could lead them. "They just thought they had to have Al Eagleson," Jim Korn said. "They thought he was the only guy who could negotiate a contract, and that was pure garbage."

In the summer of 1991, as his reign as union leader was winding down, Eagleson indulged in some revisionist history concerning how his contract was negotiated. "I gave them a blank cheque in '86 and said, 'Here, I'll stay, you fill it in. As long as the (negotiating) committee includes three players, an accountant and a lawyer, I don't give a shit what you fill in for 60 per cent of my time. Let's get that bullshit about Ziegler off the desk and let's get at it,' " Eagleson said. "Now, how many guys would sign a blank cheque? Not too fucking many. When they came back, I was happy with it." Eagleson is partly right. The contract did practically amount to a blank cheque, and not too many union members would allow their leaders to have one, let alone escape a union hall intact after such an outrageous power play.

Eagleson also took the opportunity to shake his head at some of the questions surrounding his pension. "Then (the critics) start talking about Eagleson's getting a multi-million-dollar pension. Marvin Miller's (the retired head of the Major League Baseball Players' Association) pension is $90,000 U.S., for 18 years, and the cost to the players' association was $1 million. My pension hasn't been funded yet. Had they funded it in 1987, the day I signed the contract, we could have probably put $275,000 in the bank in an annuity and that would have covered my pension for about 25 years of service. So now, when we fund it, it'll probably cost $350,000 or $400,000."

The players may have thought they saved themselves from a terrible fate at the bargaining table, but the worst was yet to come. By 1986, the rank and file among the players was looking more and more to gain the kind of freedom of movement between teams their colleagues in baseball had and the players in the National Football League were fighting for. There was a form of free agency in the NHL. A player who played out his option (an extra year on his contract that was picked up at the discretion of his team) could shop his services around. However, the compensation system in the NHL was so punitive that such signings were rare. (A team signing a free agent had to give up a player or players who were considered to be of equal value to the departing player.)

Once safely under contract, Eagleson made preliminary sounds about the players seeking to abolish the compensation system. This time they wouldn't give up so easily, as in 1979 when the remnants of the World Hockey Association joined the NHL. The league replied with its customary lament that the owners, such as Bill Wirtz in Chicago, who seldom saw anything but a sell-out in his arena, would soon be bankrupt. Ziegler's spin doctors produced figures that showed player salaries had increased dramatically. They were up 17.4 per cent for the 1984-85 season, and 18.5 per cent a year later.

Eagleson, head of what Ed Garvey called a "Mom and Pop store in a supermarket world," did not bother to provide any figures to rebut the owners' ingenuous contention. "No, there was no information handed out," Verbeek said. "All we did was talk about it, but nothing was done." If Eagleson had bothered to provide research for the players, they would have discovered their salaries were so far behind the other three major team sports (football, baseball and basketball), that their relative position to them was almost the same in 1986 as it was in 1957, when the NHL owners crushed an attempt to start a players' union. This also takes into account the fact the average hockey salary almost matched baseball's and was higher than football's in the 1970s, when the World Hockey Association was providing competition to the NHL. Of course, given Eagleson's easy acquiescence on the NHL-WHA merger, this probably would have raised more questions than Eagleson would have cared to answer.

In 1957, the average annual salary in major league baseball

was $20,000. In hockey, it was $8,000, which was 40 per cent of the baseball figure. By 1979, with the WHA-NHL war still on, the average hockey salary was $101,000, with baseball at $113,558. Hockey salaries were now 89 per cent of baseball's. In 1989, three years after Eagleson's collective bargaining sessions, the average baseball salary had shot up to $497,254, while hockey, with the WHA now just a memory, had regressed to 38 per cent of baseball's pay at $188,000. Just like the '50s all over again. Baseball, football and basketball figures are boosted by their massive television contracts, which bring in millions of dollars to each club. But research done by Ed Garvey for his 1989 report on Eagleson's leadership shows that even taking TV money into account leaves the hockey players far behind. Garvey studied salaries as a percentage of the teams' gross revenues, which would include broadcasting revenue. Garvey discovered that while Eagleson was boasting the players were paid 45 per cent of the gross revenues, NHL clubs' management were saying the players' take was "well under 40 per cent." Garvey estimated that with an average salary of $188,000, the players' take was between 20 and 28 per cent of the gross. In the National Basketball Association, where the average salary was $750,000, the players' income was 53 per cent of the gross, while in football ($300,000 average), it was 58 per cent. Baseball players' share was 55 per cent.

None of this information seemed to be taken into account, however, when Eagleson met with Ziegler to discuss the latest collective agreement. It wasn't long before Eagleson came back to the players and recommended they drop their demands for freedom in exchange for the infamous $250,000 pension bonus at age 55 for any player who reached 400 games. Eagleson told the players that too many NHL franchises were in delicate financial health, and allowing unrestricted free agents would be the death blow for teams in smaller markets like Winnipeg, Hartford, Quebec City and even St. Louis.

The players on the NHLPA executive committee (who owed their positions to their unquestioning loyalty to Eagleson) and many of the player representatives accepted this argument. But Verbeek and a few others were stunned. "I think the thing that really upset me the most is we were talking free agency at one point and, within the swing of an hour, Alan had met with Ziegler and the next thing we know, we're talking about this 400-

game package," Verbeek said. "That really upset me. How could we change our stance in so quick a time? It seemed to me that we were never serious about fighting for free agency."

Following the summer sessions with the player reps, Eagleson spent a good part of the hockey season visiting each NHL team and making a pitch for the pension deal to the players. Aside from Jim Korn, Verbeek and a few other well-educated players like Mark Johnson, most of the players thought the $250,000 was well worth giving up in exchange for their freedom. And if it wasn't, so what? They just wanted to play hockey. "Too many players just couldn't give a damn," Verbeek said.

Eagleson liked to say the pension bonus would cost the NHL owners a total of $15 million, as if they had been the ones beaten at the bargaining table. In fact, as it would later be learned — and Eagleson was forced to admit as much — the owners figured the cost would be $9.4 million. And that money came from the pension surplus.

There wasn't much else in the new five-year agreement for the players to celebrate. The compensation clause was changed to allow the awarding of draft choices depending on how long the departing player had been in the league. If the teams couldn't agree, the dispute still went to an arbitrator. The NHL minimum salary went from $20,000 to $25,000, which didn't even reflect the cost of living. Garvey's calculations showed that if the players had merely won a cost-of-living increase, the minimum salary would have been $31,100.

Even worse was that Eagleson had quietly given up the players' last remaining kick at free agency from the days of the WHA. Until 1986, players from U.S. colleges were not subject to the NHL entry draft of junior players. Nor were players who had not been drafted in their first year of eligibility. In 1985, for example, Detroit Red Wings' owner Mike Ilitch outbid several other clubs when he signed free-agent college players Adam Oates and Ray Staszak to five-year contracts at the then-princely sum of $260,000 a year. Many owners were outraged and complained that Ilitch's heavy spending would cause an escalation of salaries league-wide. To plug this free-agency loophole, the owners in the 1986 collective agreement asked for a supplemental draft to distribute anyone missed in an earlier entry draft. Eagleson and the NHLPA, without any apparent protest, agreed to this. Once again, the owners had won easily, not that the players seemed to care.

"The guys were mad at the players (Oates and Staszak) for making that kind of money," said Jim Korn, who was playing for the Toronto Maple Leafs at the time. "I don't think our top guy was making $250,000 a year. The guys said, 'Jeez, these college guys are making all this money, it's not fair.' They should have said, 'These college guys are making all this money and I should be making more.' To be honest, it was beyond me.

"So Al said, 'Yeah, it's really not fair, let's get rid of that.' What a brainstorm that was."

Although Eagleson likes to paint the 1986 agreement as a triumph for the players because of the pension bonus, the deal firmly planted the seeds of rebellion among the players. There had been coup attempts in the past, but Eagleson had always crushed them because of his tight control of the seven-man NHLPA executive committee. In 1980, Mike Milbury of the Boston Bruins, with the help of teammate Brad Park, tried to force a vote to make Eagleson commit himself full-time to the NHLPA for a salary of $200,000 per year. They were angry over his failure to fight the NHL-WHA merger. Eagleson, who had always bragged his letter of resignation was permanently on file at his office in case anyone didn't like the way he ran the show, fought back hard. Milbury had also demanded the association be operated in a more professional manner, with the members to be sent information packages on issues on a regular basis. Milbury and Park managed to conduct a vote of confidence among the NHL players, with two-thirds of the 154 who voted in favour of a full-time executive director. But Eagleson called an NHLPA meeting at the February, 1980 All-Star Game and made sure the executive committee and most of the player reps who supported him were there, along with a number of other sympathizers. While Eagleson had called the confidence vote unconstitutional because he claimed only player reps could vote on such matters, he allowed everyone present at the game to vote and easily won an endorsement to stay in the job on his terms.

Now, however, there were more and more American players like Milbury entering the game, who had been to college and who weren't afraid to ask questions. Over the next couple of years, by raising the issues of Eagleson's tactics and their poor collective bargaining agreement, Eagleson's critics began to turn the tide against him.

"I think it was a wake-up call for a few guys and I think it was the thing that got the ball rolling," Pat Verbeek said of the 1986 debacle. "Once the ball got rolling . . ."

Eagleson's move to squeeze a new contract from the players had put Verbeek squarely against him, when Verbeek was just the sort of player Eagleson always controlled. Verbeek is a scrappy forward from the small southwestern Ontario town of Sarnia. He is a product of junior hockey, with no college education, but he wasn't inclined to blindly accept the word of Eagleson. He became skeptical of Eagleson early in his hockey career when he was about to negotiate a contract with the New Jersey Devils.

"(Eagleson) was always saying that if you ever want advice on salaries, whatever, just ask," Verbeek said. "So I ended up calling him and he told me I should go for $200,000. I said, 'I'm worth more than that because I know what some guys are getting paid and I've got the same stats or better.'

"He said, 'Well, when you become an owner, you can decide that.' That's what he told me. I got off the phone and said, 'Whose side are you on?'"

Elsewhere, Mark Johnson, Jim Korn, Marty McSorley and others began asking questions. Many player agents, who had long questioned Eagleson's practices but did little about it, began talking to their clients about him. Little by little, the players as a group became more doubtful of the man who had always ruled them by intimidation.

Eagleson was well aware that the average NHL player was not inclined to question his authority. And anyone who did was quickly put in his place by a stinging personal attack. "We're Canadians, we're farm boys," Verbeek said. "We're not stupid, but I think we were intimidated by a lawyer who has a lot of education. And he knew this. His philosophy, which was spelled out in *Net Worth*, was you hit them with as much as you've got and if they still come at you, then you back off. He goes all out (on the attack) and that's what he used to do in meetings. He used to attack guys."

Thanks to the fact Eagleson drew up the sketchy NHLPA constitution, he was easily able to control the voting and the direction of the union. The executive committee was composed of six vice-presidents and a president, and most seemed to be both star players and Eagleson clients. Eagleson knew that star players carried far more clout among their peers than a 15-goal-a-year grinder. And the fact being a player representative (from whose ranks the executive was taken) was a thankless job, it was easy to persuade his clients to take an active role in the association.

"It is a lousy job," Jim Korn said. "Management comes down on you, players get mad at you, everybody comes to you with their problems."

But those players who served their terms on the NHLPA executive without controversy always seemed to pass on to their reward with NHL teams. Former NHLPA vice-presidents and presidents who are now NHL management figures include Bobby Clarke, Bob Gainey, Bryan Trottier (until he recently returned to the Pittsburgh Penguins as an assistant coach and part-time player), Tony Esposito, Phil Esposito (although he was one of the few to fight with Eagleson), Darryl Sittler and Lanny McDonald. "Yeah, you watch his clients. They all have management jobs," Verbeek said.

Those who had the temerity to get up at a meeting and question Eagleson were not tolerated. "He embarrassed me," Phil Esposito said. "If I asked a question, he'd say, 'For Christ's sake, don't be so stupid!' in front of everybody. Al's smart. He knows if he does that to me or to a Bobby Clarke, the other guys are going to say, 'Holy shit, I'm not opening my mouth.'" Lest anyone think that Eagleson was just bullying a bunch of inarticulate hockey players, it must be remembered that this was the same treatment he was giving to members of the board of Hockey Canada, businessmen who should have been able to fight back but rarely did.

Eagleson tightly controlled the agenda of the annual union meetings which were usually held at the Breakers. The hotel was luxurious, and it was not uncommon for associates like his accountant, Marvin Goldblatt, or members of his family to appear at the meetings. The players, fresh off a tough season, were more interested in recreation than business, which made it easy for Eagleson to operate the association as he pleased.

"Al wanted to keep most of the players out (of NHLPA business), make a good deal for his vice-presidents," Jim Korn said. "It was like, 'Say listen, we'll get a free trip to Florida for a week, play some golf.' One meeting, all they did was play golf. They had some meetings in the morning, Al would say 'I'm doing this, I'm doing that, let's go play golf.' Were the players going to complain? That's what most of them went down there for."

It didn't seem to occur to many of the players that it was their own money that was providing the hotel rooms, lavish dinners and golf excursions. "They certainly didn't think they were paying for it," Korn said. "It wasn't coming out of their pockets. But everybody paid union dues. When they checked out (of the hotel), they didn't get a bill to pay. That was part of the inducement. They'd come in and say we know being a player rep sucks, you take heat from the players, take heat from management. Because of this, as an inducement we're going to treat people, give them favours.

"I have no problem if he said we're going to treat the player reps because it is a lousy job. The problem I had was Al taking his family down there on my money. The bigger problem was Al running the whole show as Al Eagleson's player agency. You guys give me all this money, you guys give me all this power, I'll make all this money off international hockey. I'll pay you guys your pension in Canadian dollars, I'll take mine in American; you guys get a couple thousand dollars a year, I'll get $50,000 year (as a pension). You can pay me $200,000 a year but I'll only work 60 per cent of my time. It was crazy, absolutely crazy."

While player agents such as Rich Winter and Ron Salcer began to ask louder and louder questions about Eagleson's stewardship, few players, were standing up at meetings to ask the same questions directly. Korn, with support from Mark Johnson and a couple of others, was one of the few. An economics graduate from Providence University, Korn distrusted Eagleson from the start of his NHL career, refusing to join the NHLPA until 1986, six years after his rookie season, when the union bylaws were changed by Eagleson to require every player to pay dues even if he wasn't a member. A chance meeting with Bobby Orr during his years at Providence resulted in Korn's skepticism of Eagleson. Orr told him of his problems with Eagleson and the circumstances of their bitter split. After he had joined the union and had become a player rep, Korn decided to ask Eagleson about the Orr situation.

Rising to his feet at the annual meeting, Korn said, "Listen Al, I got a problem with what happened between you and Orr. Let's get on the phone, get him down here, and find out what's going on."

"Oh no, no, we're not doing that, he won't come down," Eagleson said quickly.

"I think if we all invited him, he'd come down," said Korn. "I know that if we all invited him, he'd come down. I just know if you won't invite him, he won't come down. So let's just call him down. He'll come down and talk about it. Just between the players."

Eagleson continued to insist Orr would not come to Florida. But when Korn persisted, Eagleson went ballistic.

"He went immediately into an attack mode on me and he had some good stuff," Korn said. "I'm an American, I'm a college player." He said, 'You weren't popular in Toronto, you wouldn't join the players' union.' I replied, 'Al, I wouldn't join the players' union because I wouldn't support you.'

"I wouldn't join the players' union, so he went down to Florida, passed a new law where you had to pay (dues). He said, 'We've got this guy who's not joining; we can't make him join but we can make him pay, so let's make everybody pay.'"

In 1988, Korn had a few more questions. He had heard that 37 Maitland Place, the building Eagleson had moved his law firm and the players' association into, was owned by one of his family's holding companies. Korn asked Eagleson why the office was moved, and who owned the building. He also wanted to know why Eagleson's son and daughter were sitting in on the players' meetings.

"Because they're interested in the association," Eagleson said.

"My mother's interested in the association, too, but she's not down here," Korn retorted.

When the matter of the rent came up, Eagleson again went on the attack, launching a verbal fusillade at Korn.

"Jimmy always had answers right back for Alan," Pat Verbeek said. "You could see the rage in Alan. He knew he was wrong, but he didn't want to get embarrassed in front of anyone. He said, 'I can't believe you have the gall to attack my integrity when you wouldn't even join the association.'"

Eagleson kept up his profane attack long enough to turn Korn's question, as was his custom in such spots, into one that cast aspersions on his own integrity thereby avoiding the issue as to who owned the office building. Without wide support around the room, Korn soon had to back off and, as Detroit Red Wings' player rep Dave Barr ruefully said later, "a perfectly good question didn't get answered."

But the questions started to grow, particularly from Winter and Salcer, who had been questioning Eagleson's methods of running the union for years. Both men had come to the profession of player-agent almost by accident. Winter, a lawyer who lives in Edmonton, had done some movie stunt work while he was a student. On the set of a television movie shot in Edmonton, Winter met the actor Darren McGavin, who encouraged him to go to Los Angeles and try the entertainment business. When his entry into show business stalled in 1983, Winter hung around the West Coast and met Dave Lewis, who was playing for the Los Angeles Kings. Lewis had just been through a bad experience with an agent, losing a lot of money, and Winter said he'd try to help. But when he called Eagleson for assistance he got nowhere. "I proposed to the NHLPA that they adopt some form of regulation of agents and Eagleson just said it's illegal. This didn't pass the smell test because there is regulation of agents by various other players' associations," Winter said. "It grew from there. I could never get pension information. He would threaten everybody. He was intimidating, tough and aggressive."

Salcer was a financial consultant who moved from New York to Manhattan Beach, Calif., where he met several Los Angeles Kings players and eventually represented Dave Taylor. Once into the business of an NHL agent, he, too, found it difficult to deal with Eagleson. "I became disenchanted because I would try to get information for players and information was never available," Salcer said. "You'd call up the players' association, a month later you'd hear back. When you finally did hear back, it was 'What can I do for you?'

"It wasn't really a position where you felt these guys were working for the players. The more I looked into it, I could see the players' salaries were not rising accordingly with what was happening around the league. Attendance was at an all-time high, but salaries weren't in line."

At first, the two men operated independently of each other, talking to players about their concerns. Then they put their heads together and decided to see if someone with expertise in the field of sports labour unions would be willing to challenge Eagleson. They first approached Marvin Miller, who had retired as head of the Major League Baseball Players' Association. He turned them down. The next choice was Wisconsin lawyer Ed Garvey, the former head of the National Football League Players' Association. Garvey told Salcer he would be interested, but only if the players wanted it done. He told Winter and Salcer to collect $100 from each interested player as a token of their commitment. Eventually, 225 players paid $100, which was the only money Garvey received for his mission, and which came nowhere close to compensating him for his time and expenses.

Garvey, Winter and Salcer went from team to team in the NHL, explaining their plans. The players were told that Garvey would investigate the operation of the NHLPA and deliver a report at their June, 1989 meeting in Florida. The three men would then call for a vote of confidence on Eagleson's leadership. At first, Garvey was skeptical of the players' enthusiasm. Then he made his first appearance in front of a team.

"I'll never forget the first meeting we had, which was with the L.A. Kings," he said. "After an hour, one of them stood up, maybe it was Kelly Hrudey, or Dean Kennedy, and said 'This is the first meeting we've had where we've been able to ask questions and nobody's yelling at us.' It was after that I said, 'Okay, it's worth taking this thing on.' This thing has been difficult, frustrating, but one of the most rewarding things I've ever done. It was very exciting."

As Garvey learned more about Eagleson's conflicts of interest, he began to raise his questions in a newsletter to the players. Called "The Players' Voice," the publication was deliberately printed in simple type and on plain white paper to drive home the point that it was time for plain, common-sense questions on the players' level. Topics included the sorry state of the pension plan, where the profits from international hockey had gone, and the chummy relationship between Eagleson, Wirtz and Ziegler. The latter was the subject of a cartoon, a drawing of Ziegler as a bird of prey, clutching a player and wearing an Eagleson mask. The character was called a Z-eagle and became a regular feature, illustrating the many areas where the interests of Eagleson and the owners blurred. "A few players told me I went too far with that one," Garvey said. "They thought it was disrespectful."

Garvey found it just as difficult as Winter and Salcer to get information out of the players' association, the NHL Pension Society and Hockey Canada. "The players deserve some kind of accounting and it was astounding to me that we could not get any members of the board of Hockey Canada and others to release those figures. Just astounding," he said.

Eagleson, too, was reluctant to show the rebel forces anything. When Garvey hired Bill Dermody, a Hamilton lawyer, to look at the NHLPA financial statements, Eagleson would only allow him to see statements from the years 1987 and 1988, and with few details.

At first, Eagleson professed publicly that he wasn't concerned. That others had tried to unseat him before and always failed. But behind the scenes, things were ugly. "When we first got started with this, (Eagleson) told me I'd better get away from it, he had me in his bull's-eye and so on and so forth," said Garvey, a man with an easy sense of humour yet not someone who can be pushed hard. "I said, 'Well, you better shoot straight you son of a bitch,' because I don't usually respond well to that kind of thing."

Winter and Salcer, too, were subjected to the worst kind of personal attacks. Eagleson would tell people that Winter was a lunatic. Given that Winter is a hard-nosed, intractable negotiator who had alienated several general managers around the league, this soon became the conventional wisdom about him. Salcer, who had built his client list by signing players who had grown disenchanted with their agents, was said to be in it just to steal players from other agents. Garvey, who had left the NFLPA after an acrimonious strike, had ruined the football union, Eagleson said.

Things took a sinister turn when Garvey discovered that someone was asking his neighbours in Madison, Wis., questions about him. While others assumed Eagleson was behind the apparent investigation, Garvey wasn't so sure. "Well, there was a guy who was asking questions. I don't know whether it was related or not, we sort of assumed it was. But Eagleson knew enough about me that he didn't have to do too much checking. My God, I've got so many enemies, one more doesn't matter. We talked about it because it came up. I think people get a little paranoid because Eagleson's trademark was to intimidate."

By April, 1989, when he travelled to Stockholm for the world championships, Eagleson had stopped scoffing. He began telling reporters that he was concerned about his future. More tangible evidence was seen late at night in the bar of Team Canada's hotel, as Eagleson and NHLPA director of operations Sam Simpson huddled often, drawing up lists of player representatives on cocktail napkins, guessing who was for or against them and counting the totals.

When the players gathered in West Palm Beach on June 2, the tension was crackling throughout the hockey community. The dividing lines that would mark the weekend meetings were evident from the start, when more than 80 players began arriving, along with a crowd of agents, reporters and a few curious observers from the NHL community.

Eagleson, his supporters and the player representatives stayed at the posh Breakers. It had seen kings, queens and presidents pass through its doors. It was also the hotel of choice for the NHL owners when they held their semi-annual meeting in December. Ed Garvey laughed and said, "A union that holds its meetings at the Breakers — that's a statement in itself."

A mile or so down the road was the more down scale Hilton, which the rebel forces adopted as their headquarters. Former NHL goaltender Denis Herron was the hotel's sales manager, and he provided his colleagues with good rates and moral support. "When I retired I phoned Alan several times for advice. He never returned my calls," Herron said.

Also on the scene were Bill Wirtz, Bob Pulford and Lou Nanne. They were there to show the flag for their good friend Alan Eagleson and lobby on his behalf. This in itself should have been an educating sight for any player. The dour Pulford (of whom another NHL executive once said, "I was in a bar and they asked Pulford to leave so they could start the happy hour") even made an effort to chat up a few reporters. Other owners, worried about losing a compliant labour leader, were lobbying the player representatives by telephone. "They were so terrified. What is going to happen to Alan? They're terrified to this day," said Bruce McNall, owner of the Los Angeles Kings who was new to the league at the time.

When the meeting opened on a Saturday morning, the tension was palpable. The rebel forces and the loyalists took positions on opposite sides of the room. The agents, too, took sides. Rich Winter and Ron Salcer, of course, were firmly on the rebel side. So was Herb Pinder, a Saskatchewan lawyer and agent who had been offering them quiet support. In the middle of the room were Rick Curran, an ex-Eagleson employee, and Bob Goodenow, a Detroit labour lawyer with a burgeoning client list. On Eagleson's side of the room, in fact sitting right behind him, was Don Meehan, a Toronto lawyer who was quickly becoming the top agent in the league. As the day went on, and Garvey scored his points, there was some movement among the agents. "It was interesting to see people's positions change as the day went on," said one man who was in the room. "Meehan moved from behind

(Eagleson) and down the side of the room. Ricky moved down the side, too."

One man of particular interest was Goodenow, whose practice was growing thanks to his fellow Harvard law school grad, Brian Burke. When Burke took a player personnel job with the Vancouver Canucks (he is now the NHL's Director of Hockey Operations), he passed his client list on to Goodenow. Goodenow would make his first major impact on the game a year later, in June, 1990, when he negotiated a $7.2-million contract for Brett Hull that opened the door for people other than the game's two superstars — Wayne Gretzky and Mario Lemieux — to make six-figure salaries.

Goodenow started his career as a labour lawyer, usually acting for management in strike negotiations. He was also a consummate politician, which quickly became apparent at the Breakers. While being careful not to align himself publicly with either side, Goodenow appeared to be active behind the scenes. Two of the player representatives were his clients — Kelly Miller of the Washington Capitals and Peter Taglianetti of the Winnipeg Jets — and both were considered anti-Eagleson. During the breaks Miller and Taglianetti would huddle with Goodenow, who was emphatically offering advice.

One observer thought that even then, Goodenow had his eye on the NHLPA executive director's chair. "I watched Bobby, he was very clever. He had nothing to say, he had no profile, and after every break in the sessions slid into a room with Miller and Taglianetti. Obviously, he was being told what was going on and giving marching orders. Well, when I say marching orders that's a bit unfair, because (Miller and Taglianetti) are bright guys. He was giving them assistance, moral support. Those guys handled themselves well."

Eagleson was so confident of beating back Garvey's report that did not contest his right to speak, even though Eagleson had tightly controlled the agenda in the past. "He thought it would be a big showcase, where he got everybody in the room and had me at the microphone and he would argue me out of all these positions," Garvey said.

It was just the first of many mistakes Eagleson would make on this day.

After Garvey was granted the floor, he warmed to his task by tangling with Edgar Sexton, a corporate lawyer with a somewhat haughty demeanor who was sitting next to Eagleson. He asked Sexton what he was doing there. Sexton said he was representing Eagleson because Rich Winter had threatened to sue him. Garvey pointed out that no lawsuit had ever been filed and that, in any case, the threat had nothing to do with the meeting. "Why did you have to be here, and at whose expense?" Garvey asked. Sexton declined to answer.

Later, Sexton tried to strike back, but he embarrassed himself when he forgot a lawyer's basic tenet. He asked Garvey who he represented and immediately, dozens of players' hands came up. "This hot-shot litigator broke the first rule of cross examination, the rule you learn the first day of civil procedure in law school," said Herb Pinder. "Don't ask a question you don't know the answer to. Litigators only ask questions they know the answer to. It was one of the funniest things I've ever seen."

Then Garvey bore in on Eagleson. His report was devastating. It detailed all of the abuses the players had suffered over the years. The summary of findings at the front of his report was an indictment of Eagleson's operation of the NHLPA:

1. With the exception of a few players hand-picked by Alan Eagleson, players have little or no voice in the operations of the NHLPA. The NHLPA is the least democratic labour union in sports.

2. Players have virtually no ability to get detailed information about the operations of their union, their pension, international hockey, decision-making in the NHL, salaries, the economics of the NHL or any other important matter impacting on their careers.

3. No benefits of any significance have been achieved in the entire decade of the '80s through collective bargaining. In fact, the organization has gone backwards while sports unions in all other sports have made major gains. You are last in salaries, benefits, percentage of the gross, and in information. As a matter of fact, you might well be better off without a union.

4. The NHLPA staff provides little or no help to players or their agents in the negotiation of individual contracts because the staff is small, Alan Eagleson is a part-time director who does not reach out to help his competitors — other agents — and he is not available to answer questions half the time.

5. The NHLPA provides few services to players despite high dues and other revenues.

6. Alan Eagleson's conflicts of interest negatively impact on almost every aspect of your profession.

7. Alan Eagleson refuses to provide information that is required by law to be made available to all union members. . . . His refusal to provide backup data on the expense money he receives and large expenditures on such items as "gifts and awards" should be investigated.

8. In practice, the officers are appointed, not elected; the collective bargaining agreements have never been approved by secret ballot; and the executive director does little to even educate members about the NHL collective bargaining in advance of the meetings.

9. Finally, Alan Eagleson may well be the most overpaid executive in the labour movement in North America. Not even the president of the two-million-member Teamsters union comes close to Alan in wages, benefits, pension and expense accounts.

For more than two hours, Garvey hammered away at Eagleson as he sank lower and lower in his chair. "What we found can only be described as a scandal," Garvey said in his report, as he detailed the ways in which Eagleson operated the association "as a private preserve rather than a union for players." For the first time, the players heard details of their pension plan, the use of the surplus, the fact that they had no representation on the NHL Pension Society. They were also told about the lack of controls on Eagleson's spending, how he moved the association into a build-ing owned by Jialson Holdings Ltd., his own company, and of the many conflicts of interest between his job as player-agent, union chief, international hockey czar and real estate lawyer. "You have moved into a conflict position that is so deep it would be nearly impossible to untangle you," Garvey said.

Eagleson's legendary arrogance and aggressiveness, which probably led him to give Garvey the floor so easily, had vanished. At one point, when he attempted to explain something, Jim Korn jumped up and said, "No, no. You didn't say that, Al. I heard you. I was there in the room and this is what you said."

This time, there were no profane putdowns, but just a man who practically wilted in his chair. The transformation was electrifying for the players. It was so complete, even those committed to his firing felt involuntary pangs of sympathy. "I don't know how to explain it. He'll surprise you. One minute he's this tough guy, but then he'll be as meek as a mouse if you've got him by the balls. You feel sorry for him. It's ridiculous," said Pat Verbeek.

"I really think a lot of the players were just afraid of Alan Eagleson," Ed Garvey said later. "I think the players had felt there was just no way you could get to him because of this myth that he was so powerful in Canada. That meeting down in Florida was a classic. It was something to remember.

"It was the first time that he had been confronted by someone who had as much background as him, who wasn't intimidated by him. He had all his lawyers there, his entourage, including a vice-president of the NHL (Ken Sawyer). It was going to be a big showcase for him. But we knew a lot more than he anticipated." Garvey was not without weapons of his own. One of the most formidable was Bobby Orr, with whom he held frequent telephone conversations over the weekend.

What Eagleson didn't anticipate was handing Garvey some of the most damaging information himself. When Garvey was questioning Eagleson about the mortgage loans, the name Ungerman came up. The name didn't mean anything to Garvey, but John Agro, a lawyer and former head of the Canadian Football League Players' Association who was helping the Garvey team, pointed out the connection with Eagleson. Garvey was then able to get Eagleson to admit he had made some of the loans to his law partner, Howard Ungerman, which were intended for Ungerman's father, Irving, a good friend of Eagleson. Despite Eagleson's pious rejoinder that "no commissions or fees have been charged to the NHLPA with respect to any of these mortgages," Garvey was able to establish that his law firm, Eagleson Ungerman, collected legal fees from the borrowers.

"In my entire law practice I've never heard such a stunning admission to what's clearly improper," Garvey said. "I said to Agro, 'I can't believe this. He's taking pension money, loaning it to his clients, taking a fee and he's in charge of the money?' This sort of hubris was the cause of his downfall."

Eagleson and his supporters argued that the investments brought a good return, but as Garvey told Mike Liut, an NHLPA vice-president and staunch Eagleson supporter, "Mike, that's not the issue."

During the breaks in the morning meeting, there was almost as much action in the corridors as there was during the session. At one point, Rich Winter laid into fellow agent Don Meehan for not doing more to support the anti-Eagleson forces. He also delivered a tongue-lashing to union lawyer Larry Latto, who was also considered an Eagleson booster. The incidents did nothing to soften reporters' impressions (many of them formed by chats with Eagleson) that Winter was a hothead.

By the time Garvey finished his tour de force, Eagleson knew his job was in jeopardy. He huddled with his entourage at the lunch break in Sam Simpson's suite at the Breakers, which is where Herb Pinder found him. The player agent suggested they go for a walk, and Eagleson quickly accepted. Pinder hinted there was a graceful way out for him. But Eagleson was adamant that he would not resign outright. "I have to go back to Toronto as head of the association."

Pinder then had a suggestion for him: tell the players you will step down in a set period of time, after an assistant has been hired who will be considered your eventual successor. Offer to stay on as the union's international hockey representative. Eagleson eagerly embraced this proposal, no doubt because it allowed him a connection with international hockey, and his dignity.

In the afternoon Eagleson offered the players his apologies along with Pinder's proposed face-saving exit. The players asked everyone else to leave the room, and they began to debate the future of the man who had ruled them for 22 years. At one time, such a scene would have been unthinkable.

But Eagleson had not entirely lost all his cunning. During the players-only sessions, Darryl Sittler went back and forth between their room and Simpson's. Sittler, a long-time client of Eagleson's, had been retired since 1982, and some had thought he and Eagleson had once had a falling out. Now, Sittler was obviously lobbying the players on Eagleson's behalf and delivering reports on their deliberations. Finally, an agent challenged him. "Darryl, what are you doing? It's players only in there. You're not a player." As one of the best NHL players of his era, Sittler was not used to being spoken to in such a fashion. He looked at his questioner in shock and failed to reply.

There was also some urgent lobbying going on over the telephone. Wayne Gretzky, the most important player in the NHL, was an honourary vice-president of the NHLPA. As the reigning superstar of the game, he had enormous clout both with the players and management. If either side could land his vote, and make it known in advance, it would almost certainly mean victory. Like Goodenow, Gretzky was also a smart politician. He did not declare himself for either side, but said prior commitments would prevent him from attending. This was a rather transparent excuse, and some among the rebel forces resented the fact Gretzky would not publicly join the fight against Eagleson. Rich Winter accused Gretzky of refusing his requests to become involved in that issue, as well as the pension lawsuit later on. However, others involved in the pension lawsuit did not feel Gretzky's presence was desperately needed. The players understood Gretzky's position completely, since becoming publicly involved in a controversial issue could harm the pristine image that brought him so much endorsement income. But one player had some reservations.

"I don't think there was a whole lot in it for Wayne," Jim Korn said. "He had everything to lose and nothing to gain. But I did feel that if he accepted the position (the NHLPA) had given him, he should have been involved.

"I didn't see anything necessarily wrong with what he was doing. I thought he should have just backed out of the whole thing, to be honest with you. He kind of did that, but it allowed Eagleson to say, 'This guy's a vice-president; he's not here and we need his vote.' So then you've got all this lobbying over the phone. I'm sure Eagleson got hold of him directly and that's not fair. How does he know what's going on in Florida when he's at home in California?"

Almost all of the telephone lobbying was done by Marty McSorley, Gretzky's teammate with the Kings and an Eagleson foe, and Kevin Lowe, his ex-teammate with the Edmonton Oilers. McSorley was squarely with the rebels, while Lowe was an Eagleson loyalist. In the end, only a couple of people knew which way Gretzky went, and they have been silent to this day.

Hockey's other great superstar, Mario Lemieux, made a surprise appearance at the meetings. His presence, though, was less than inspirational. One person present at the meeting said Lemieux fell asleep on the first day, and didn't show up at all on the second day when the vote of confidence was taken. Apparently, the meeting conflicted with a golf date, although it should be noted that Lemieux was not a player representative and thus did not have a vote.

By the end of the day, the players had decided that if Eagleson got through the confidence vote, he could keep his job, but only under a new set of conditions. He had to agree to a search for a deputy executive director who, as Pinder suggested, would eventually replace him; he would give up his player agent business; his contract would be renegotiated; he would submit his tax returns for the past several years for review by the players; and he would allow an independent audit of the NHLPA's finances. Eagleson would also be retained as the NHLPA's international hockey representative after he stepped down as executive director. A follow-up meeting was planned for July in Toronto to make sure the conditions were going to be met.

The vote was held the next day. With the six vice-presidents plus NHLPA president Bryan Trottier all firmly on Eagleson's side, the vote of confidence carried 16-12. As there were only 28 votes, it seems that in the end Gretzky abstained, as he was a seventh vice-president.

Despite the restrictions now placed on him, and the fact he had made the commitment to stepping down, Eagleson was able to claim a victory. His relief was evident.

"When we had the vote and he was back in, you should have seen him," Pat Verbeek said. "He was almost in tears. 'Oh,' he says, 'this is a great day. I vow to do this, boom, boom, boom.'

"The way the question (the vote was taken on) was worded, it made people give Alan another chance. If it was 'Is Alan in or out,' then he would have been out. But they worded it in such a way, that if Alan can submit to all these rules, all these guidelines, fine. But you knew Alan could never abide by them."

Verbeek was right. Once he was back in Toronto, the old fire burned bright. He cancelled the July meeting at the last minute, then re-scheduled it for late August when it just happened that several of his enemies couldn't make it because of commitments to getting ready for training camp. All of his supporters were able to clear their schedules to attend, however.

The players had hired William Dovey, an accountant with Price Waterhouse's Toronto office, to conduct the audit of the finances. His investigation covered the years 1987 through 1989. Instead of complete access to the NHLPA books, Eagleson was able to limit Dovey to only the bare-bones financial statements and Eagleson's monthly expense accounts. He broke his promise on tax returns, refusing to give them up for inspection.

On the day of the meeting, Dovey's report was brief, and offered no judgments on whether or not Eagleson's handling of union funds was appropriate. This allowed Eagleson to claim he was vindicated. But, like his claim about the *Dermody Report* absolving him of impropriety in his handling of the players' money, it was a trifle overstated.

Thanks to the opposition being outmaneuvered, Dovey's report was never studied in detail by the players. In fact, it was never distributed widely among them. If it had, there might have been another storm to rival the one in June.

Russ Conway obtained a copy of the audit. He revealed that Dovey wrote that because he was limited in examining NHLPA documents, he was unable to decide if the spending "was necessary to or appropriate for the NHLPA." He did say that no expenses were "clearly inconsistent" with operating the association.

But an examination of Dovey's report does not offer the complete vindication Eagleson claimed. The years 1987 to 1989 show a union leader who enjoyed a luxurious lifestyle and showered friends and associates with gifts, meals, drinks, theatre tickets and sports event tickets, all paid for by the players' association.

Since none of the above matters was studied in detail by the players, Eagleson did not have to face another round of unpleasant questions at the Toronto meeting. In the absence of a strong opposition lobby, another vote of confidence was taken and Eagleson won, 29-0 (perhaps Gretzky's vote was finally registered). Eagleson could legitimately claim another victory, although he was still committed to a search for a successor and stepping aside by 1992.

"We felt down in Florida that we lost part of the battle but we won the war," Ed Garvey said. "Total victory would have been Eagleson losing or resigning. But in agreeing to step aside and eliminate conflicts of interest, and making it one team, one vote (in NHLPA affairs), we felt we brought democracy to the union."

The big winners were the players, who received an abrupt education in the value of taking an interest in their association.

"You know what they say, knowledge is power," said Pat Verbeek. "The players are more knowledgeable now. When you're knowledgeable, (Eagleson) doesn't scare you. You can't pull the wool over our eyes any more."

Eagleson's enjoyment of his victory was short-lived. It wasn't long before official complaints by several retired players to authorities in the Boston area resulted in the FBI and grand jury investigations. Then the RCMP went from assisting the American investigation to launching one of its own.

Bob Goodenow, who played his cards so well in Florida, was hired to be Eagleson's successor and was installed in office by the summer of 1990. More than one agent close to the scene said Eagleson and his cronies did their best to make Goodenow uncomfortable at Maitland Place. While Goodenow himself never complained, others (such as Rich Winter) charged that Eagleson was having his communications monitored. Eagleson fiercely denied this.

"That's asinine, ridiculous, bullshit lies," Eagleson said in 1991. "The fucking faxes come in at 50 pages a day. Does Bob have to stand over the fax machine to make sure I don't read it when it's coming in from Rich Winter? Shit, Bob works with me and we share every piece of paper."

Nevertheless, Goodenow moved quickly to take charge of the union. He established himself in sole control of the 1991 negotiations for a collective bargaining agreement, although Eagleson told people it was his idea to bow out of the talks. The offices were moved from Eagleson's building to a downtown Toronto office tower. Eagleson stuck to his retirement date of December 31, 1991, although at least one NHL insider said it was enforced by Goodenow's "encouragement." And as the investigations mounted over 1992 and 1993, Eagleson lost his cherished post as the NHLPA's international negotiator. Goodenow quietly let it be known in early 1993 that he had added that portfolio to his duties.

The final, cathartic break with the Eagleson era came on April 1, 1992, when the players voted 560-4 to strike over a new collective agreement. The 11-day walkout was the NHL's first since a brief, ill-supported strike by the Hamilton Tigers in the 1920s. When it was over, the players did not win free agency or any other startling concession. But they made one huge gain that will pay off at every future bargaining session: they won the owners' respect.

Chapter Thirteen

THE LEGACY

THE RESIGNATION of R. Alan Eagleson from Hockey Canada marked the end of an era in hockey. Following Eagleson's departure, John Ziegler and Bill Wirtz also lost their positions of power.

Ziegler resigned his post as NHL president in June, 1992 when it became clear that many NHL club's owners were angry with his handling of the player strike. After a fierce attempt to hang on (with Eagleson helping to lobby the owners), Ziegler realized it was a lost cause and negotiated a million-dollar golden handshake for himself.

Wirtz saw that a new, more progressive faction of owners was seizing power, and he gave up his post as chairman of the NHL's board of governors. But at the NHL meetings in June, 1992, when the owners were planning the leadership transition, Wirtz had a change of heart. He let it be known he would run again for chairman, but backed off when he realized his peers would vote him out of office. As chairman, Wirtz was the acknowledged leader among the governors, who often would follow his lead in matters of league policy. Since Wirtz's ideas of marketing were rooted in the 1950s, which it meant merely hanging out a sign that said "Game Tonight," the NHL's business strategy had remained in that era.

The trio of Wirtz, Ziegler and Eagleson represented the NHL's last link with hockey's feudal era, the days of Big Jim Norris, when the league was known derisively in some quarters as the "Norris House League." In those days, the players were paid little, had few bargaining rights or benefits and were met harshly when they made even the mildest demands. Jim Norris and Arthur Wirtz were co-owners of the Blackhawks, and Bill learned the business under the tutelage of his father who assumed sole ownership of the team after Norris's death. In the 1970s, Ziegler rose through the ranks as legal counsel for the Detroit Red Wings, owned by the Norris family. It is no coincidence that both Ziegler and Bill Wirtz came to power while they were associated with the powerful Norris clan. The Norris link then passed through Ziegler and Wirtz to Eagleson, as he developed a close friendship with the management figures.

Eagleson met Wirtz, the prototypical hockey establishment figure from the 1960s to the 1990s, through his work for the players. The same with Ziegler, a well-groomed, sleek lawyer whose appearance belied his bumbling term in office. The attraction of befriending Wirtz and Ziegler, the successor to Clarence Campbell, proved far too strong for the young hustler from the working-class neighbourhood of New Toronto. Somewhere along the way, the lines between labour and management became blurred. Perhaps it was aboard Bill Wirtz's yacht off the coast of Florida, where Eagleson liked to hang out with his pals.

"Whether it was right or wrong, the perception was he became far too close to the people he was meeting across the table and increasingly remote from the people he was dealing on behalf of," said fellow agent Herb Pinder. "Anywhere you'd go, you'd go to the Olympic Games, he was sitting with John Ziegler at centre ice. But he didn't have time to talk to players or their representatives. In that respect, I think it was time for him to move on."

Before he became so firmly entangled with the hockey establishment, Eagleson did accomplish much for both the game and the players. He did form the first successful players' union; he did, to a degree, improve working conditions for players who had been exploited for so long it was the stuff of a Dickens novel.

His greatest achievements came in the field of international hockey. While Eagleson did try to usurp the credit for putting the historic 1972 Canada-Soviet Union Summit Series together, it still could not have happened without him. Eagleson may not have brought the Soviets to the party, but he twisted the arms of the NHL owners to let the players come to the big dance. Then there is the Canada Cup. If there is one thing Eagleson can rightly claim as his, it is this tournament. The Canada Cup has its flaws — by playing every important game in Canada and with NHL officials it is not a true World Cup, like the pride of soccer, and is too heavily weighted in favour of Canada — but it has been the best hockey competition in the world. The game has never been played at a higher level than what was seen at the 1987 final between Canada and the Soviet Union.

But, like everything else Eagleson did, these accomplishments came with a huge caveat. The triumphs in international hockey came at the cost of collective bargaining gains by the players, while Eagleson and his companies made enormous amounts of money from them.

"You can't lose sight of one thing. Alan Eagleson is the only person in the history of this game to become a millionaire out of it," said one of his former employees, indulging in a bit of hyperbole (Conn Smythe is another rags to riches figure in hockey). "A lot of them in (hockey) were millionaires before they got into it. Nobody went into the game a pauper and came out of it a millionaire but Alan Eagleson. The other thing he loses sight of is that the players paid his ticket."

Losing sight of that undoubtedly caused his downfall. Too many times, calls to the NHLPA from players were ignored, particularly if the caller did not retain Alan Eagleson as his agent. Given the players' astounding willingness to accept almost anything Eagleson told them, it could be argued that if he had just been a little more solicitous with the union membership, he may not be facing nearly as many problems. He might even have held on to his job as executive director of the NHLPA.

The owners certainly weren't going to make any moves against Eagleson. Why get rid of someone who kept the workers docile at contract time, and lined the owners' pockets at the same time? "Eagleson generated the money (from international hockey) and the owners didn't have to put anything into the pension," said a former Eagleson associate. Hockey Canada wasn't about to say anything. For Eagleson was the goose that laid golden eggs that supported such programs as the resurrection of the Olympic hockey team in 1980. "As long as he was making money, (the

Hockey Canada directors) weren't complaining," the ex-associate said.

It was easy for those involved to overlook the excesses of Eagleson, for they could tell themselves Eagleson was still advancing hockey. But it has to be asked just how many of the "gains" Eagleson brought to hockey would have happened even if he hadn't been there to guide them along.

Eagleson's friends in the media often called him the great emancipator, the man who freed the players. However, by the 1960s, Marvin Miller was on the scene, organizing the Major League Baseball Players' Association into the strongest union of its kind. It was the baseball players who, in 1976, first won the right to unrestricted free agency. That was the same year Eagleson gave away free agency by agreeing to a compensation formula that would reward any NHL team losing a free agent to another NHL team with a player or players of equal value. It hardly seemed a coincidence that Eagleson needed the owners to release the players for the Canada Cup in 1976, and once the WHA died in 1979, the compensation clause choked off any freedom of movement for most players.

The same can be said for international hockey. The Canadian public was demanding that our best hockey players play the best from the Soviet Union in order to assuage the collective psyche that Canadians were still the masters of the game. The Summit Series didn't happen because Alan Eagleson strode to the negotiating table (if you believe his version) or because he controlled the players. One of the key players, the late Joe Kryczka, believed the series came about because of the Russians. "In retrospect, I'm convinced that even before we arrived in Prague (to conduct the final negotiations for the series), the Soviets had decided privately that their hockey team was good enough to beat the NHL," Kryczka told Jim Coleman. "They strung out those meetings to get every possible concession concerning the rules under which the games would be played." Perhaps, if someone other than Alan Eagleson was negotiating on behalf of the players, they might have ended up playing for more than a token salary and the right to offset the NHL owners' pension contributions.

In the late 1970s, athletes were reaping the financial benefits of free agency in baseball, from a WHA-NHL bidding war, and the explosion of television money that came from American networks in the form of rights fees for various events. Through the 1980s, though, hockey players regressed in salaries, because of the death of the WHA and the reluctance of Alan Eagleson to fight for the rights of the players. This eagerness to support the status quo hurt not only the players, but the game as well. Without any strong incentives to search for more revenue to pay for what should have been booming salaries, the NHL owners kept hockey as a regional sport. This was how John Ziegler referred to the game in the late 1980s when he explained the league's decision not to pursue a deal with one of the major American networks. The league's last such exposure ended in 1976, with the expiry of a CBS deal. Instead, Ziegler said the NHL's television strategy would be to look to the cable networks, both regionally and nationally, for its broadcast revenue.

The shortsightedness of the NHL owners was dramatically demonstrated in 1988, when they rejected a modest contract offer from their existing U.S. broadcaster, the ESPN cable network, in favour of the quick cash of a three-year, $51-million deal from the smaller SportsChannel America. The contract was greeted with universal scorn by the press, and for good reason. While ESPN was available on cable in every major U.S. television market, with a potential audience of 50 million homes, SportsChannel America was actually a cobbled-together group of regional broadcasters which could only reach 11 million homes. It wasn't even available in several NHL cities. The cash grab was a miscalculation by a league that needed exposure. Despite the network's promise to expand quickly to reach at least 50 million homes, it never happened. By the time the deal expired, in 1991, SportsChannel hadn't even hit 25 million homes. With ESPN still angry over its rejection, and poor ratings giving it no clout, the league was forced to renew with SportsChannel for one year at a mere $5.5-million for 1991-92. The NHL finally got back on ESPN just after the departure of Ziegler, when a five-year, $80-million deal was signed that also included ABC, the parent company of ESPN, which eventually agreed to carry several playoff games. The payoff is modest compared to other sports, but the five-year deal gives the league a chance to build a national audience in the United States. The rapid expansion of the league in 1992 and 1993 predicts the audience is there.

David Cruise, co-author of *Net Worth*, has a theory that the same, small-time attitude has hindered the league since 1957, when the owners managed to smash an attempt by the players to form a union. Cruise believes hockey has stagnated since that time, because without an aggressive union driving up salaries, the NHL owners did not need to bother hustling an American television contract. They were content to depress players' salaries and rake in healthy profits from the live gate along with some television, as well as concessions and parking revenue, since most of them owned the arenas as well. With American networks discovering just how profitable sports programming was in the 1960s, hockey missed out on the boom and has been playing catch-up ever since. When Eagleson came along, his tame union just helped perpetuate the status quo.

By 1980, despite the fact it had no enormous TV contract, the NHL was in better shape than the National Basketball Association, which shared many of the same cities and arenas with the hockey league. But thanks to a new commissioner, David Stern, who had the vision to market the game's stars, such as Magic Johnson, Michael Jordan and Larry Bird, as well as aggressively court television, the NBA has surged to become the most popular sport among people under 24 years of age. In the meantime, hockey regressed, despite having the sort of demographics advertisers love: its core audience was white, middle class and affluent. Hockey also had the good fortune to have the two of the greatest players in its history playing in their prime through the late 1980s — Wayne Gretzky and Mario Lemieux.

Hockey in the mid-1960s was ripe for a man such as Alan Eagleson. In 1967, players were unhappy with their plight, but they weren't ready to engage in all-out labour war. Alan Eagleson stepped in, formed a players' association and scored some small gains. This earned him the undying loyalty of the players who were, for the most part, small-town Canadian boys who were raised not to question authority. In time, the unquestioned authority became Eagleson.

"Athletes are trusting in general and I think hockey players are more trusting in general because they're mostly Canadian, and Canadians are just nice people, they have no reason to mistrust anybody," said Jim Korn, an American who had a habit of asking Eagleson annoying questions about union finances.

Eagleson saw that the support of the star players in the NHL was the key to establishing the union. Without them, the owners could easily break the association. In the union infancy of other major sports, players who became prominent labour activists, even those who just became player representatives, tended to be traded. But an owner would soon enrage the fans if he began trading away his stars. As the top player agent in the NHL in the 1960s and 1970s, Eagleson had many of the NHL's top stars as clients and many of them, such as Darryl Sittler and Lanny McDonald, became NHLPA vice-presidents. As those who questioned Eagleson discovered, this practice had a beneficial effect for Eagleson, too.

"Al was smart that way, he always aligned the top players," Korn said. "That gave him a power base. You could have 15 average, run-of-the-mill hockey players as player reps challenging the six NHL All-Star vice-presidents, and you were gonna lose every time. It didn't make sense, they didn't have any more votes than we did, but it's hard to attack a guy who's got that prestige in the league.

"(The stars) deserve (the prestige) on the ice, but I don't think they necessarily deserve it in a union meeting where you're talking about issues unrelated to your abilities on the ice. I think I was in a better position to talk to Al about some of the issues we were discussing than an NHL All-Star who happens to be quite a good hockey player but may not be quite as aware of some of the issues."

Yet it was those star players who could protect the union. "Sure, because what would it cost a team to summarily dump me?" Korn said. "No one had to relate it to my union activities. They could just say I wasn't good enough, anyway. You can't do that to a star player, to a guy who's clearly got the ability to play."

When the owners saw just how tame the union could be, they dropped any ideas of fighting with the players. "I shudder to think what would have happened to the NHL if we had a Marvin Miller or Ed Garvey as head of our players' association," Clarence Campbell once said. "They have been militantly hostile to management. Eagleson hasn't been a tooth fairy. But when chips are down he has acted like one." Campbell was referring to a $600,000 NHLPA loan that Eagleson, without telling the players, gave the NHL to prop up the financially comatose Cleveland Barons. The Barons, owned by Gordon and George Gund, members of one of the wealthiest families in the U.S., refused to save the team. It failed anyway. The Barons merged with the Minnesota North Stars in 1978, and the NHLPA loan was repaid.

It was these kinds of deals that increasingly drew Eagleson closer to the owners rather than the players. Given his attitude toward them, perhaps this was inevitable. "I'm not sure Al really likes players and I'm not sure he really understands them," said someone who was once close to Eagleson. "There are certain ways you have to treat them and he could be a little more compassionate with them rather than call them dumbos. There's more to them than meets the eye. So some of them aren't formally well educated. But they have feelings and they make their decisions in a rational fashion. When they do make them, they don't want to be ridiculed in front of the Canadian public because of it."

Eagleson's curt manner with the players came to be the way he dealt with anyone who he saw as getting in the way. As he became more powerful in hockey, his arrogance grew in proportion. Derek Holmes, who worked with Eagleson at Hockey Canada, said it would never occur to Eagleson that any of his actions were wrong or that he couldn't do something because it was improper. "Fuck you, just watch me," Eagleson would say when Holmes would tell him he couldn't do something. If Hockey Canada's directors didn't like it, they soon acquiesced under an Eagleson attack.

At the same time, this man, who could be the definition of vulgar, could be compassionate with his employees, and still hold the strong religious beliefs he acquired in childhood. Eagleson once said he taught Sunday school for 15 years. "He's a very religious man, although you'd never know that," said an ex-friend. "He always had a genuine concern for your family and how they were doing."

There is a theory that Eagleson, despite all the conflicts of interest and odd dealings, may have been able to hang on to his position if he had been just a little more upfront about his motives. "I think the only mistake Al made was that he told everybody he was going to make Mike Walton and Bobby Orr millionaires and it didn't work out. If he'd kept his mouth shut, I don't think anyone would have (thought ill of him)," said a former associate. "It's the same problem (with international hockey). He tells everybody he volunteers his time to Hockey Canada. I mean really. If he'd just keep his mouth shut when it comes to volunteering there wouldn't be a problem. I mean, not too many of us volunteer.

"Now he's got a problem because people are saying , 'Hey, you're making a million off this deal and it's a volunteer position.' Now if he hadn't said anything, the guy's entitled to that. The guy's put the Canada Cup together, he's done a lot of great things. He's entitled to be paid. But don't go around telling people you're not being paid."

Eventually, "the hubris was his downfall," Ed Garvey said. However, it was not a learning experience for Eagleson, once he was burned by his own arrogance. In 1989, well after Ed Garvey's report exposed his many conflicts and Eagleson had promised to end such practices in order to keep his job, Eagleson was engaged in yet another egregious conflict of interest. And again, he apparently never informed the players. This time, he was after a $1-million payoff from Compuware CEO Peter Karmanos who wanted to become one of the NHL owners, the very people Eagleson was supposed to be fighting on behalf of the NHLPA. The compulsion to set up a deal, to hustle a dollar, was too much, despite the fact he was under more scrutiny than at any time in his career.

Eagleson was viewed by Karmanos as the ideal agent to assist him in buying a team because of his close relationship with NHL owners, particularly Ziegler and Wirtz. "I thought, and still think, he was the finest guy to be representing us in that situation, because of his abilities and his contacts," Karmanos said.

Eagleson's job was to gather information on teams that might be for sale and report his findings to Karmanos. He embarked on his assignment with enthusiasm and filed several comprehensive reports. In an October, 1988, letter to Karmanos, Eagleson suggested that Karmanos buy the Toronto Maple Leafs. He concluded that they would be of "excellent value, even at an exorbitant price."

In a follow-up letter, Eagleson gave reasons for pursuing the Toronto franchise and profit strategies:

(a) The team makes money with bad management and a bad team.
(b) Toronto controls the Hamilton franchise. One could buy Toronto and sell off the rights to the Hamilton (Ontario) market.
(c) Buy Toronto and move Toronto to Hamilton and keep Toronto area rights.

The notion of the Leafs, a famous Canadian team, being moved to Hamilton was outrageous, and Karmanos says he did not seriously consider Eagleson's recommendation. "I can assure you, I had no intention of buying the Leafs. I said, 'Alan, it's foolish.' I mean, the Leafs are a Canadian institution."

Eagleson also filed reports containing gossip on NHL owners. Of Harold Ballard, the late owner of the Leafs, and his companion Yolanda Ballard, Eagleson wrote: "She has apparently co-habited with Ballard for a 3-5 year period. Ballard has an apartment in the Maple Leaf Gardens building and Yolanda stays overnight more often than not. She and her daughter have both officially changed their names to 'Ballard'. Yolanda is a convicted felon and served more than a year in jail for conspiracy to defraud."

Of Peter Pocklington, the owner of the Oilers, Eagleson wrote: "Can be an asset if handled properly. . . . He will be a valuable source of information. Peter and I have been friends for 15 years through business affiliations and politics. We have come to know each other very well over the last 10 years because of hockey.

"Peter insists the Oilers are not for sale. The fact that he sold Gretzky to Los Angeles suggests otherwise."

In profiling New Jersey Devils' owner John McMullen, Eagleson advised Karmanos: "He has an intense dislike for Ziegler. Wants to be NHL president or commissioner (he must think I am crazy).

"Spent $32 million for franchise and TV cable rights (paid to Flyers, Rangers and Islanders). He has complained to anyone who will listen that the NHL owners screwed him on the deal."

Eagleson ended up earning about $37,000 for his efforts on behalf of Karmanos, but he missed out on the big payoff. The million-dollar bonus that was on the table was contingent on Karmanos buying a team at a good price and, by the end of 1989, any hope of that had ended when, in December, the NHL announced that it was expanding by two teams and would be charging $50 million for each franchise. Karmanos was shocked. He, and many others, felt the price was far too high and had been posted at that amount to the artificially inflate the value of the other NHL teams.

"The drums of expansion had started to beat and these fellows all were doing the dance of the sugar plum fairy," Karmanos said, with a colourful mix of metaphors. "They thought that somehow, by magically announcing a $50-million expansion tag, they were going to artificially create value for floundering hockey teams. They thought that because expansion was $50 million, all other teams were anointed with this $50-million price tag.

"We just threw up our hands and said the owners were bonkers if they thought their franchises were all worth that much. The owners, the wheeler-dealer ones, were hoping somebody would come along and offer something over $50 million for a franchise such as the Hartford Whalers or the Winnipeg team, and there's no way on God's green earth they're worth that much."

Karmanos's pursuit of an NHL team effectively ended on January 7, 1990 at the Chicago Stadium during an exhibition hockey game, organized by Eagleson, between Wirtz's Chicago Blackhawks and the Soviet Central Red Army team. Eagleson arranged for Karmanos and Compuware's director of hockey operations, Jim Rutherford, to attend and speak with Wirtz and Ziegler, but the meeting did not go well. In fact, it turned into a disaster.

During an intermission, Eagleson, Wirtz, Ziegler, Karmanos and Rutherford gathered in the Blackhawk offices. Wirtz and Eagleson stayed close by, but were not directly involved in the discussion. According to Karmanos, Ziegler had been drinking and was in a surly mood. Any pretense of cordiality ended when Karmanos asked Ziegler about the cost of a new franchise.

"I had the temerity, I guess, to ask John how they arrived at a $50-million price," Karmanos said. "He shouted at me that it was none of my goddamn business. Then I said in the same conversation that I'd just like to understand the logic in coming up with that kind of price, because the highest price ever paid for a team up to that time had been $30 million for the Hartford Whalers. And now they were asking $50 million for an expansion team.

"John started screaming at me. He almost lost control. After we were able to settle him down, Jimmy and me, I asked him if there was any hope of a national TV contract. He said, 'We're not going to get a national TV contract; we're a regional sport.' In the course of shouting at me, he said, 'The NBA thinks that it charged enough for its franchises.' I said, 'A franchise in the NBA was $32.5 million for Charlotte and Orlando, but coming with that was a five-year TV contract worth $8 million a year and the NHL has nothing of the equivalent.' Again, he started shouting at me. Later, Al and Bill Wirtz apologized for Ziegler's behaviour. They came in and helped settle John down a little bit."

Despite the failure of Karmanos's quest for an NHL team, he says he came away with a high opinion of Eagleson. "He was a good union representative. As far as getting good solid ownership in the league, that only enhances the players' position. He's very, very good. He's getting an awful lot of criticism, but I think he did a marvellous job of getting the players as much as they did."

*   *   *

In the years since the players revolted in 1989, since the FBI and grand jury started their investigations in 1991, Eagleson has virtually dropped out of sight, both on the orders of his lawyers and because he is now largely shunned by the hockey world. Once Eagleson dreamed aloud of spending his last years in hockey as the international strongman for both Hockey Canada and the NHLPA. There was also the chance of heading the International Ice Hockey Federation, which Eagleson allowed might interest him, as long as it came with a salary, unlike the IIHF's president's post held by his friend Gunther Sabetzki. All of those jobs are out of reach now. As one of Eagleson's good friends and business associates said in early 1993, "He's finished. It doesn't matter what comes out of all this. He's finished." That was evident to some in June, 1993 at a reception to mark the opening of the new Hockey Hall of Fame in downtown Toronto. Eagleson and Ziegler, who are members of the Hall of Fame, turned up together. One person present said the pair was not ignored completely by the other guests, which included most of the NHL establishment, but it was obvious Ziegler and Eagleson were trying mightily, and failing, to once again be the centre of attention. It was Gary Bettman's party now.

Eagleson, citing his lawyers' orders, refuses to comment on anything under investigation. But during off-the-record chats with friendly reporters, Eagleson has said the investigations have become a strain on himself and his family, but he wasn't about to fall to pieces. Those close to him say the distress has been extreme, far more than he will ever admit.

While the fall of Eagleson and Ziegler, and the retreat by Bill Wirtz to ordinary team owner, have brought about cataclysmic changes in the NHL, not everything has changed. There are still controversies and conflicts of interest surrounding some agents.

The NHLPA under Bob Goodenow has started a register of player-agents, but it still does not regulate them like the baseball and football unions. Don Meehan, who has the biggest client list of any agent operating in the NHL, still represents both management figures and players. Rick Curran, another top agent, was caught in a nasty fight with the Lindros family after he was dropped as the agent for their son, Eric, who is expected to follow Wayne Gretzky and Mario Lemieux as the next great NHL superstar. One of the reasons cited by Carl and Bonnie Lindros for firing Curran was that he used a contract Eric Lindros had signed with Score, a player card company, to enlist the company's help in obtaining a mortgage for his home.

Curran has not denied this, but there are extenuating circumstances. When Curran shifted his business from Toronto to a suburb of Philadelphia in 1992, he was a stranger to the bankers in the area. Curran didn't know anyone who could vouch for him for a housing loan, so he turned to Score, with which he had done business on behalf of Lindros. The card company acted as guarantor on a bank mortgage, which was for 8 per cent, consistent with rates at the time. "In no way was Eric's Score agreement compromised by the company helping me," Curran said. "The family was aware of the arrangement." Curran had negotiated a contract for Eric Lindros that paid him $3.5 million a year from the Philadelphia Flyers in 1992-93, the highest-ever salary for a rookie. It was also more than Wayne Gretzky's salary from the Los Angeles Kings. Curran and the Lindros family settled their differences out of court.

The aftermath of the Eagleson-Ziegler-Wirtz years has left the NHL reeling, with new commissioner Gary Bettman left to pick up the pieces. Thanks to decisions made while those three men were in office, the league is facing litigation that could last into the next century. The NHL has already lost upwards of $40 million in the pension lawsuit, although it is under appeal. The league may wind up before the Supreme Court of the United States since the retired players in the U.S. have appealed the decision of a federal court that it did not have the jurisdiction to hear the case.

There could more yet. A group of players is considering the possibility of a collusion lawsuit against the NHL owners, that might involve Eagleson as well. The lawsuit would allege a conspiracy to keep NHL salaries low. One of the players explained it this way: "Let's say since 1972, each team saved $2 million on salaries. That's 21 teams times two, so $42 million. Multiply that by 20 years and you've got about $840 million."

Another group may launch a class-action lawsuit against the league and possibly the NHLPA over difficulties in obtaining disability insurance settlements. "We haven't been fighting dirty yet," said one retired Hall of Famer. "What would they say if we started bringing the guys in wheelchairs and the guys who are destitute and bringing them up front for everybody to see?"

In the summer of 1991, before the forces of the American justice system, and the tardy Canadian authorities had borne down on Eagleson and the players' grievances were still muted, Eagleson was his usual defiant self. "If they have any complaint, and think there's been an impropriety, go to the authorities. That's what we have the police for."

Two years later, one of the authorities had an answer. "Mr. Eagleson is a wealthy man and I'm sure he'll hire the best lawyers he can," said Paul Kelly, the assistant U.S. attorney in charge of the Eagleson case. "Like any citizen, if he is indicted he will get his day in court."

Endnotes

Chapter One/ **The Antagonists**

Page 16: In 1982, Brad Park, then a Bruin defenceman: *The Eagle-Tribune*, Feb. 22, 1993.

Page 18: "This all came from Bobby Orr": *Toronto Sun*, March 2, 1993.

Page 26: "I can't say I really knew anything about it": *The Globe and Mail*, Feb. 20, 1993.

Chapter Two/ **The Legend**

Page 28: "If the rest of the class took 30 minutes": *Eagle: The Life and Times of R. Alan Eagleson*, p. 26.

Page 30: "There's my permit": *Net Worth*, p. 156.

Page 30: "Al told me that he worked on the premise": *Net Worth*, p. 155.

Page 31: "He was a belligerent little rooster": *Net Worth*, p. 159.

Page 33: Eagleson called the Diefenbaker-led Tories, "a beautiful ride 'em cowboy contrast": *Power Play: The Memoirs of Hockey Czar R. Alan Eagleson*, p. 64.

Page 34: "We took 'em, went door to door": *The Eagle-Tribune*, Sept. 22, 1991.

Page 35: "Can he play hockey?": *Net Worth*, p. 164.

Chapter Three/ **The Emancipator**

Page 43: "a tall, slender bespectacled man": *James Norris and the Decline of Boxing*, p. 64.

Page 47: During the 1955-56 season, for example, CBS paid four American teams: *Net Worth*, p. 89.

Chapter Four/ **The Brothers**

Page 53: had assets totalling $456,600. His taxes, legal and accounting bills amounted to $469,550: *The Eagle-Tribune*, Sept. 26, 1991.

Page 55: "We wouldn't trade Bobby Orr": *Bobby Orr: My Game*, p. 31.

Page 57: "He could thread a needle with the puck": *The Toronto Star*, Aug. 5, 1990.

Page 70: Between 1971 and 1979, Orr withdrew from BOE: *Toronto Sun*, Sept. 4, 1990.

Page 71: "Al was looking after everything": *The Toronto Star*, Aug. 5, 1990.

Chapter Five/ **The Patriot**

Page 74: The Hockey Canada organization was handed a two-fold mandate: *Hockey Is Our Game*, p. 114.

Page 74: "with an ironic twinkle in his eye": *Hockey Is Our Game*, p. 116.

Page 75: "not one of the Canadian delegates: *Hockey Is Our Game*, p. 117.

Page 76: "Between 1969 and 1972 I kept pushing the Canada-Soviet series idea": *Power Play: The Memoirs of Hockey Czar Alan Eagleson*.

Page 76: "tell them every fucking word": *Net Worth*, p. 218.

Page 76: the negotiations in Prague: *Net Worth*, p. 217.

Page 77: "Oh, my wife and I": *Net Worth*, p. 217.

Page 77: "The credit — the credit doesn't really matter": *Net Worth*, p. 218.

Page 79: "turned that $750,000 into a $1.2-million profit": *Eagle: The Life and Times of R. Alan Eagleson*, p. 130.

Page 81: "Al delivers us the players": *Sports Illustrated*, July 2, 1984.

Page 83: "verbally smacked and frozen out": *The Eagle-Tribune*, Sept. 24, 1991.

Page 83: "in whatever way that was necessary": *The Eagle-Tribune*, Sept. 24, 1991.

Chapter Six/ **The Hockey Czar**

Page 86: "Neither I nor any member of my family": *The Eagle-Tribune*, Sept. 23, 1991.

Page 89: Harnett and Eagleson go back to the early 1960s: *Eagle: The Life and Times of R. Alan Eagleson*, p. 131.

Page 90: In 1972, after Eagleson formed Ballard-Orr Productions Ltd.: *The Eagle-Tribune*, Sept. 23, 1991.

Page 91: "As a radio-TV person": *Eagle: The Life and Times of R. Alan Eagleson*, p. 131.

Page 91: "Well, no, not to Eagleson": *Sports Illustrated*, July 2, 1984.

Page 91: "They say that before Harnett coughs in the morning": *Sports Illustrated*, July 2, 1984.

Page 94: If he has a difference of opinion with you": *Eagle: The Life and Times of R. Alan Eagleson*, p. 165.

Page 99: Furthermore, Russ Conway discovered the owners: *The Eagle-Tribune*, Sept. 24, 1991.

Chapter Seven/ **The Mortgage Man**

Page 103: "I have not made my money": *The Eagle-Tribune*, Feb. 23, 1993.

Page 105: In 1982, the NHLPA gave Irving Ungerman: *The Eagle-Tribune*, Feb. 23, 1993.

Page 105: In the early 1980s, builder and developer Norman Donaldson: *The Eagle-Tribune*, Feb. 23, 1993.

Page 107: "It's no contest that as far as the loans were concerned": *The Eagle-Tribune*, Sept. 23, 1991.

Page 107: "The players (Mr. Eagleson and Mr. Donaldson) knew one another": *The Eagle-Tribune*, Feb. 23, 1993.

Page 108: "What that does is minimize the investor's outlay": *The Eagle-Tribune*, Sept. 23, 1991.

Page 108: "I still do not see": *The Eagle-Tribune*, Feb. 23, 1993.

Page 110: Alan Eagleson sold the television advertising rights to Harcom: *The Eagle-Tribune*, Sept. 23, 1991.

Page 110: "directly with Eagleson": *Sports Illustrated*, July 2, 1984.

Page 115: "any currently owned": *The Eagle-Tribune*, Feb. 23, 1993.

Page 115: A company called New Leaf Florists: *The Eagle-Tribune*, Feb. 23, 1993.

Page 115: In October of 1981, the NHLPA gave Tesson Developments: *The Eagle-Tribune*, Feb. 23, 1993.

Page 115: "despite the fact no interest had been paid": *The Eagle-Tribune*, Feb. 23, 1993.

Page 116: Tesson was an even bigger headache: *The Eagle-Tribune*, Feb. 23, 1993.

Page 116: "Mr. Eagleson has indicated that you may need some extra time": *The Eagle-Tribune*, Feb. 23, 1993.

Page 116: "in response to your request": *The Eagle-Tribune*, Feb. 23, 1993.

Page 117: "Investment committee?": *The Eagle-Tribune*, Feb. 23, 1993.

Page 117: The players "didn't know a thing": *The Eagle-Tribune*, Feb. 23, 1993.

Page 118: "mentioned there were monies": *The Eagle-Tribune*, Feb. 23, 1993.

Page 118: "That appraisal is worth nothing": *The Eagle-Tribune*, Sept. 23, 1991.

Page 118: "Net worth and 60 cents": *The Eagle-Tribune*, Sept. 23, 1991.

Page 118: "That's an absurd statement": *The Eagle-Tribune*, Sept. 23, 1991.

Page 119: When Walton, Casey and the other investors defaulted on the mortgages: *Toronto Sun*, Sept. 9, 1990.

Page 120: "He read the text of my report": *The Eagle-Tribune*, Feb. 23, 1993.

Chapter Eight/ **The Union Boss**

Page 122: "Let's get Paul Desmarais out of bed": *Power Play: The Memoirs of Hockey Czar R. Alan Eagleson*, p. 162.

Page 122: In 1988, he billed the NHLPA $4,928 for a large dinner party: *The Eagle-Tribune*, Feb. 22, 1993.

Page 128: "I remember that as clear as a bell": *Sports Illustrated*, July 2, 1984.

Page 129: "Did you guys think you had anything to do with the merger?" *Sports Illustrated*, July 2, 1984.

Chapter Nine/ **The Hat Tricks**

Page 135: "I left figuring (Harrison) was still with the team": *The Eagle-Tribune*, Sept. 23, 1991.

Page 137: "He wanted to dictate whether benefits should be paid": *The Eagle-Tribune*, Sept. 25, 1991.

Page 137: "Nobody jumped up from the players' association": *The Eagle-Tribune*, Sept. 25, 1991.

Page 142: "I liked Eagleson very much": *Sports Illustrated*, July 2, 1984.

Page 145: These are kings' ransoms: *The Eagle-Tribune*, Sept. 24, 1991.

Page 147: Dozens of former and current players: *The Eagle-Tribune*, Sept. 24, 1991.

Page 148: Conway also couldn't find any players: *The Eagle Tribune*, May 9, 1993.

Page 148: "It is regrettable": Carl Brewer, *et al.*, to John Ziegler, May 12, 1991.

Page 152: He pointed out that his investigation: Ed Garvey in his report to the players, June 3, 1989.

Page 153: On December 11, 1990, a group of 93 former NHL players: *Net Worth*, p. 83.

Page 153: "The owners donated the players' own wages to fund their pension plan": *Net Worth*, p. 83.

Page 153: "The league could do whatever they wanted with the pension fund": *The Eagle-Tribune*, Sept. 24, 1991.

Page 154: In the spring of 1976: *Eagle: The Life and Times of R. Alan Eagleson*, p. 178.

Page 155: "They never asked for it.": *The Eagle-Tribune*, Sept. 24, 1991.

Page 155: "I had been elected to a positon with the Pension Society": *The Eagle-Tribune*, May 9, 1993.

Page 155: "Whether or not it didn't get from the club to him, I don't know": *The Eagle-Tribune*, May 9, 1993.

Page 156: "But that hasn't happened": *The Toronto Star*, Sept. 1992.

Page 156: "When (the governments' tax departments) agree within our tax counsel's position": *The Toronto Star*, Sept. 1982.

Page 157: "I cannot see how they could not deem it as a pension plan.": *The Eagle-Tribune*, Feb. 23, 1993.

Page 159: "(Eagleson) then said, "I understand Mark Zigler"": David Forbes, in a letter to Carl Brewer, Dec. 14, 1990.

Page 162: Jim Fox, a player rep for the Los Angeles Kings at the time: *The Eagle-Tribune*, Sept. 24, 1991.

Page 163: "the consequences of these actions, in my opinion, represent a gain to the benefit of the NHL clubs": *The Eagle-Tribune*, Sept. 24, 1991.

Page 163: was *"not* to look after retired players": *The Eagle-Tribune*, May 9, 1993.

Page 163: "all hockey players who participate": *The Eagle-Tribune*, May 9, 1993.

Page 164: "I never saw that letter, was never aware of it until now": *The Eagle-Tribune*, May 9, 1993.

Page 164: "Absent of the approval of the players": *The Eagle-Tribune*, May 9, 1993.

Chapter Eleven/ **The Watchers**

Page 166: "Jesus, you must be a communist": *Tales of an Athletic Supporter*.

Chapter Twelve/ **The Siege**

Page 181: "It was the surprise and the fear": *Net Worth*, p. 297.

Page 181: "Now they don't have to worry": *Net Worth*, p. 297.

Page 183: "well under 40 per cent": Ed Garvey, in his report to the players, June 3, 1989.

Page 185: But Eagleson called an NHLPA meeting at the February, 1980 All-Star Game: *Net Worth*, p. 291.

Page 187: "He embarrassed me": *Sports Illustrated*, July 2, 1984.

Page 189: "a perfectly good question didn't get answered": *Net Worth*, p. 304.

Page 193: "They were so terrified": *Net Worth*, p. 308.

Page 195: The summary of findings at the front of his report: Ed Garvey in his report to the players, June 3, 1989.

Page 197: "No, no. You didn't say that, Al. I heard you. I was there in the room and this is what you said.": *Net Worth*, p. 315.

Page 198: "I have to go back to Toronto as head of the association.": *Net Worth*, p. 317.

Page 201: "was necessary to or appropriate for the NHLPA": *The Eagle-Tribune*, Feb. 22, 1993.

Chapter Thirteen/ **The Legacy**

Page 209: "I shudder to think what would have happened to the NHL": *Net Worth*, p. 276.

Page 212: "She has apparently co-habited with Ballard": *The Eagle-Tribune*, Feb. 21, 1993.

Bibliography

Books

Clayton, Deidra. *Eagle: The Life and Times of R. Alan Eagleson.* Toronto: Lester & Orpen Dennys Ltd., 1982.

Coleman, Jim. *Hockey Is Our Game.* Toronto: Key Porter Books, 1986.

Cruise, David, and Alison Griffiths. *Net Worth.* Toronto: Viking, 1991.

Eagleson, R. Alan, and Scott Young. *Power Play: The Memoirs of Hockey Czar Alan Eagleson.* Toronto: McClelland and Stewart, 1991.

Ferguson, Bob. *Who's Who in Canadian Sport.* Toronto: Summerhill Press Ltd., 1985.

Frayne, Trent. *The Tales of an Athletic Supporter.* Toronto: McClelland and Stewart, 1990.

Harris, Billy. *The Glory Years.* Toronto: Prentice-Hall Canada Inc., 1989.

Houston, William. *Ballard: A Portrait of Canada's Most Controversial Sports Figure.* Toronto: Summerhill Press Ltd., 1984.

Howe, Colleen, and Gordie Howe and Charles Wilkins. *After the Applause.* Toronto: McClelland and Stewart, 1989.

Nagler, Barnie. *James Norris and the Decline of Boxing.* New York: Bobbs-Merrill Co. Inc., 1964.

Orr, Bobby, and Mark Mulvoy. *Bobby Orr: My Game.* Boston: Little, Brown and Company, 1974.

Smythe, Conn, and Scott Young. *Conn Smythe: If You Can't Beat 'Em in the Alley.* Toronto: McClelland and Stewart, 1981.

Magazines

Maclean's, Toronto
Quest, Toronto
Rinkside Magazine, New York
Sports Illustrated, New York
The Hockey News, Toronto
Toronto Life, Toronto

Newspapers

The Citizen, Ottawa
The Eagle-Tribune, Lawrence, Mass.
The Gazette, Montreal
The Globe and Mail, Toronto
The Toronto Star, Toronto
Toronto Sun, Toronto
The Vancouver Province, Vancouver

Index

Campbell, Clarence, 41, 43, 50-52, 74, 153, 204, 209
Campbell, Kim, 22, 23
Canada Cup, 31, 80, 81, 82, 83, 86, 87, 88, 90, 97-98, 100, 101,   110, 122, 127, 130, 154, 156, 167-168, 169, 179, 205, 206, 211
Canadian Amateur Hockey Association (CAHA), 24, 56, 74, 76, 102
Canadian Football League Players' Association (CFPLA), 197
Canadian Inter-University Athletic Union, 74, 82
Can-Am Enterprises, 71
Canning, Gordon, 111
Cannon, Mike, 78
Carling-O'Keefe Breweries, 90, 110
Caron, Jacques, 45
Casey, Dan, 119
Cashman, Wayne, 58
Cavallini, Paul, 99
Chapman, Blair, 131, 133, 138
Cheevers, Gerry, 58, 78
Christopher Lang and Associates, 87
Clancy, King, 35, 41
Clarke, Bobby, 187
Clayton, Deidra, 28, 33, 46, 60, 172, 176
Coleman, Jim, 74, 206
Columbia Broadcasting System (CBS), 47
Compuware, 25, 211
Conway, Russ, 16-18, 20, 24, 25, 71, 72, 90, 99, 103, 105, 106,   107, 110, 115-120, 129, 129, 136, 137, 141, 142, 148, 155, 158, 162, 174, 175, 201

Cooke, Jack Kent, 46, 60
Cotton, Harold, 56
Crawley Warren, 141
Cruise, David, 30, 124, 173, 207-208
Cumberland, J.D.W., 32
Curran, Rick, 62, 88-89, 100-101, 124, 193, 215

Davey, Keith, 121
Davis, William, 142
Daw, Richard, 94, 95
Dawson, Earl, 74
Dermody, Bill, 92, 104, 105, 107, 112-113, 117, 120, 191
Desmarais, Paul 121, 122
Desruisseaux, Paul, 36
Dingwall, David, 22
Dionne, Marcel, 58
Donaldson, Marie, 115
Donaldson, Norman, 105, 107, 108, 110, 111, 112, 115, 116, 117
Dovey, William, 105, 200-201
Dowbiggin, Bruce, 20, 21, 24-25, 163, 174, 175
Dumart, Woody, 159
Dunnell, Milt, 168, 171, 173

Eagleson, Agnes, 28
Eagleson, James Allen, 28
Eagleson, Jill, 32, 35, 62, 112-114, 143
Eagleson, Nancy (Fisk), 32, 34, 62, 111, 120, 122, 143, 176
Eagleson, Trevor Allen, 32, 89, 97, 98, 112
Eagleson Ungerman, 60, 89, 103, 113, 118, 142, 197
Ellis, Lynda, 157
Elston, Murray, 163, 164

Emms, Hap, 55, 56
Employee Retirement Income Security Act (ERISA), 14
ESPN, 207
Esposito, Phil, 13, 16, 58, 65, 128, 129, 156, 187
Esposito, Tony, 187
Estey, Willard "Bud", 121

Federal Bureau of Investigation (FBI), 16-18, 20, 21-22, 24, 50, 175, 202, 214
Ferguson, John, 78
Fisher, Douglas, 43, 73, 74, 76, 77, 176-177
Fisher, Red, 168, 171, 173, 174
Fiske, Donald, 133
Fleming, Reggie, 146
Fletcher, Cliff, 126
Flynn, Michael, 132, 138
Forbes, Dave, 148, 151, 152, 158, 159
Fox, Jim, 162, 180
Francis, Emile, 139
Frayne, Trent, 166-167, 169
Fuhr, Grant, 167, 168
Fung, Robert, Jr., 113

Gainey, Bob, 187
Gallinger, Don, 41
Garvey, Ed, 14, 72, 92, 104, 114, 148, 152, 153, 162, 182, 183, 190-198, 201, 209, 211
Giguere, Louis, 51
Godfrey, Paul, 121, 176, 177
Goldblatt, Marian, 113
Goldblatt, Marvin, 27, 59, 88, 90, 94, 95, 98, 111, 113, 140, 187
Goodenow, Bob, 101, 102, 120, 162, 165, 193, 194, 199, 202, 215
Gordon, Larry, 129
Graham, George, 27
Graves, Hilliard, 67

Green, Ted, 57, 58
Greene, Nancy, 36
Gretzky, Wayne, 101, 130, 167, 168, 194, 198-199, 200, 208, 215
Griffiths, Alison, 30, 124, 173
Gross, George, 171, 173
Gund, George, 209
Gund, Gordon, 209

Haggert, Bobby, 59, 78
Hamilton, John, 33
Hampton, Howard, 20
Harcom, 59, 90, 91, 93, 108, 109, 110
Harnett, Arthur, 59, 89, 90, 91, 93, 94, 104, 110
Harris, Bill, 58
Harris, Billy, 27, 33, 34, 37, 38 148
Harrison, Jim, 134-136
Harrison, Liz, 135
Harvey, Doug, 47, 49
Hatskin, Ben, 129
Havlicek, John, 153
Hay, Bill, 93, 103
Hay, Charles, 73, 74, 75, 76, 77, 83
Hayes, George, 146
Hayes, Judy, 146
Hayter, Evan, 91
Healy, Mike, 138
Henderson, Paul, 58, 145, 150-151
Herron, Denis, 193
Hewitt, Foster, 28
Hockey Canada, 22-24, 26, 73, 74-84, 85, 86, 87, 88-93, 101, 102, 110, 124, 127, 130, 142, 174, 177, 179, 187, 191, 202, 205-206, 207, 210, 214
Hockey Hall of Fame, 44, 215
Hodge, Ken, 58, 65
Holmes, Derek, 76, 77, 79-80, 81-83, 84, 95-96, 97, 210
Howe, Gordie, 20, 48, 49, 53, 54, 57, 145, 146, 148, 149, 152, 153, 155

233

235

Photo Credits

Photographs used in this book are courtesy of the following sources.

The Stan Fischler Archives.
H. Robinson, Jack Dobson, John McNeill, Thomas Szlukovenyi, Randy Velocci, Fred Lum courtsey of The Globe and Mail.
Brent Nicasto/Photographer courtsey of Garvey & Bauer
Legal Services.